BlackBerry® Pearl™ 3G

FOR DUMMIES®

by Robert Kao and Dante Sarigumba

WILEY

Wiley Publishing, Inc.

BlackBerry® Pearl™ 3G For Dummies®
Published by
Wiley Publishing, Inc.
111 River Street
Hoboken, NJ 07030-5774
www.wiley.com

Copyright © 2011 by Wiley Publishing, Inc., Indianapolis, Indiana

Published by Wiley Publishing, Inc., Indianapolis, Indiana
Published simultaneously in Canada

WILEY

106627

About the Authors

Robert Kao is one well-rounded professional. His ability to translate his technical knowledge and communicate with users of all types led him to cowrite *BlackBerry For Dummies* and *BlackBerry Pearl For Dummies*. He started out as a BlackBerry developer for various financial firms in New York City, that truly global city. Kao is currently the founder of a mobile software start-up. A graduate of Columbia University, with a Computer Engineering degree, he currently lives in South Brunswick, New Jersey.

Dante Sarigumba is a long-time user of BlackBerry, a gizmo enthusiast, and coauthor of *BlackBerry For Dummies* and *BlackBerry Curve For Dummies*. He is a software developer and lives in South Brunswick, New Jersey, with his wife, Yosma, and two sons, Dean and Drew.

Dedication

I would like to thank my father (MHK), my mother (SYT), and the rest of the Kao family for everything they've done for me. I wouldn't be here without their kindness and understanding. I would also like to thank my lovely wife, Marie-Claude, and little Jade for all their support. In addition, thanks to Manon Lalancette and the rest of the Gamelin family for all your cheers!

—Robert Kao

As always, this book is for Yosma, Dean, and Drew: my greatest treasures. Thank you for your thoughts, understanding, and support.

—Dante Sarigumba

Authors' Acknowledgments

Collectively, we want to give a big thanks to our acquisition editor Katie Mohr and our editor Susan Pink for making us look good! In addition, we'd like to thank Carol McClendon, our agent, for presenting our proposal to the right people, and Victoria Berry, PR of Research In Motion, for getting us access to the proper channels at the right time. In addition, we thank the rest of the Wiley staff. Without you all, this book would not have been possible.

—Rob and Dante

Publisher's Acknowledgments

We're proud of this book; please send us your comments at http://dummies.custhelp.com. For other comments, please contact our Customer Care Department within the U.S. at 877-762-2974, outside the U.S. at 317-572-3993, or fax 317-572-4002.

Some of the people who helped bring this book to market include the following:

Acquisitions and Editorial

Project Editor: Susan Pink

Acquisitions Editor: Katie Mohr

Copy Editor: Susan Pink

Technical Editor: Richard Evers

Editorial Manager: Jodi Jensen

Editorial Assistant: Amanda Foxworth

Sr. Editorial Assistant: Cherie Case

Cartoons: Rich Tennant (www.the5thwave.com)

Composition Services

Project Coordinator: Patrick Redmond

Layout and Graphics: Joyce Haughey, Lavonne Roberts

Proofreaders: Laura Albert, Toni Settle

Indexer: Estalita Slivoskey

Publishing and Editorial for Technology Dummies

   Richard Swadley, Vice President and Executive Group Publisher

   Andy Cummings, Vice President and Publisher

   Mary Bednarek, Executive Acquisitions Director

   Mary C. Corder, Editorial Director

Publishing for Consumer Dummies

   Diane Graves Steele, Vice President and Publisher

Composition Services

   Debbie Stailey, Director of Composition Services

Contents at a Glance

Table of Contents

Introduction

· ·

*H*i there, and welcome to *BlackBerry Pearl 3G For Dummies*. This is a great book to have around if you want to discover new features or need something to slap open and use as a quick reference. If you don't have a BlackBerry Pearl yet and have some basic questions — such as "What is a BlackBerry Pearl?" or "How can a Pearl help me be more productive?" — you can benefit by reading this book cover to cover. Regardless of your current BlackBerry User Status — BUS, for short — we're here to help you get the most out of your BlackBerry.

Right off the bat, we can tell you that a BlackBerry Pearl is not a fruit you find at the supermarket nor a jewel. Rather, it is a feature-packed always-connected smartphone that has e-mail capabilities with a built-in Internet browser and advanced media features and a camera. With your BlackBerry, you are in the privileged position of always being able to receive e-mail, browse the Web, and have fun listening to music and taking pictures.

On top of that, a BlackBerry has all the features you'd expect from a personal organizer, including a calendar, to-do lists, and memos. Oh, and did we mention that a BlackBerry also has a mobile phone built in? Talk about multitasking! Imagine being stuck on a commuter train: With your BlackBerry by your side, you can compose e-mail while conducting a conference call — all from the comfort of your seat.

In this book, we show you all the basics but then go the extra mile by highlighting some of the lesser-known but still handy features of the Pearl. Your Pearl can work hard for you when you need it as well as play hard when you want it to.

About This Book

BlackBerry Pearl 3G For Dummies is written as a comprehensive user guide as well as a quick user reference. This book is designed so that you can read it cover to cover if you want, but you don't need to. Feel free to jump around while you explore the different functionalities of your BlackBerry. We cover basic and advanced topics, but we stick to those areas that we consider the most practical and frequently used. If you use or want to use a certain function of your BlackBerry, it's likely covered here.

Foolish Assumptions

In writing this book, we tried to be considerate of your needs. But because we've never met you, we had to create an image of you:

- You have a BlackBerry Pearl, and you want to find out how to get the most from it. Or you don't have a BlackBerry Pearl yet, and you're wondering what one can do for you.

- You want to take advantage of the many fun features of your BlackBerry Pearl, including taking pictures, listening to music, and watching video clips.

- You're looking for a book that doesn't assume you know all the jargon and tech terms used in the smartphone industry.

- You want a reference that shows you, step by step, how to do useful and cool things with a BlackBerry without bogging you down with unnecessary background or theory.

- You're tired of hauling your ten-pound laptop with you on trips, and you're wondering how to turn your BlackBerry into a miniature traveling office.

- You no longer want to be tied to your desktop system for the critical activities in your life, such as sending and receiving e-mail, checking your calendar for appointments, and surfing the Web.

- You like to have some fun, play games, and be entertained from a device but don't want to carry an extra game gadget in your bag.

How This Book Is Organized

BlackBerry Pearl 3G For Dummies consists of five parts, and each part consists of chapters related to that part's theme.

Part 1: Getting Started

Part I starts with the basics of your BlackBerry Pearl. You know: What it is, what you can do with it, and what the parts are. We also show you how to personalize and express yourself through your BlackBerry. This part wraps up with must-knows about security and how to customize your BlackBerry Pearl to suit your needs.

Part II: Getting Organized

Part II deals with the fact that your BlackBerry is a feature-packed phone and also a full-fledged organizer. We show you how to get your BlackBerry to keep your contacts in its Contacts app as well as how to manage your appointments and meetings in Calendar. You also find out how to use the Clock app to set an alarm, set a timer, and set your device to bedside mode. You explore how to use the Password Keeper app to centralize your passwords. Knowing that a big use of Pearl is for calling, in this part you'll find all the ways of using the Phone app, from simple dialing to multitasking while in a call. And finally, you see that most BlackBerry apps interconnect, working hard for you.

Part III: Getting Online

Part III shows you how you what made BlackBerry what it is today: always-connected e-mail. We also get into another strength of the BlackBerry — Web surfing functionality — but we don't stop there. We point out how you can use other forms of messages, specifically text messaging, instant messaging, PIN-to-PIN messages, and BlackBerry Messenger messages.

Part IV: Getting the Fun Stuff

You find the fun stuff in Part IV. Navigate using the BlackBerry GPS. Rock your world and use your BlackBerry Pearl to play music, watch videos, and take pictures. You also get the scoop on how to record videos and sample ring tones. Plus you get timesaving shortcuts when using the Media apps.

Part V: Getting Hooked with BlackBerry Desktop

In Part V, we detail BlackBerry Desktop Software and BlackBerry Desktop Manager and show you some of the hoops you can put the programs through with your Pearl, including making backups and installing BlackBerry apps from your desktop to your Pearl. Readers with a PC (sorry Mac users) also find out how to port data from older devices — BlackBerry or not — to their new Pearl. And we didn't forget to cover important stuff such as data syncing your appointments and contacts with desktop apps such as Outlook.

Part VI: The Part of Tens

All *For Dummies* books include The Part of Tens at the end, and this book is no different. In Part VI, we show you where to get cool BlackBerry accessories, how to know the popular games, download useful apps, and find Web sites suited for your BlackBerry Pearl.

Icons Used in This Book

This book rarely delves into the geeky, technical details, but when it does, this icon warns you. Read on if you want to get under the hood a little, or just skip ahead if you aren't interested in the gory details.

Here's where you can find not-so-obvious tricks that can make you a BlackBerry power user in no time. Pay special attention to the paragraphs with this icon to get the most out of your BlackBerry.

Look out! This icon tells you how to avoid trouble before it starts. A paragraph with this icon explains consequences you may not like on certain actions you do on your BlackBerry Pearl.

This icon highlights an important point that you don't want to forget because it just may come up again. We'd never be so cruel as to spring a pop quiz on you, but paying attention to these details can definitely help you.

Where to Go from Here

If you want to find out more about the book, visit `www.dummies.com/cheatsheet/blackberrypearl3g`. Now you can dive in! Give Chapter 1 a quick look to get an idea of where this book takes you, and then feel free to head straight to your chapter of choice.

Part I
Getting Started

The 5th Wave   By Rich Tennant

"This model comes with a particularly useful function — a simulated static button for breaking out of long-winded conversations."

In this part . . .

The road to a happy and collaborative relationship with your BlackBerry Pearl starts here. Chapter 1 covers all the nuts and bolts — how things work, the Pearl's look and feel, and connectivity. Chapter 2 discusses how you can navigate with ease to the world of BlackBerry Pearl, offering timesaving shortcuts. Finally, Chapter 3 shows you how to customize Pearl and make it your own.

Chapter 1

Your BlackBerry Is Not an Edible Fruit

. . . .

In This Chapter

▶ Checking out your BlackBerry behind the scenes

▶ Seeing what your BlackBerry can do

▶ Managing memory

. . . .

*W*ith all the talk about how the BlackBerry can change the way you work, communicate, and are entertained, you probably have an idea of what the device is — although it's okay if you don't (as long as you're not trying to eat it). Before we jump in to how the BlackBerry can change your lifestyle, we're curious — what convinced you to buy this particular handheld mobile device? Was it BlackBerry Messenger, or always-connected e-mail, or the multimedia player that replaces your iPod or iPhone, or a good app you saw on a friend's BlackBerry? For whatever reason you bought your BlackBerry, congratulations: You made an intelligent choice.

The same smarts that made you buy your BlackBerry Pearl are clearly at it again. This time, your native intelligence led you to pick up this book, perhaps because your intuition is telling you that there's more to the BlackBerry than meets the eye. Your hunch is right. For example, your BlackBerry is a whiz at making phone calls and checking e-mails, but it's also a social networking do-it-all smartphone that can update your Facebook account and let you instant chat with your business partner in another continent. And, of course, you can surf the Web and download apps at an amazing speed.

But that's not all. With the BlackBerry, help is always at your fingertips instead of sitting on some desk at home or at the office. You can use your BlackBerry to

✔ Check the reviews of that restaurant on the corner

✔ Find out — right now — what's showing at your local movie theater, or the weather forecast for tonight, or the best place to shop the sales

✔ Retrieve news headlines and check stock quotes

> ✔ Get directions to that cozy bed-and-breakfast
>
> ✔ Chat or view photos online
>
> ✔ Network with your old classmates

You can also improve your productivity, become better organized, and increase your cool factor. Watch out, world! Person bearing a BlackBerry Pearl coming through!

How the Pearl Works

For those of you who always ask, "How do they do that?" you don't have to go far; this little section is just for you.

The role of the network service provider

Along with wondering how your BlackBerry actually works, you may also be wondering why you didn't get your BlackBerry from RIM instead of a network service provider such as Cingular or T-Mobile. Why did you need to go through a middleman? After all, RIM makes BlackBerry.

Here's a quick-and-dirty answer. RIM needs a delivery system — a communication medium, as it were — for its technology to work. Not in a position to come up with such a delivery system all by its lonesome, RIM partnered (and built alliances across the globe) with the usual network service providers — the big cell phone companies.

These middle-providers support the wireless network for your BlackBerry so that you have signals to connect to the BlackBerry Internet Service — which means you can get all those wonderful e-mails (and waste so much valuable

time surfing the Internet). See Figure 1-1 for an overview of this process.

Network service providers don't build alliances for nothing, right? In return, RIM gave them the right to brand their names on the BlackBerry they offer for sale. For example, a T-Mobile Pearl may look different from a similar model you would get from Vodafone. Which leads to another question: Do BlackBerry functionalities differ from phone model to phone model? Quick answer: In the core BlackBerry apps (such as Tasks and Address Book), you find no major differences. However, some BlackBerry features, such as instant messaging, might or might not be supported by the network service provider. (See Chapter 8 for details on instant messaging.)

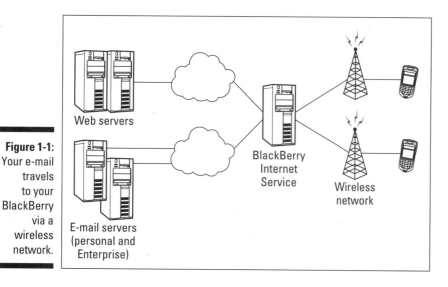

Figure 1-1:
Your e-mail
travels
to your
BlackBerry
via a
wireless
network.

Connecting to your personal computer

A personal computer is a household necessity, so it should come as no sur-prise that BlackBerry works hand-in-hand with your PC or Mac. The USB cable that comes with your BlackBerry does more than just charge your device. All the chapters in Part IV are dedicated to guiding you in making use of this important connection with the help of BlackBerry Desktop Manager and all the utilities that come with it. You find discussions in Chapter 17 on how to sync your device with the personal information manager data that you keep in your PC or Mac. Chapter 19 guides you on how to back up almost anything in your BlackBerry, down to your desktop. Lastly, Part V shows you what accessories to buy and which apps will help you be most productive!

Oh, the Things You Can Do!

Always-connected e-mail is likely first in the long list of reasons you got your device. And, if you need to go global, you can use your BlackBerry in more than 100 countries. Just hop off your flight, turn on your BlackBerry, and voilà: You can receive and send e-mails whether you're in Hong Kong, London, or Paris. Your significant other can get in touch with you wherever you are — just to say hi or to remind you that you promised Aunt Edna a bottle of Chanel No. 5.

Social networking

Want to update your Facebook page so your fans know your whereabouts? Tweet about the latest stock news? Upload your quick snapshot to Flickr? Have other buddies with BlackBerry phones? You and your buddies will never be out of touch with BlackBerry Messenger (see Chapter 10). You can be socially connected all the time with your BlackBerry. (Is that such a good thing? Well, that's up to you!)

All-in-one multimedia center

Previously, many people hesitated to buy a BlackBerry due to its lack of multimedia functions. Now, however, BlackBerry has a high-resolution camera and a memory slot for a microSD chip, so your BlackBerry can function as

- A music player
- A video player
- A portable flash drive
- Your personal photo collection

Internet at your fingertips

With the new BlackBerry Web browser, you can surf the Net nearly as smoothly on your smartphone as you can on a desktop computer. Even better, you can continue chatting with your friends through Instant Messenger, as though you never left your office. You can get an alert when your stock is tanking. True, that isn't fun, but you want this information as fast as possible.

Intrigued? Read how BlackBerry can take full advantage of the Web in Chapter 11.

Me and my great personal assistant

You might be saying, "But I'm a busy person, and I don't have time to browse the Web. What I *do* need is an assistant to help me better organize my day-to-day tasks." If you can afford one, go ahead and hire a personal assistant. The next best thing is a personal *digital* assistant (PDA).

Whip out that BlackBerry of yours and take a closer look. That's right; your BlackBerry is also a full-fledged PDA, helping you

- ✔ Remember all your acquaintances (see Chapter 4)
- ✔ Manage your appointments (see Chapter 5)
- ✔ Keep a to-do list (see Chapter 6)

Me and my chatty self

Your Pearl is also a full-featured phone. With voice dialing and the capability to carry out conference calls with you as the moderator, your Pearl isn't like other cell phones out there. To find out more about your Pearl phone, see Chapter 7.

Look, Dad, no hands!

Your BlackBerry is equipped with an earphone that doubles as a microphone for hands-free talking. This accessory is your doctor's prescription for preventing the stiff neck that comes from wedging your BlackBerry against your ear with your shoulder. At the minimum, it helps free your hands so that you can eat Chinese takeout.

Some places require you by law to use an earphone while driving and talking on a cell phone. We recommend that you avoid using your cell phone while driving, hands-free or not.

RIM didn't stop with just your standard wired earphones. BlackBerry also supports cool wireless earphones based on Bluetooth technology. How can a bizarrely colored tooth help you here? *Bluetooth* is the name for a (very) short-distance wireless technology that connects devices. See Chapter 7 for how to connect your BlackBerry to a Bluetooth headset.

Final BlackBerry Tidbits

The main concerns most of us have when buying a product are quality and reliability. Will the product last? Will it perform as the flier says? Will I regret having bought this item six months down the road? This section looks at some of the hardware features that make buying the BlackBerry Pearl a wise purchase.

Power efficiency

Now, anyone who has had an ear to the ground regarding BlackBerry knows its reputation as a highly efficient little machine when it comes to power consumption. Even with the addition of color and high-resolution screens, the Pearl still has an 18-day *standby time* (how long a single battery charge will last on your Pearl without actively using it) and close to 5½ hours talk time. So, when the salesperson offers you a special deal on a second battery, simply tell him or her that you'll think about it. With the Pearl's standard battery, you'll have more than enough power.

Memory management

When you first receive your BlackBerry Pearl, the device definitely has ample free memory. However, you're stuck with a fixed amount of memory, which can prove limiting over time as you download apps. In fact, you could eventually run out of memory altogether.

Don't confuse this fixed amount of memory with the memory available through the microSD slot. A microSD chip can store MP3s, portable videos, and pictures that you download or load from your computer.

Does your device die when you run out of memory? No, thank goodness. Your BlackBerry monitors the free memory on your device. If you're ever in danger of reaching your upper limits, the BlackBerry has a memory management tool that cleans house to free this limited resource.

BlackBerry apps right out of the box are capable of figuring out what data isn't that important. For example, the BlackBerry Browser caches data to enhance your experience when browsing the Web. *Caches* use local copies of Web pages to speed up the reloading of previously visited Web sites, so they are generally good things to have around. However, the cache also takes up space. When the OS tells Browser that the device is reaching its upper memory limit and it needs to do some house cleaning, Browser deletes this cache. In addition, the Message app deletes e-mails you've already read, starting from the oldest and working its way backward, when the Pearl is short on memory.

Curious about how much available space your device has? From the Home screen, press the Menu key. Select Options (wrench icon), and then select Status. In the Status screen, the File Free field tells you how much space is left.

Sentry on duty

As the history of human existence shows, humans are capable of some nasty things. Unfortunately, the virtual world is not exempt; every day, a battle is fought between those who are trying to attack a system and those who are trying to protect it. Included among those attacking the system are people who are trying to steal corporate data for their advantage or steal personal data to carry out identity theft.

A computer connected to the Internet faces an extra risk of being hacked or becoming infected by a computer virus intent on simply annoying the heck out of you or (even worse) wreaking havoc on your computer. Fortunately, security is one of the strong points of the BlackBerry. RIM has built in to its software features that allow companies to curtail activities for their BlackBerry users that they deem risky, such as installing or running a third-party app. Data transmitted on and from the device is encrypted to prevent snooping. RIM also has a Signature process for app developers, which forces developers to identify themselves and their programs if they are developing any apps running on the BlackBerry platform that need to integrate with either BlackBerry core apps or the OS.

The security measures RIM implemented on the BlackBerry platform have gained the trust of the U.S. government as well as many of the Forbes Top 500 enterprises in the financial and health industries.

Although mobile viruses pose no immediate threat to your BlackBerry, spyware can redirect your e-mails and SMS messages to another destination without your knowledge. Spyware is usually installed without the user knowing, which is why we recommend that you set a password with a security timeout (see Chapter 3). In addition, you can install third-party software such as SmrtGuard to perform a spyware scan.

Chapter 2

Navigating the Pearl

*T*he new BlackBerry Pearl has a brighter and higher-resolution screen. But what makes it fundamentally different than previous versions of the Pearl is its trackpad.

What? No more trackball? Where is the trackpad? What can you do with it? We answer these questions (and others) in this chapter. Bear with us, and you will be master of your BlackBerry Pearl in no time.

Anatomy 101

Together with the trackpad, a few important keys will help you master navigating your BlackBerry Pearl. Figure 2-1 labels all the Pearl's major keys and elements.

Your Pearl has the following major features:

- **Display screen:** The screen is the graphical user interface (GUI) of your BlackBerry Pearl.

- **SureType keyboard:** You use the keyboard for input.

- **Escape key:** This key cancels a selection or returns to a previous page in an app (such as Browser).

- **Menu key:** You press this key to display the full menu of the app you're using (see Figure 2-2, left).

    If you owned a BlackBerry before, you may have noticed that the Menu key is new. The Menu key basically replaces the trackwheel click.

- **Trackpad:** You navigate the display screen of your BlackBerry Pearl with the trackpad. You have four directional movements. When you press on the trackpad, a short menu of the app you're using appears (see Figure 2-2, right).

✔ **Left and right convenience keys:** By default, the left convenience key brings up the voice dialing app. The right convenience key brings up the camera. In Chapter 3, you find out how to program these two keys so they display the programs you use the most.

✔ **Media keys:** The three media keys are play/pause, next track, and previous track. These keys allow you to quickly access and control media.

✔ **MicroSD slot:** Although it's hidden inside your BlackBerry Pearl and can be revealed only by removing the battery cover, the microSD slot is a crucial element to your media experience on your Pearl.

Figure 2-1:
Your new
BlackBerry
Pearl.

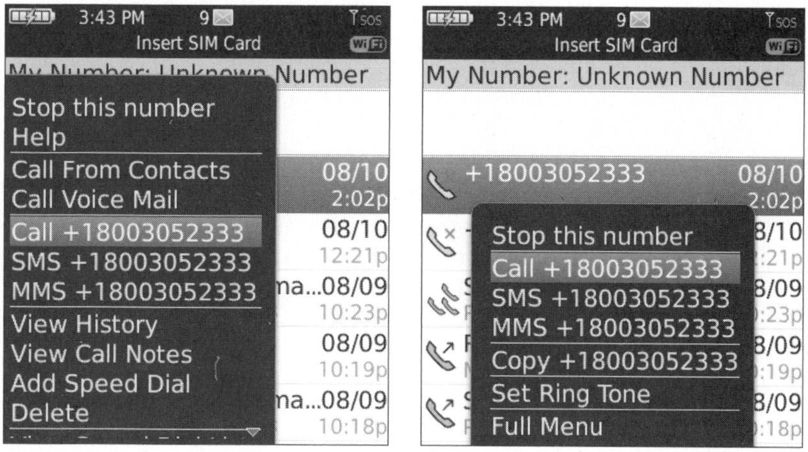

Figure 2-2:
A full menu
(left) and a
short menu
(right) in the
Message
app.

Display screen

When you first turn on your Pearl, the display screen displays the *Home screen,* which is your introduction to the GUI of your BlackBerry Pearl. The five icons represent the different apps in your BlackBerry Pearl. Refer to

Figure 2-3 for examples of what your Home screen might look like.

Depending on the theme you're using, you might see apps listed in text form rather than as icons. How your GUI looks depends on how you want it to look, because the font and theme are customizable. For more on personalizing your BlackBerry, see Chapter 3.

Figure 2-3:
Your
BlackBerry
Pearl Home
screen.

SureType keyboard

The Pearl doesn't have a full QWERTY keyboard. Rather, it works with a QWERTY-based keyboard known as the *SureType* keyboard. Many keys share letters (refer to Figure 2-1), and the SureType technology is smart enough to learn what key combinations are necessary for the words you want. Basically, with SureType, you can now type with only one thumb, and your BlackBerry Pearl learns the words that you use frequently.

Here are tips to speed up the learning curve when using SureType technology:

- ✔ **Lock in correct characters as you type.** This way, you get to what you want to type faster. See Figure 2-4. If a character is wrong, delete it and then continue typing. The locked-in characters appear in bold.

- ✔ **If SureType got the word you're typing correct on the first try, use the Space key to move on instead of clicking the trackpad or pressing Enter.**

- ✔ **Take advantage of Custom Wordlist, which is a list of words defined by you.** We describe this feature in a moment.

- ✔ **Type! Type! Type!** Because SureType learns how you type, the more you use it, the smarter it becomes in adapting to your style.

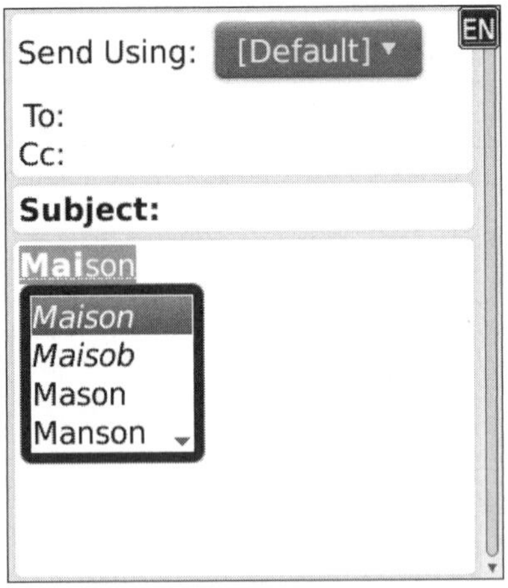

Figure 2-4: Lock in partially correct characters.

Send Using: [Default] ▾   EN
To:
Cc:
Subject:
Maison
Maison
Maisob
Mason
Manson

SureType versus multitap

You can type on your Pearl not only with SureType but also in *multitap* mode. The regular way — at least we think of it as the regular way — is the multitap approach. Suppose you want to type an *h* character on your Pearl. You search out the *h* on your keyboard but then notice to your dismay that the *h* shares a key with the letter *g*. What's a person to do? Do you really want to go through life writing *GHello* for *Hello?*

Your problem has an easy solution. To get to the letter *g*, you tap the GH key once. To get the letter *h* — the second letter in the key's pair — you tap the key twice — hence, the term *multitap*.

TIP

If you want to switch between multitap and SureType while you're typing, press the * key.

What about SureType? When you're in SureType mode, your Pearl tries to help you do the communication thing by figuring out what word you're typing. For example, if you want to type the word *hi*, you start by pressing the GH key and then the UI key. Doing so prompts SureType to display a list of words it thinks you may be aiming for, as shown in Figure 2-5.

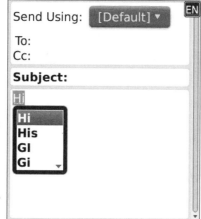

Figure 2-5: Now, did you want to type *hi* or *gi*?

If the first listed word is what you want, simply press the Space key. The word is automatically selected, and you can continue to type. If what you really wanted to type appears a little later in the list, simply scroll to it using the trackpad and select it by pressing the trackpad. Over time, SureType learns the words you're most likely to use and sticks those at the front of the list. Yup, that's right — it gets smarter the more you use it.

Custom Wordlist

SureType keeps all the words it learns in a safe place — a Wordlist, to be precise. You can review your SureType Wordlist — and even add to it — using the Custom Wordlist option. (Using this option to add words or proper names to the list means that SureType doesn't have to learn them while you're typing.)

To see or add words using the Custom Wordlist option, follow these steps:

1. From the Home screen, press the Menu key and select Options.

2. **Select Custom Wordlist.**

   The Custom Wordlist appears, and you see all the words that SureType has learned. (If you just got your BlackBerry, the list may have no words or only a few.)

3. **Press the Menu key and select New.**

   A dialog box appears, prompting you to type a new word, as shown in Figure 2-6.

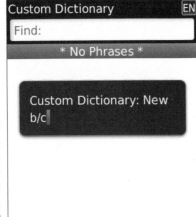

Custom Dictionary   EN

Find:

* No Phrases *

Custom Dictionary: New

b/c

Figure 2-6:
Adding
b/c to the
Custom
Wordlist.

4. **Type a custom word that you want to add, and then press the trackpad.**

   Your word is saved to Custom Wordlist.

SureType has a tough time getting people's names right, but thankfully, SureType can automatically learn all the names in your Address Book as follows:

1. **From the Home screen, press the Menu key and select Options.**

2. **Select Language.**

   You see the Language option screen, where the handy Input Option button makes its home.

3. **Scroll to the Show Text Input Options button and select it.**

   The Input Options screen appears with the following options:

   • **Frequency Learning:** If turned on, the word used most frequently appears first in the SureType word list while you type.

   • **Auto Word Learning:** If turned on, SureType learns as you type.

   • **Use Contacts as Data Source:** If turned on, SureType learns all the names in your Contacts.

4. **Make sure the Use Contacts as Data Source option is turned on.**

   If it isn't, scroll to this field, press the trackpad, and select On from the drop-down list.

5. **Save your changes by pressing the Menu key and selecting Save.**

Trackpad

You can perform two functions with the trackpad: scrolling and pressing down. When you scroll with the trackpad, you can navigate the display screen in four directions. In a text-filled screen such as the body of an e-mail, you can usually navigate through the text in four directions.

Depending on where you are on the screen, different situations determine what happens when you press the trackpad, also called the *trackpad click:*

✔ **Display a drop-down list:** When you're in a choice field, pressing the trackpad displays a drop-down list of choices for that field.

✔ **Confirm a choice:** The trackpad can function as a confirmation key. For example, to select the highlighted choice in a drop-down list, press the trackpad.

✔ **Display a short menu:** In a text-filled screen (the body of an e-mail or a Web page), press the trackpad to display an abbreviated version of the full menu (refer to Figure 2-4, right). To see the full menu, press the Menu key.

Menu key

As mentioned, you press the Menu key to display the full menu for the app you're using. When you're on the Home screen, pressing the Menu key displays a list of apps installed on your BlackBerry. If you want to change the order of the apps in the list, see Chapter 3.

If you press and hold the Menu key for two seconds, you can switch between apps while multitasking.

MicroSD slot

Your BlackBerry Pearl comes with 128 megabytes of memory, but a good chunk of that is taken up by apps that came with your Pearl. If you're a music or video fan, no need to worry. The folks at Research in Motion have incorporated a microSD slot in your Pearl so you can add extended memory and store all the media files you want.

To insert a microSD card, remove the battery cover. The microSD slot is located at the top.

Navigation Guidelines

Throughout the book, we show you application-specific shortcuts. In this section, however, we go over general navigational guidelines and shortcuts. Whether you're on a Web page full of text or in an e-mail message, you can perform the tasks in this section.

Following are navigational basics while reading a text-filled page or a list of items, such as a list of e-mail in the Message app:

- **Move to the top of the page:** Press the ER key
- **Move to the bottom of the page:** Press the CV key
- **Move to the next page:** Press the M or Space key
- **Move to the previous page:** Press the UI key
- **Move to the next line:** Press the BN key
- **Move to the previous line:** Press the TY key

Following are some editing basics:

- **Select a line:** Press and hold the Shift key and use the trackpad to scroll horizontally.
- **Select multiple lines:** Press and hold the Shift key and use the trackpad to scroll vertically.
- **Copy selected text:** Press the Alt key and the trackpad together.
- **Cut selected text:** Press the Shift and Del (delete) keys together.
- **Paste text:** Press the Shift key and the trackpad together.
- **Insert an accented letter:** Hold down a letter key and horizontally scroll the trackpad. As you scroll, that single letter changes on your screen. When you release the letter key, a list of all accents for that letter appears. You can scroll through the list and confirm the accented letter of your choice.
- **Insert a symbol:** Press the Symbol (SYM) key and select the desired symbol from the pop-up screen that appears.
- **Num lock:** Press the Shift and Alt keys together.
- **Switch between multitap and SureType:** When typing in a text field, press and hold the * key.

Switching apps

When you're navigating inside an app, you can quickly change apps. Just press and hold the Menu key for two seconds and select the app you want to switch to, as shown in Figure 2-7. In addition, the full menu always has the Switch Application option, which displays a list of apps you can switch to. Yet another way to switch apps is by pressing Alt and Escape.

Figure 2-7:
Change
apps with
the Switch
Application
menu.

Changing options

The easiest way to change the value in an option field is to first scroll to the field using the trackpad. Next, press the trackpad to see the drop-down list of choices, and then press the trackpad again on the option of your choice.

Chapter 3

Tweaking Your Pearl

*Y*our Pearl should look and sound unique, by reflecting your personality and fashion, not someone else's. In addition to customizing your BlackBerry Pearl so that it expresses the inner you, you should keep it in tip-top shape by watching out for battery life and information security. This chapter fills you in on all you need to know to keep your Pearl shiny, tuned, and quirkily personal.

Making Your BlackBerry Pearl Yours

Close to 60 million BlackBerry smartphones are serving the needs of people like you. Because of this fact, we're certain that finding ways to distinguish your BlackBerry from your colleagues' is high on your list of priorities.

Branding your BlackBerry Pearl

Like any number of electronic gadgets that you could possibly own, your BlackBerry Pearl comes to you off the shelf fitted with a collection of white-bread factory settings. This section helps you put your name on your Pearl, both figuratively and literally. You can start by branding your BlackBerry Pearl:

1. **From the Home screen, press the Menu key and select Options (the wrench icon).**

2. **Select the Owner setting.**

   You see spaces for entering your information.

3. **In the Name field, enter your name. In the Information field, enter your contact information.**

The idea here is to phrase a message (like the one shown in Figure 3-1) that would make sense to any possible Good Samaritan who might find your lost BlackBerry and want to return it to you.

If you lock or don't use your BlackBerry Pearl for a while, the standby screen comes on, displaying the owner information that you entered into the Options (Settings) screen. Read how to lock your BlackBerry Pearl, either manually or by using an auto setting, in "Keeping Your BlackBerry Safe," later in this chapter.

4. **Confirm your changes by pressing the Menu key and choosing Save.**

```
Owner
Name: Robert Kao
Information:
If found please contact
Rob.Kao@gmail.com
```

Figure 3-1:
List your
owner info
here.

Choose a language, any language

Branding your BlackBerry Pearl with your own John Hancock is a good start, but setting the language to your native tongue so you don't need to hire a translator to use your Pearl is equally important — and equally easy. You can also set your input method of choice here, which can affect whether AutoText shows up. Don't worry. We explain what that means.

Here's how to change the language setting:

1. **From the Home screen, press the Menu key and select Options (the wrench icon).**

2. **Select the Language setting.**

3. **Select the Language field. In the drop-down list that appears, select your native tongue.**

   Depending on your network provider, as well as your region (North America, Europe, and so on), the language choices you have vary.

Most handhelds sold in North America default to English or English (United States).

If your network provider supports it, you can install more languages in your BlackBerry Pearl by using Application Loader in the BlackBerry Pearl Desktop Manager. For installing more languages on your BlackBerry Pearl, contact your network service provider.

4. **Confirm your changes by pressing the Menu key and selecting Save.**

Isn't it great when you can actually read what's on the screen? But don't think that you're finished quite yet. You still have some personalizing to do.

Typing with ease using AutoText

Your BlackBerry Pearl comes equipped with an *AutoText feature,* which is a kind of shorthand that can help you cut down on how much you have to type. AutoText works with a few default abbreviations plus a pool of abbreviations that you set up. You then type an abbreviation to get the word you associated with that abbreviation. For example, if you set *b/c* as an AutoText word for *because,* anytime you type **b/c**, you automatically get *because* onscreen.

Here are some useful default AutoText entries:

- ✔ **mypin:** Displays your BlackBerry PIN

  We're talking about your BlackBerry Pearl PIN here — your device's unique identifying number — and not the PIN someone would use to empty your checking account with the help of one of those automated tellers. For more on BlackBerry PINs, see Chapter 9.

- ✔ **mynumber:** Displays your BlackBerry phone number
- ✔ **myver:** Displays your BlackBerry model number and OS version

The whole AutoText thing works only if you set up your own personal code, mapping your abbreviations to their meanings. (This is why we're discussing AutoText as part of our personalization discussion.) To set up your own code, do the following:

1. **From the Home screen, press the Menu key and select Options (the wrench icon).**

2. **Select the AutoText option.**

   Here, you can choose to see (or search for) existing AutoText words or create new ones.

3. **Press the Menu key and select New.**

   The AutoText screen appears.

4. **In the Replace field, enter the characters that you want to. Then, in the With field, type what replaces your characters.**

   In Figure 3-2, we entered *b/c* in the Replace field and *because* in the With field.

5. **In the Using field, choose SmartCase or Specified Case.**

   SmartCase capitalizes the first letter when the context calls for that, such as the first word in a sentence. Specified Case replaces your AutoText with the exact text found in the With field.

   For example, suppose that you have the AutoText *bbg* set up for the term *blackberryGoodies.com*, and you want it to appear as is, in terms of letter cases (the first *b* is not capitalized). If you were to choose SmartCase for this AutoText, it would be capitalized when it was the first word in a sentence, which is not what you want. On the other hand, if you use Specified Case, your AutoText always appears as *blackberryGoodies.com,* no matter where it is in the sentence.

6. **Confirm your changes by pressing the Menu key and selecting Save.**

Figure 3-2:
Create
AutoText
here.

```
AutoText: New
Replace:
b/c
With:
because|
Using:       [ SmartCase ▼ ]
Language:    [ All Locales ▼ ]
```

Establishing your dates and times

Having the correct date, time, and time zone is important when it comes to your BlackBerry Pearl for obvious reasons, we hope. When it comes to having the correct time, the easiest way is to let BlackBerry Pearl adjust it for you. How? Your Pearl can automatically set its time by using your network provider's server time. This way, you need not worry about daylight saving time.

However, even when using your network service provider's time, you still need to set up your time zone properly. Follow these steps:

1. **From the Home screen, press the Menu key and select Options (the wrench icon).**

2. **Select the Date/Time setting.**

   The Date/Time screen appears.

3. **Select the Time Zone field. In the drop-down list that appears, select Change Option.**

4. **In the Auto Update Time Zone field, select Prompt.**

   When you travel across different time zones, your BlackBerry can detect the time zone.

5. **For the Set Time field, select Manual.**

   By selecting Manual, your date and time source is set to your service provider's server time (see Figure 3-3), so the time will always be accurate.

   If you always set the time a few minutes earlier than the actual time (so you won't be late for those important meetings), set this field to No.

6. **For the Time and Date fields, select the proper date, hour, and minutes.**

   Here, you adjust the date and time to the current hours and minutes. These fields appear only if you selected Manual in Step 5.

7. **Confirm your changes by pressing the Menu key and selecting Save.**

   Doing so saves your date and time settings in perpetuity — a really long time, in other words.

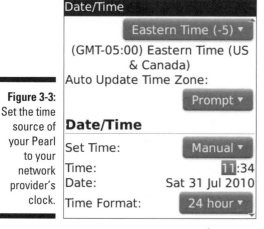

Figure 3-3:
Set the time source of your Pearl to your network provider's clock.

Customizing your screen's look and feel

Right up there with making sure that your date and time settings are accurate is getting the display font, font size, and screen contrast to your liking. Now we know that some of you don't give a hoot if your fonts are Batang or Bookman as long as you can read the text, but we also know that some of you won't stop configuring the fonts until you get them absolutely right. For all you tweakers out there, here's how you play around with your BlackBerry Pearl fonts:

1. **From the Home screen, press the Menu key and select Options (the wrench icon).**

2. **Select the Screen/Keyboard setting.**

   The Screen/Keyboard screen appears with various customizable fields, as shown in Figure 3-4.

Figure 3-4: The Screen/ Keyboard screen, waiting for personalization.

Screen/Keyboard	
Font Family:	BBAlpha Sans ▾
Font Size:	8 ▾
Font Style:	Plain ▾
The quick brown fox jumps over the lazy dog.	
Backlight Brightness:	100 ▾
Backlight Timeout:	30 Sec. ▾
Automatically Dim Backlight:	
	On ▾

3. **Select the Font Family field. In the drop-down list that appears, select the font you want.**

   The list contains three to ten fonts, depending on your provider.

4. **Select the Font Size field. In the drop-down list that appears, select the font size you want.**

   The smaller the font size, the more you can see onscreen; however, a smallish font is harder on the eyes.

   Note: As you scroll up and down the list of fonts and font sizes, notice that the text "The quick brown fox jumps over the lazy dog" takes on the look of the selected font and size so that you can preview the font.

5. **Confirm your changes by pressing the Menu key and selecting Save.**

Tuning Pearl navigation

With fonts out of the way, it's time to fine-tune the Pearl so that it navigates the way you want it to. To help you get to the apps that you need the most, the folks at Research in Motion have created two convenience keys that open apps.

To configure these convenience keys, follow these steps:

1. **From the Home screen, press the Menu key and select Options (the wrench icon).**

2. **Select the Screen/Keyboard setting.**

   The Screen/Keyboard screen appears with its various customizable fields (refer to Figure 3-4).

3. **Select the Right Side Convenience Key Opens field. In the drop-down list that appears, select the app you want.**

   For example, instead of the default camera, you can have the right side convenience key launch your browser.

4. **Select the Left Side Convenience Key Opens field. In the drop-down list that appears, select the app you want.**

   Select what you want your left side key to open when you press it.

   If you often multitask on your BlackBerry Pearl, you can configure one of your convenience keys to be the Application Switcher. This way, you can easily switch from, say, e-mailing to browsing.

5. **Select the Trackpad Horizontal Sensitivity field. In the drop-down list that appears, select an option.**

   This option determines how sensitive you want the trackpad to be horizontally. You can choose anywhere from 20 to 100 for this option, where 20 is the least sensitive and 100 is the most sensitive.

6. **Select the Trackpad Vertical Sensitivity field. In the drop-down list that appears, select an option.**

   This option is like the preceding one, only it determines the trackpad's vertical movement. Keep in mind that if your trackpad is too sensitive, it will be hard to control. On the other hand, if your trackpad is not sensitive enough, you may find it slow.

   Think of trackpad sensitivity settings as the mouse sensitivity on the PC. The correct sensitivity can be helpful for making the trackpad go exactly where you want it. Play around with vertical and horizontal sensitivities and adjust them to your liking.

7. **Confirm your changes by pressing the Menu key and selecting Save.**

Choosing themes for your BlackBerry

Your BlackBerry Pearl is preloaded with different themes depending on your provider, as shown in Figure 3-5. Themes can add flair to how your BlackBerry screen looks by way of fonts, color schemes for the text and screen background, wallpaper, and even how the Home screen icons are arranged.

To change your theme, follow these steps:

1. **From the Home screen, press the Menu key and select Options (the wrench icon).**

2. **Select the Theme setting.**

   You see a list of available themes.

3. **Select the theme you want.**

   You see a preview of the theme you've selected.

4. **Select Activate from the context menu that appears.**

   You see the change immediately.

Unlike the figure on the left in Figure 3-5, your BlackBerry Pearl, out of the box, probably doesn't come with a theme that lists all apps on the Home screen. To see the list of apps installed on your BlackBerry Pearl, you need to press the Menu key to see the app list, as shown in Figure 3-6. We know what you're thinking: What if you don't like the order in which apps are listed in the app list? Don't worry, you can change that order — and hide apps you don't often use.

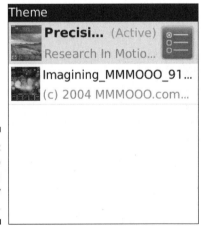

Figure 3-5:
Two
themes on a
BlackBerry
Pearl.

Figure 3-6:
Pop-up
showing a
list of apps.

To change the order of the apps in the app list, do the following:

1. **From the Home screen, press the Menu key.**

   You see a list of apps.

2. **Highlight the desired app, press the Menu key, and select Move Application.**

3. **Move the trackpad up and down to place the app into the desired order, as shown in Figure 3-7, and then press the trackpad.**

   You've completed the ordering of the app you selected in Step 2.

To hide an app, select Hide Application instead of Move Application in Step 2. A dimmed icon means it is currently hidden.

Figure 3-7:
Moving the
Browser
app.

The first five apps listed in the app list screen are the ones accessible from your Home screen. So choose your top five listed apps based on what you do the most on your BlackBerry Pearl.

Wallpaper for your BlackBerry

Like your desktop PC, you can customize your BlackBerry to have personalized wallpaper for your Home screen. You can set an image to be your BlackBerry Home screen background by using the BlackBerry Media app, as follows:

1. **From the Home screen, press the Menu key twice.**

2. **Select the Options menu.**

   You see the "Home Screen Preferences" screen.

3. **Select the Wallpaper field.**

4. **Select the picture you want to use for your home screen background**

   The selected picture appears in full-screen view.

5. **Press the Menu key and select Set as Wallpaper.**

   The picture is set as your new wallpaper.

6. **Press the Menu key and select Save.**

After you have your BlackBerry's look and feel just the way you want, there's just one thing left to do before you can move on: getting your BlackBerry to *sound* the way you want it to.

Letting freedom ring

The appeal of the BlackBerry is the idea that this little electronic device can make your life easier. One of the ways it accomplishes this is by acting as your personal reminder service — letting you know when an appointment is coming up, a phone call is coming in, an e-mail has arrived, and so on. Your BlackBerry is set to bark at you if it knows something it thinks you should know, too. Figure 3-8 lists the kinds of things your BlackBerry considers bark-worthy, ranging from browser alerts to task deadlines.

Different people react differently to different sounds. Some BlackBerry barks may be greatly appreciated by certain segments of the population, whereas other segments may react to the same sound by pitching their BlackBerry under the nearest bus. The folks at Research in Motion are well aware of this and have devised a great way for you to customize how you want your BlackBerry to bark at you — they call it your *profile*.

Figure 3-8:
Set atten-
tion-needy
apps here.

You can use a predefined profile, or you can create your own profile. We look at both approaches in this section. Whether you create your own profile or customize a predefined profile, each profile is divided into several categories that represent the app for which you can define alerts.

Profiles can be found in the Sound app. Items in the Sound app are organized into the following categories:

- ✔ **Phone:** Alerts you if you have an incoming call or voice mail.

- ✔ **Messages:** Alerts you if you have an incoming e-mail, SMS, MMS, or BlackBerry PIN message. Additionally, you can set different alerts for each individual e-mail account.

- ✔ **Instant Messages:** Alerts you if you have any BlackBerry Messenger alerts. If you have third-party instant messaging (such as Google Talk) installed, you can set its alerts here as well.

- ✔ **Reminders:** Alerts you if you have set up calendar reminders, tasks reminders, or e-mail follow-up flags (see Chapter 8).

- ✔ **Other:** Alerts for third-party app, such as Facebook, as well as the Browser app can be found here.

You can personalize all the listed apps according to how you want to be alerted. Because how you customize them is similar, we use one app, Messages, as an example in the text that follows.

After this, we go over creating a profile from scratch. You may be wondering why you need to create a profile if you can personalize the predefined ones. If your needs are different from the predefined settings, creating a profile is the way to go.

Customizing a predefined profile

If you want to customize a predefined, factory-loaded profile, just do the following:

1. **From the BlackBerry Home screen, select the Sound app.**

   A pop-up screen appears, listing different profiles (Silent, Vibrate, Normal, Loud, Medium, Phone Calls Only, All Alerts Off).

2. **Select Edit Profiles, which appears at the end of the list.**

   A screen appears, listing different profiles.

3. **Highlight the Normal profile in the list, press the Menu key, and then select Edit.**

   The Normal screen appears, listing the apps with alert capabilities mentioned in the preceding section (refer to Figure 3-6).

4. **Expand the Messages heading by clicking the trackpad once and then select an e-mail account.**

   A screen appears with options to set the ring tone, LED, and vibration.

5. **For Ring Tone, you can set the following options:**

   - **Ring Tone:** The ring tone you want.

   - **Volume:** The loudness of the ring tone, from Silent to 10 (the loudest).

   - **Count:** The number of times the ring tone repeats, from 1 to 3.

   - **Play Sound:** Whether the ring tone plays while your BlackBerry is in or out of the holster or whether it will always play.

6. **For LED, set it to On or Off.**

7. **For vibration, set it to On, Off, or Custom.**

   If you choose Custom, you have the following options:

   - **Length:** How long each vibration lasts: Short, Medium, or Long.

   - **Count:** The number of times the vibration occurs; you can choose 1, 2, 3, 5, or 10.

   - **Vibrate:** Whether the vibration will occur while your BlackBerry is in or out of holster or will always vibrate.

8. **Press the Menu key and then select Save.**

If you're like us and get more than 200 e-mails daily, you probably don't want your BlackBerry sounding off more than 200 times a day. You can set up your Pearl so that it notifies you only if an e-mail has been marked urgent, requiring your immediate attention. Begin by setting the notification for your Messages app to None (see Steps 4 and 5 in the preceding list) for both In

Holster and Out of Holster. Then, in the Level 1 option (refer to Figure 3-6), set your desired notification for both In Holster and Out of Holster. That way, you conveniently filter any unnecessary e-mail notifications, leaving just the urgent stuff to sound off to you.

Creating your own profile

You need to know which apps on your BlackBerry have alert capabilities because then you can personalize each "Hey, you!" to your liking. You can have your BlackBerry so personalized that you can tell whether you have a phone call or an incoming message just by how your BlackBerry sounds. As we mention earlier, you can personalize the predefined profiles that come with your BlackBerry. However, if you like to keep the predefined profiles the way they are, create a new profile by following these steps:

1. **From the BlackBerry Home screen, select the Sound app.**

   A pop-up screen appears, listing different profiles.

2. **Select Edit Profiles, which appears at the end of the list.**

   A screen appears, with Add Custom Profile and a list of profiles.

3. **Select Add Custom Profile.**

   A New Custom Profile screen appears, prompting you to name your profile.

4. **In the Name field, enter a name for your profile.**

   For this example, just type **MyOwnProfile**.

5. **Configure your new profile.**

   To customize each category of apps, refer to "Customizing a predefined profile," Steps 3–7.

6. **Press the Menu key and then select Save.**

   Your newly created profile appears on the Profile screen.

7. **Select My Profile.**

   You can start to use your newly created profile.

You can switch between your current profile and the Quiet profile by pressing and holding the # key.

Regardless of whether the ring tone is for an incoming call or an incoming e-mail, you can download more ring tones to personalize your BlackBerry. Additionally, you can use any MP3 file in your Media app as your personalized ring tone. Follow these steps:

1. **From the Home screen, press the Menu key and then select the Media app.**

2. **In Media, select the Music category.**

   You see various music classifications, such as Artist, Album, and Genres.

3. **Highlight the music file you want to use for your ring tone.**

4. **Press the Menu key and then select Set as Phone Tune.**

   This sets the music file as your new phone tune.

5. **Press and hold the Escape key to return to the Home screen.**

Keeping Your BlackBerry Safe

The folks at Research in Motion take security seriously, and so should you. Always set up a password on your BlackBerry Pearl. If your Pearl hasn't prompted you to set up a password, you should do so immediately. Here's how:

1. **From the Home screen, press the Menu key and select Options (the wrench icon).**

2. **Select the Password setting.**

3. **Select the Password field. In the drop-down list that appears, select Enabled.**

   All this does for now is enable the Password feature. You won't be prompted to type a password until you save the changes you just made.

4. **Confirm your changes by pressing the Menu key and selecting Save.**

   You are prompted for a password.

5. **Type a password and then type it again for verification.**

   From this point on, whenever you lock your BlackBerry Pearl and want to use it again, you have to type the same password. How to lock your BlackBerry? Good question. Keep reading.

Make sure to remember what your password is and not just which key you press. You need the same password if you link your BlackBerry Pearl with BlackBerry Desktop Manager for synchronization. For more on BlackBerry Desktop Manager, please refer to Chapter 16.

Setting up your password is a good first step, but just having a password won't help you much if you don't take the further step of locking your BlackBerry when you're not using it. (You don't want people at the office or sitting at the table next to you at the coffee shop checking out your e-mails or phone history when you take a bathroom break, do you?) So, how do you lock your BlackBerry? Let us count the ways. We came up with two.

You can go the Autolock After Timeout (also known as Security Timeout) route:

1. **From the Home screen, press the Menu key and select Options (the wrench icon).**

2. **Select the Password setting.**

3. **Select the Security Timeout field. In the drop-down list that appears, select the desired time.**

   The preset times range from 1 minute to 1 hour.

4. **Confirm your changes by pressing the Menu key and selecting Save.**

 To lock your Pearl on demand, simply press and hold the asterisk (*) key when you're on the Home screen. You probably would lock your Pearl if you want to prevent others from accessing your data or before you put your Pearl into your pocket.

No matter what route you take to lock your Blackberry Pearl, you use your (newly created) password to unlock it when you get back from wherever you've been.

Blocking Spam

You can block certain e-mails, SMS numbers, or BlackBerry PINs from getting to your inbox. To set up your personal spam blocker, follow these steps:

1. **From the Home screen, select the Options (wrench) icon.**

2. **Select the Security option.**

3. **Select the Firewall option.**

   The Firewall screen appears.

4. **Highlight the Status field and select Enable.**

   This enables the spam blocker.

5. **Under Block Incoming Message, select what you want to block:**

   - **SMS:** Blocks SMS messages.

   - **PIN:** Blocks BlackBerry PIN messages.

   - **BlackBerry Internet Service:** Blocks e-mail messages (for example, the e-mail account that you set up from Google or Yahoo! Mail).

   - **Enterprise Email:** Blocks enterprise e-mail (if you're in a corporate e-mail network).

6. **In the Except Messages From area, select the desired options:**

- **Contact:** Blocks everything except the e-mails and phone numbers in your Contacts.

- **Specific Address:** Blocks everything specified by you (you can set up the list described in Steps 7 and 8).

7. **Press the Menu key and then select Configure Exception.**

This opens the Firewall exception screen.

8. **Press the Menu key and then select the desired options:**

- **Add Email:** Specify the e-mail you want to block by selecting this check box.

- **Add PIN:** Specify the BlackBerry PIN you want to block by selecting this check box.

- **Add Phone Number:** Specify the SMS number you want to block by selecting this check box.

9. **Press the Menu key and select save to confirm your changes.**

Part II
Getting Organized

The 5th Wave
By Rich Tennant

"Don't be silly - of course my passwords are safe."

In this part . . .

Find out how to use your BlackBerry Pearl to its fullest to get — and remain — organized. Peruse Chapter 4 to find out how to use Contacts. See in Chapter 5 how to use the Calendar app to keep appointments. In Chapter 6, you use the Clock app to set alarms, use the timer, and switch to bedside mode, as well as use Password Keeper to keep your passwords safe and easy to retrieve. Finally, in Chapter 7, you see how to take advantage of the many features of the Phone app.

Chapter 4

Remembering and Locating Your Acquaintances

The Contacts app on the BlackBerry Pearl serves the same function as any address book: an organizational tool that gives you a place to record information about people. From one central place, you can retrieve information for reaching your contacts through phone, cell phone, e-mail, snail mail, or the speedy messaging of PIN, SMS, MMS, or BlackBerry Messenger.

In this chapter, we show you how to make your BlackBerry Pearl a handy, timesaving tool for managing your contacts' information. Specifically, you find out how to add, change, and delete contacts as well as how to locate them later. You'll be amazed at how well Contacts is integrated with all the other BlackBerry features you've come to know and love — phoning contacts, adding invites to your meetings, adding contacts to BlackBerry Messenger, and composing e-mails. You can even sync your BlackBerry contacts and Facebook friends, so you'll always get the profile updates to your BlackBerry.

Accessing Contacts

The Contacts icon, shown in Figure 4-1, looks like an old-fashioned address book. Opening Contacts couldn't be simpler: Select the Contacts icon from the Home screen. You can open Contacts also by pressing the Menu key and choosing Contacts.

Figure 4-1:
You can
move icons
to a new
location.

You can also access Contacts from the Phone, Messages, BlackBerry Messenger, and Calendar apps. For example, if you are using the Calendar app and you want to invite people to one of your meetings, Contacts is in the menu, ready to lend a helping hand.

Working with Contacts

Now that you have a new BlackBerry Pearl, the first thing you'll want to do is call or e-mail someone, right? But wait a sec — you don't have any contact information yet, which means you're going to have to type someone's phone number or e-mail address each time you want to reach him or her — what a hassle.

Most of us humans — social creatures that we are — maintain a list of contacts somewhere, whether in an old cell phone, or maybe on a piece of paper tucked away in a wallet. The trick is getting that list into your BlackBerry Pearl so that you can access the info more efficiently. The good news for you is that the getting contact info into your BlackBerry isn't difficult. Stick with us, and you'll have it down pat by the end of this chapter.

Often the simplest way to get contact information into your BlackBerry Pearl is to enter it manually. However, if you've invested a lot of time and energy in maintaining some type of contacts application on your desktop computer, you may want to sync that data into your BlackBerry. For more on synchronizing data, check Chapter 17.

Creating a new contact

Do you have to chant someone's phone number because you can't scare up a writing implement? Not if you have your handy BlackBerry device with you. With BlackBerry in hand, follow these steps to create a new contact:

1. **On the BlackBerry Home screen, select the Contacts app.**

   As mentioned, you can access Contacts also from different apps. For example, see Chapter 8 to find out how to access Contacts from Messages.

2. **Press the Menu key and select New Contact.**

   The New Contact screen appears, as shown in Figure 4-2 (left).

3. **Use the keyboard to enter contact info in the appropriate fields.**

   While entering an e-mail address, press the Space key to insert an at symbol (@) or a period (.). BlackBerry is smart enough to figure out that you need an @ or a period.

4. **(Optional) For contacts with more than one e-mail address, do the following:**

   a. **Press the Menu key and select Add Email Address.**

      A new, blank Email field appears.

   b. **Enter the additional information.**

      You can have up to three e-mail addresses for each contact.

5. **When you finish entering contact information, press the Menu key and select Save.**

   Your new contact is added to the list, as shown in Figure 4-2 (right).

Figure 4-2: Create a new contact (left), and Contacts after adding Jane Doe (right).

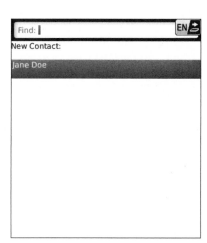

The importance of contact info

We don't think you can overdo it when entering a person's contact information. Enter as much info as you possibly can. The benefit may not be obvious now, but when your memory fails or your boss needs a critical piece of info that you just so happen to have at the ready, you'll thank us for this advice.

Here's something slick to know when you're entering phone information for a contact: BlackBerry can also dial an extra number after the initial phone number. That extra number can be someone's extension, or a participant code on a conference number, or simply your voice mail PIN. When you're entering the contact's phone number, type the primary phone number, press the Alt key and X, and then add the extension number. Suppose you enter 11112345678X1111; when you tell your BlackBerry to call that number, it will dial 11112345678 first. When a call is established, you'll see a prompt asking you to continue or skip dialing the extension. If you don't respond to the prompt after a short delay, the extension is dialed automatically.

Although the menu is always available through the Menu key, we prefer to use the trackpad, which displays a shortened menu list based on where you are.

Adding notes

The Notes field on the New Contact screen (you may need to scroll down a bit to see it) is useful for adding a unique description about your contact. For example, use the field to hold info to refresh your memory with tidbits such as *Knows somebody at ABC Corporation* or *Can provide introduction to a Broadway agent.* Or perhaps your note is something personal, such as *Likes golf; has 2 children: boy, 7, & girl, 3; husband's name is Ray.* It's up to you. Again, the more useful the information, the better it will serve you.

Customizing with your own fields

Perhaps your contact information really doesn't fit into any of the available fields. Although you can't create additional fields from scratch, you can commandeer one of the User fields for your own purposes.

The User fields are located at the bottom of the screen — you have to scroll down to see them. You can use these fields any way you want, and you can even change the field's name. (Face it, *User field* is not a descriptive title.) For example, you could rename a User field to capture suffixes (such as MD, PhD, and so on). Or how about profession, birth date, hobbies, school, or nickname? You decide what information is important to you.

Changing the field name for this particular contact changes it for all your contacts.

To rename a User field:

1. **Scroll to the bottom of the screen and place your cursor in a User fields.**

2. **Press the Menu key and select Change Field Name.**

   The Change Field Name selection appears only if the cursor is in a User field.

3. **Use the keyboard to enter the new User field name.**

4. **To save your changes, press the trackpad or the Enter key.**

Adding a picture

Like most phones, your BlackBerry can display a picture of the caller. Here's how to add a photo for a contact:

1. **Get a digital picture of the person, and then transfer that photo to your Blackberry.**

   See Chapter 13 for more about taking photos with your BlackBerry. You can send the picture through e-mail, copy it to the microSD card, or copy it to the built-in memory of BlackBerry. For information on using the microSD card, see Chapter 15, your gateway to managing media files.

2. **From the Home screen, select the Contacts icon.**

3. **Highlight a contact, press the Menu key, and then select Add Picture, as shown in Figure 4-3.**

Figure 4-3:
Add a pic-
ture here.

4. **Use the trackpad to navigate to the drive and folder that contains the picture. Then select the picture.**

   You can use multiple locations for storing media files, such as pictures. Chapter 15 gives you the scoop. When you select the pic, it is displayed in full onscreen, with a rectangle over it.

5. **Use the trackpad to position the rectangle on the face, then click the trackpad and select Crop and Save.**

Contacts uses a tiny image, just enough to show the face of a person. The rectangle you see here within the full picture indicates how the app crops the image.

6. **Press the Menu key and then select Save.**

Assigning a tone

Oh, no, your ringing BlackBerry has woken you. Ring tones help you decide whether to ignore the call or get up. Switch to Sleep mode if you decide to ignore the call.

Follow these steps to assign a ring tone to one of your contacts:

1. **While editing a contact on the Edit Contact screen, scroll to the Ring Tones/Alerts section.**

   (See the "Editing a contact" section for info on editing.) In the Ring Tones/Alerts section, you see Phone and Messages. You can customize the ring tone when you receive a call and when you have a new message, such as an e-mail or an SMS.

2. **Select Phone and then customize the ring tone on the screen that follows.**

   You see and can change the following options:

   • **Ring Tone:** Select a ring tone from a list of tones here.

   • **Volume:** Control the volume. The default is set to use the Active Profile settings. Other values are 1 to 10; 10 is the loudest.

   • **Play Sound:** Control in what state to play the tone. Values are Active Profile, In Holster, Out of Holster, and Always; the default is set to Active Profile.

   • **LED:** Use the LED to indicate a call.

   • **Vibration:** Enable vibration as a way of notification. Choices are Active Profile, Off, On, and Custom. The default is Active Profile. Choosing Custom allows you to control how long you want the vibration to last.

   • **Vibrate with Ring Tone:** Choose between vibrating and playing the tone. Choices are Active Profile, On, and Off. The default value is Active Profile.

3. **Press the Escape key.**

   You're back to the Edit Contact screen.

4. **Select Messages.**

   You are presented with the Messages screen, which allows you to customize the ring tone when you receive a message. You can do all the customizations listed in Step 2 plus the following:

   • **Notify Me During Calls:** Toggle notification while you're actively on a call. Your choices are Yes or No, and the default is No.

5. **Press the Escape key.**

6. **Press the Menu key and then select Save.**

Spend a little time adding your own contact record(s). We recommend adding at least one record for your business contact info and one for your personal contact info. This step saves you from having to type your own contact information every time you want to give it to someone. You can share your contact record by sending it as an attachment to an e-mail. (See the later section "Sharing a Contact.")

Adding contacts from other BlackBerry apps

When you get an e-mail message or a call, that person's contact information is in Messages or Phone. It's just logical to add the information. You may have noticed that the Phone app lists only outgoing numbers. That's half of what you need. You can access incoming phone calls in Messages:

1. **On the BlackBerry Home screen, select Messages.**

2. **In Messages, press the Menu key and then select View Folder.**

3. **Select Phone Call Logs.**

A phone log entry stays only as long as you have free space on your BlackBerry Pearl. When BlackBerry runs out of space (which could take years, depending on how you use it), it deletes read e-mails and phone logs, starting from the oldest.

You can view your device memory information by selecting Options (the wrench icon) from the Home screen and then selecting Memory. The screen shows you three types of memory: application memory, device memory, and media card. Pay close attention to application memory because this is where your apps are installed, including data from out-of-the-box apps such as Contacts, Messages, and Calendar. Your BlackBerry has a limited amount of application memory, and you should see how much is free on this screen. If free application memory drops below 10MB, your device may slow down a bit, and if it approaches 0MB, your device may lag. At this point, you need to free some space:

✔ Pull the battery to immediately net some space because apps that are running and using memory will close.

✔ Delete unused apps.

✔ Remove unnecessary bloatware that comes preloaded on the device (such as movie trailers and sample photos).

Creating a contact from an existing e-mail address or phone number in Messages is easy:

1. **On the BlackBerry Home screen, select Messages.**

2. **In Messages, select the e-mail address or the phone number.**

3. **Select Add to Contacts.**

   A New Contact screen appears, filled with that particular piece of information.

4. **Enter the rest of the information you know.**

5. **Press the Menu key and then select Save.**

The best solution for capturing contact information from e-mail is an app called gwabbit. The app has the intelligence of detecting contact information and gives you a quick and easy way to add the info to Contacts. You can purchase gwabbit for $9.99 a year and download the app from its Web site at www.gwabbit.com.

Viewing a contact

Suppose that you just entered your friend's name, *Jane,* into your BlackBerry, but you have a nagging thought that you typed the wrong phone number. You want to quickly view Jane's information. Here's how you do it:

1. **On the BlackBerry Home screen, select Contacts.**

2. **In Contacts, scroll to and highlight the contact name you want and then press the trackpad.**

   Pressing the trackpad or the Enter key while a name is highlighted is the same as opening the menu and choosing View — just faster.

   View mode displays only information that's been filled in, as shown in Figure 4-4. It doesn't bother showing blank fields.

Jane Doe

Email: jane.doe@blackberryfordummies.com
Work: 212-111-2222

Figure 4-4:
View mode
for a
contact.

Editing a contact

Change is an inevitable part of life. Given that fact, your contact information is sure to change as well. To keep current the information you diligently put in Contacts, you have to do some updating now and then.

To update a contact, follow these steps:

1. **On the BlackBerry Home screen, select Contacts.**

2. **Scroll to and highlight a contact name, press the Menu key, and then select Edit.**

   The Edit Contact screen for that contact makes an appearance.

   In Contacts (or any BlackBerry app, for that matter), displaying a menu involves a simple press of the Menu key. The Edit option is on the menu right below View.

3. **Scroll through the various fields of the Edit Address screen, editing the contact information as you see fit.**

   If you want to replace only a few words or letters located in the middle of a field (rather than replace the entire text), hold down the Alt key while scrolling the trackpad to position your cursor precisely on the text you want to change. Then make your desired changes.

4. **Press the Menu key and select Save.**

   The edit you made for this contact is saved.

When you're editing information and want to totally replace the entry with a new one, it's much faster to first clear the contents, especially if the old data is long. When you're in an editable field (as opposed to a selectable field), just press the Menu key and select the Clear Field option. This feature is available in all text-entry fields and for most BlackBerry apps.

Deleting a contact

When it's time to eradicate someone's contact information (whether a case of duplication or a bit of bad blood), BlackBerry makes it easy:

1. **On the BlackBerry Home screen, select Contacts.**

2. **Scroll to and highlight a contact name you want to delete, press the Menu key, and then select Delete.**

   A confirmation screen appears, as shown in Figure 4-5.

3. **Select Delete.**

   The contact is deleted and disappears from your Contacts list.

Dealing with the Confirmation screen can be a pain if you want to delete several contacts in a row. If you are 100 percent sure that you want to ditch a number of contacts, you can suspend the Confirmation feature by setting the Confirm Delete option to No in the Contacts Options screen. See the "Setting preferences" section, later in this chapter, for more on Contacts options.

Figure 4-5:
The con-
firmation
screen
when you're
about to
delete a
contact.

Copying Contacts from Desktop Applications

Most people use desktop applications to maintain their contacts — you know, Microsoft Outlook, IBM Lotus Notes, or Novell GroupWise. A word to the wise: Maintaining two address books is a recipe for disaster. Luckily,

Research in Motion makes it easy for you to get your various contacts —
BlackBerry, desktop, laptop, whatever — in sync.

Your BlackBerry comes with a collection of programs called BlackBerry
Desktop Manager, one of which is Synchronize. You can use Synchronize to

✔ Sync between your device and the PC software for managing contacts,
such as Outlook.

✔ Set up and configure the behavior of the program, including how the
fields in the desktop version of Contacts map to the Contacts fields in
your BlackBerry.

Chapter 17 shows you how to use Synchronize.

Looking for Someone?

Somehow — usually through a combination of typing skills and the shuttling
of data between electronic devices — you've created a nice long list of contacts in your Contacts. Nice enough, we suppose, but useless unless you can
find the phone number of Rufus T. Firefly at the drop of a hat.

That's where the Find screen comes in. When you open Contacts, the first
thing you see is the Find screen, as shown in the left screen in Figure 4-6.

You can conveniently search through your contacts by following these steps:

1. **In the Find field, start typing the name you want to search for.**

   Your search criterion is the name of the person. You can enter the last
   name or first name or both.

   The list is usually sorted by first name and then last name. As you type,
   notice that the list starts shrinking based on the matches on the letters
   you enter. The right screen in Figure 4-6 illustrates how this works.

2. **Using the trackpad, scroll and highlight the name from the list of matches.**

   If you have a long list in Contacts and want to scroll down a page at a
   time, just hold down the Alt key (it's located to the left of the Z key) and
   scroll. You get where you need to go a lot faster.

3. **Press the Menu key and select from the possible actions listed on the
   menu that appears.**

   After you find the person you want, you can select from the following
   options, some of which are shown in Figure 4-7:

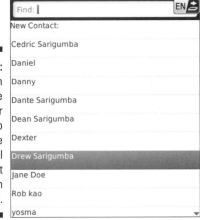

Figure 4-6: Your search starts here (left). Enter letters to shorten the potential contact list search (right).

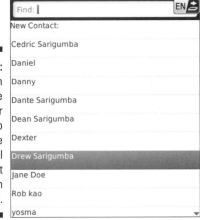

Figure 4-7: Options for the selected contact.

- **Activity Log:** Opens a screen listing e-mails, calls, and SMS messages you've made to the contact.

- **View Work Map:** Appears only if you have filled in work address information. This option allows you to map a location using Maps.

- **Email:** Starts a new e-mail message. See Chapter 8 for more information about e-mail.

- **PIN:** Starts a new PIN-to-PIN message, which is a messaging system unique to BlackBerry. With PIN-to-PIN, you can send someone who has a BlackBerry a quick message. See Chapter 9 for more details about PIN-to-PIN messaging.

- **Call:** Uses the phone to dial the number.

- **SMS:** Starts a new SMS message. SMS is short for *Short Messaging Service,* which is used in cell phones. See Chapter 9 for more details about SMS.

- **SIM Phone Book:** This menu option enables you to view contacts saved on the SIM card.

- **MMS:** Starts an MMS message. MMS is short for *Multimedia Messaging Service,* an evolution from SMS that supports voice and video clips. See Chapter 9 for details about MMS. The MMS item appears in the menu only if you've filled in the contact's Mobile field.

- **Send as Attachment:** Starts a new e-mail message with the contact as an attachment. See Chapter 8 for more information.

- **Forward Contact:** Allows you to forward this contact to one of your BlackBerry Messenger contacts. (This option appears only if you have BlackBerry Messenger installed.)

If you have a finger-fumble and press a letter key in error, press the Escape key once to return to the original list (the one showing all your contacts), or press the Menu key once and select View All.

You aren't hallucinating: Sometimes `Email <contact name>` or `Call <contact name>` appears on the menu, and sometimes it doesn't. Contacts knows when to show those menu options. If a contact has a phone number, `Call <contact name>` and `SMS <contact name>` show up, and the same is true for e-mail and the personal identification number (PIN). In fact, this list of actions is a convenient way to find out whether you have particular information — a phone number or an e-mail address — for a particular contact.

In a corporate environment, your BlackBerry Enterprise server administrator may disable PIN-to-PIN messaging because it doesn't go to the corporate e-mail servers and, therefore, can't be monitored. If this is the case, the menu option `PIN<contact name>` won't appear, even though you entered PIN information for your contacts. You can still receive a PIN-to-PIN message, but you won't be able to send one.

Organizing Your Contacts

You've been diligent about adding your contacts to Contacts, and your list has been growing at a good clip. It now has all the contact info for your business colleagues, clients, and (of course) family, friends, and relatives.

Imagine that you just saw an old acquaintance, and you want to greet the person by name. You know that if you saw the name, you'd recognize it. The trouble is that your list has 300-plus names, which would take so long to scroll through that this acquaintance would surely come right up to you in the meantime, forcing you to hide the fact that you can't remember his name. (How embarrassing.) In this scenario, the tried-and-true Find feature wouldn't be much help. What you need is a smaller pool of names to search.

Simply do one of the following:

- ✔ **Organize your contacts into groups.** Using groups (as every kindergarten teacher can tell you) is a way to arrange something (in your case, contacts) to make them more manageable. How you arrange your groups is up to you. For example, you can place all your customer contacts in a Clients group and place family members and relatives in a Family group.

- ✔ **Set up your contacts so that you can filter them.** Use the Filter feature in combination with BlackBerry's Categories. (Using *Categories,* you can label your contacts to make it easy to filter them.) The Filter feature can narrow the Contacts list to such an extent that all you have to do is scroll down and find your contact — no need to type search keywords, in other words.

Whether you use the Group or Filter feature is up to you. You'll find out how to use both methods in the next sections.

Creating a group

A BlackBerry group in Contacts — as opposed to any other kind of group you can imagine — is a simple filter or category. In other words, a *group* arranges your contacts into subsets without affecting the content of your contact entries. In Contacts, a group shows up in the contact list just like any other contact. The only wrinkle here is that when you select the group, the contacts associated with that group — and *only* the contacts associated with that group — appear onscreen.

Need some help visualizing how this works? Go ahead and create a new group, following these steps:

1. **On the BlackBerry Home screen, select Contacts.**

2. **Press the Menu key and select New Group.**

   A screen similar to that shown on the left of Figure 4-8 appears. The top portion of the screen is where you type the group name, and the bottom portion is where you add your list of group members.

3. **Type the name of the group in the New Group field.**

   You can name the group anything. We named it Poker Buddies.

4. **Click the trackpad and then select Add Member.**

   The main Contacts list shows up in all its glory, ready to be pilfered.

5. **Select the contact you want to add to your new group list, click the trackpad, and then select Continue from the menu that appears.**

   Everyone knows a Rob Kao, so select him. Doing so places Rob Kao in your Poker Buddies group list, as shown to the right of Figure 4-8.

The contact must have at least an e-mail address or a phone number if you simply want to add the contact to a group and not necessarily use the group as a distribution list. (Contacts is strict on this point.) If you need to skirt this roadblock, edit that contact's information and put in a fake (and clearly inactive) e-mail address, such as `notareal@emailaddress.no`.

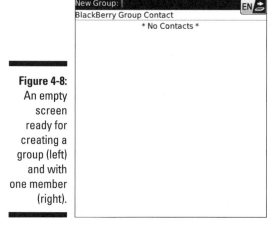

Figure 4-8: An empty screen ready for creating a group (left) and with one member (right).

6. **Repeat Steps 4 and 5 to add more friends to your list.**

7. **Press the Menu key and select Save Group.**

   Your Poker Buddies group is duly saved, and Poker Buddies is listed on your main Contacts list.

Groups is a valuable tool for creating an e-mail distribution list. When adding members to a group, make sure that you select an e-mail address field for your members instead of a phone number. Also, use a naming convention to easily distinguish your group in the list. Appending *-DL* or *-Distribution List* to the group name can quickly indicate a distribution list.

You can quote me on this one

You create groups so that you can easily scroll through your contacts, right? Assuming that you have a long list, your Family group can be buried in the middle of it — given where *F* falls in the alphabet. Or, you may not even remember one of the group names you used.

(How embarrassing.) One simple technique to make a group appear at the very top of your contact list is to enclose it within single quotes. For example, instead of naming your group *Friends,* you could name it *'Friends.'*

Using the Filter feature on your contacts

Are you a left-brainer or a right-brainer? Yankees fan or Red Sox fan? An innie or an outie? Dividing up the world into categories is something everyone does (no divisions there), so it should come as no surprise that BlackBerry divides your contacts into distinct categories as well.

By default, two categories are set for you on the BlackBerry: Business and Personal. But why stop at two? BlackBerry makes it easy to create more categories. In this section, you first find out how to categorize a contact and then you see how to filter your Contacts list. Finally, you find out how to create categories.

Categorizing your contacts

You create a contact or edit an existing contact in Edit mode. Getting into Edit mode is simple:

1. **On the BlackBerry Home screen, select Contacts.**

2. **Highlight the contact, press the Menu key, and then select Edit.**

   Contacts is now in Edit mode for this particular contact, which is exactly where you want to be.

3. **Press the Menu key and then select Categories.**

   A Categories list appears, as shown in Figure 4-9. By default, you see only the Business and the Personal categories.

4. **Click the trackpad or the Space key to select the check box next to Personal.**

5. **Press the Menu key and then select Save.**

   You're brought back to the Edit screen for this particular contact.

6. **Click the trackpad and select Save (again) from the menu that appears.**

Select Category
Business
Personal

Figure 4-9:
Default
categories.

Filtering your contacts

You now have one — count 'em, one — contact with Personal as its category, which means you can filter your Contacts list by using a category. Here's how:

1. **On the BlackBerry Home screen, select Contacts.**

2. **Press the Menu key and then select Filter.**

    Your Categories list appears.

    If you haven't added any categories in the meantime, you see only the default Business and Personal categories.

3. **Select the Personal check box.**

    Your Contacts list shrinks to just the contacts assigned to the Personal category, as shown in Figure 4-10.

As you add more contacts to a category, you can also use Find and enter the first few letters of the name to further narrow the search for a contact. If you need a refresher on how Find works, see the "Looking for Someone?" section, earlier in this chapter.

Adding a new category

Whoever thought the default categories (Business and Personal) were enough for the complexities of the real world didn't have many acquaintances. It's easy to add categories, so you can divide your world as much as you like:

1. **On the BlackBerry Home screen, select Contacts.**

2. **Press the Menu key and select Filter.**

    You get a view of the default categories (refer to Figure 4-9).

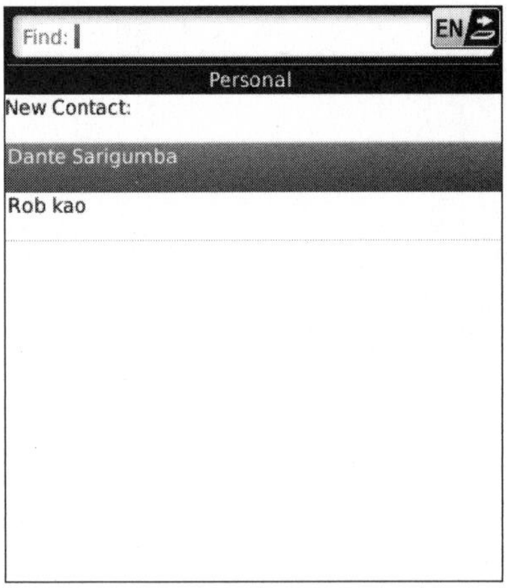

Find:	EN

Personal

New Contact:

Dante Sarigumba

Rob kao

Figure 4-10:
The
Contacts
list after
applying a
filter.

3. **Press the Menu key and select New.**

A pop-up screen asks you to name the new category.

4. **In the Name field, type the name of the category and then press the trackpad.**

The category is automatically saved. The Filter screen lists all the categories, including the one you just created.

5. **To get back to the Contacts main screen, press the Escape key.**

Setting preferences

Vanilla, anyone? Some days, you'll wish that your Contacts list was sorted differently. For example, there's the day when you need to find the guy who works for ABC Company but has a foreign name that you can hardly pronounce, let alone spell. What's a body to do?

You're in luck. Contacts Options navigates some out-of-the-ordinary situations. Figure 4-11 shows the Contacts Options screen, which, despite its simplicity, provides four important options that change the behavior of Contacts:

✔ **Sort By:** Changes how the list is sorted. You can use First Name, Last Name, or Company. Use the Space key to toggle among the choices. Remember that guy from ABC Company? You can use the Sort By option to sort by company so that all contacts from ABC Company are listed next to one another. With any luck, the guy's name will jump out at you.

✔ **Separators:** Changes the dividers in the Contacts list. It's purely an aesthetic change, but check it out — you may like the stripes.

Figure 4-11:
Choose your
sort type
here.

✔ **Allow Duplicate Names:** Self-explanatory. If you turn on this option, your Contacts list can contain multiple people who happen to share the same name. If you disable this option, you get a warning when you try to add a name that matches one already on your list. Maybe you are tired and are mistakenly trying to add the same person twice. Then again, sometimes people just have the same name. We recommend keeping the default value of Yes, allowing you to have contacts with the same names.

✔ **Confirm Delete:** Displays a confirmation screen for all contact deletions.

Always keep the Confirm Delete feature turned on for normal usage. You can inadvertently delete someone from your Contacts in many ways, so this feature minimizes accidents.

How do you change any of these options? The fields behave like any other field in a BlackBerry app. You simply highlight the field, press the trackpad to display a menu from which you can select the possible values. For example,

Figure 4-12 shows the possible Sort By fields.

Sharing a Contact

Suppose you want to share your contact information with a friend who also has a BlackBerry. A *vCard* — virtual (business) card — is your answer and can make your life a lot easier. In BlackBerry land, a vCard is a contact in Contacts that you send to someone as an attachment to an e-mail.

At the receiving end, the BlackBerry (being the smart device that it is) recognizes the attachment and informs the BlackBerry owner that he or she has the option of saving it, making it available for his or her viewing pleasure in Contacts.

Contacts Options

Views

Sort By:

First Name ▼
Last Name
Company ▼

Separators:

Actions

Allow Duplicate Names: Yes ▼

Confirm Delete: Yes ▼

Figure 4-12:
The Sort
By field
options.

Sending a vCard

Because a vCard is nothing more than a Contacts contact attached to an e-mail, sending a vCard is a piece of cake. (Of course, you do need to make sure that your recipient has a BlackBerry device to receive the information.)

Here's how you go about sending a vCard:

1. **On the BlackBerry Home screen, select the Messages app.**

2. **Press the Menu key and select Compose Email.**

   A screen where you can compose a new e-mail appears.

3. **In the To field, start typing the name of the person to whom you want to send this vCard.**

4. **When you see the name in the drop-down list, highlight it and then click the trackpad.**

   You see an e-mail screen with the name you just selected as the To recipient.

5. **Type the subject and message.**

6. **Press the Menu key and then select Attach Contact.**

   Contacts opens.

7. **Highlight the name of the person whose contact information you want to attach and then click the trackpad.**

   The e-mail composition screen reappears, and an icon that looks like a book indicates that the e-mail now contains your attachment. Now all you have to do is send your e-mail.

8. **Click the trackpad and select Send from the menu that appears.**

   You just shared the specified contact information. (Don't you feel right neighborly now?)

Receiving a vCard

If you get an e-mail with a contact attachment, you can save it to your Contacts as follows:

1. **On the BlackBerry Home screen, select Messages.**

2. **Select the e-mail that contains the vCard.**

   The e-mail with the vCard attachment opens.

3. **Scroll down to the attachment. When the cursor is hovering over the attachment, click the trackpad and select View Attachment from the menu that appears.**

   The vCard makes an appearance onscreen.

4. **Press the Menu key and select Add to Contacts.**

   The vCard is saved and is available in Contacts.

Searching for Someone outside Your Contacts

Does your employer provide your BlackBerry? Do you use Outlook or Lotus Notes on your desktop machine at work? If you answer yes to both questions, this section is for you.

BlackBerry Contacts allows you to search for people in your organization using any of the following programs, which contain employee databases:

- ✔ Microsoft Exchange (for Outlook)
- ✔ IBM Domino (for Lotus Notes)
- ✔ Novell GroupWise

Exchange, Domino, and GroupWise facilitate e-mail delivery in a corporate environment and enable access to a database of names: Global Address Lists (GALs) in Exchange, Notes Address Books in Domino, and GroupWise Address Books in GroupWise.

To search for someone in your organization through a database of names, simply follow these steps:

1. **On the BlackBerry Home screen, select Contacts.**

2. **Press the Menu key and select Lookup.**

   Some corporations may not enable the Lookup feature. Please check with your IT department for more information.

3. **Type the name you're searching for and then click the trackpad.**

   You can enter the beginning characters of a person's last or first name. You are searching your company's database, not Contacts, so this step may take some time.

   For big organizations, we recommend being more precise when searching. For example, searching for *Dan* yields more hits than searching for *Daniel.* The more precise your search criteria, the fewer hits you'll get, and the faster the search will be.

   While the search is in progress, you see *Lookup* and the criteria you put in. For example, if you enter **Daniel,** the top row reads Lookup: Daniel. After the search is finished, BlackBerry displays the number of hits, or matches — for example, 20 matches: Daniel.

4. **Select the number of matches.**

   A header at the top of this screen details the matches displayed in the current screen as well as the total hits. For example, if the header reads something like Lookup Daniel (20 of 130 matches), 130 people in your organization have the name Daniel, and BlackBerry is displaying the first 20. You have the option of fetching more by clicking the trackpad and choosing Get More Results from the menu that appears.

   You can add the listed name(s) to your Contacts by using the Add command (for the currently highlighted name) or the Add All command for all the names in the list. (As always, click the trackpad to call up the menu that contains these options.)

5. **Select the person whose information you want to review.**

   The person's contact information is displayed on a read-only screen (you can read the info but not change it). You may see the person's title; e-mail address; work, mobile, and fax numbers; and snail-mail address at work. Any of that information gives you confirmation about the person you're looking for. Of course, what shows up depends on the availability of this information in your company's database.

Synchronizing Facebook Contacts

Do you network like a social butterfly? You must be using one of the popular social networking applications, such as MySpace or Facebook, and want to copy the contact information of your tons of friends to your BlackBerry. Individual networking sites have their own way to achieve this task. In this section, we show you how to get your Facebook contacts into your BlackBerry Pearl.

The latest Facebook app (version 1.8.0.49 as of this writing), makes it easy to get Facebook contacts into your BlackBerry. The Facebook app also allows you to synchronize information between your BlackBerry and your friend's information in Facebook.

Adding a Facebook friend's info to Contacts

As mentioned, pulling down your friend's information from Facebook is easy:

1. **On the BlackBerry Home screen, select the Facebook icon.**

   The Facebook application is filed under the Downloads folder.

2. **Press the Menu key and then press F.**

   Your friend's list shows up in the screen similar to Figure 4-13, left.

3. **In the Find field, start typing your friend's name.**

   This narrows the list, as shown in Figure 4-13, right.

Figure 4-13: Select Facebook friends to add to Contacts here.

4. **Highlight the friend you want to add to Contacts, press the Menu key, and then select Connect to BlackBerry Contact.**

   A dialog box appears, as shown in Figure 4-14, allowing you to choose whether to connect this Facebook friend to an existing contact or add the friend as a new contact to your BlackBerry. In this case, you want to add.

Figure 4-14: Connect a Facebook friend to an existing contact or add a new contact here.

If the same person exists in your BlackBerry and in Facebook, you can simply link the contact here. Also, see the next section to get an automatic update on your BlackBerry whenever your friend changes his or her profile in Facebook.

Connect in the Facebook application means telling the app which contact is associated with a Facebook friend. After the app records this linkage, it knows which contact to update when information in Facebook changes.

5. **Select New Contact.**

   A progress screen appears momentarily, telling you that the Contacts app is getting the contact information from Facebook. When the transfer is finished, a new contact is added to your BlackBerry with the contact info shown on the screen.

6. **Press the Escape key.**

   The Facebook app displays a prompt, requesting the contact's phone numbers. This is a default behavior even if your friend's phone numbers are already in your BlackBerry. If you select Yes to this prompt, your Facebook friend will receive a Phone Numbers Request notification in Facebook. Your friend needs to reply to that notification with his or her phone numbers before Facebook syncs the phone numbers.

7. **Select either Yes or No in the prompt to request for phone number.**

   You're back to the previous Facebook screen, and an Address Book icon is added to the right of your friend's name (see Figure 4-15), indicating that this friend is now connected, or linked, to a BlackBerry contact.

Figure 4-15:
The Address Book icon shows that your Facebook friend is connected to a BlackBerry contact.

Automatic syncing between Facebook profiles and Contacts

When running the Facebook application for the first time, you're asked to enable synchronization. You can choose from the following Facebook and BlackBerry connections:

✔ **BlackBerry Message app:** When enabled, you'll see new Facebook notifications in your Messages app.

✔ **BlackBerry Calendar app:** When enabled, a calendar item is automatically created in your BlackBerry whenever you have a new Facebook event.

✔ **BlackBerry Contacts app:** When enabled, your BlackBerry contacts are periodically updated with the latest Facebook information, including the profile pictures. For this to happen, your BlackBerry contacts also will be sent to Facebook.

If you opted out of these options the first time you ran Facebook, you can still enable them from the Facebook Options screen. The following steps enable Contacts synchronization:

1. **On the BlackBerry Home screen, select the Facebook icon.**

   The Facebook app is filed under the Downloads folder.

2. **Press the Menu key and select Options (the wrench icon).**

   The Options screen appears. This screen contains a lot of information and text, and you have to scroll down to see all the options. For synchronizing contacts, refer to the first two pages of the screen, which look similar to the ones shown in Figure 4-16.

Figure 4-16:
Enable the synchronization of Facebook friends with Facebook Options.

3. **Add a check mark to the BlackBerry Contacts app.**

   Explanatory text appears below this check box. If you scroll down, you should see another check box, which allows you to synchronize Facebook profile photos with Contacts photos.

4. **Add a check mark to the option titled Update Existing Photos in Your BlackBerry Contacts List with Facebook Friend Profile Photos (see Figure 4-16, right).**

5. **Press the Escape key, and select Yes for the Save Changes prompt.**

   Your Contacts will now be periodically updated with Facebook friends.

Chapter 5

Keeping Appointments

*T*o some folks, the key to being organized and productive is mastering time management (and we're not just talking about reading this book while you're commuting to work). Many have discovered that there is no better way to organize their time than to use a calendar — a daily planner tool. Some prefer digital to paper, so they use a planner software program on their PC — either installed on their hard drive or accessed through an Internet portal (such as Yahoo!). The smartest of the bunch, of course, use their BlackBerry Pearl handheld because it has the whole planner thing covered in handy form with its Calendar app.

In this chapter, we show you how to keep your life (personal and work) in order by managing your appointments with your BlackBerry Pearl Calendar. What's great about managing your time on a BlackBerry Pearl versus your PC is that your Pearl is always with you. Just remember that you won't have any more excuses for forgetting that important quarterly meeting or Bertha's birthday bash.

Accessing the BlackBerry Pearl Calendar

The BlackBerry Calendar is one of the Pearl core apps, such as Address Book or Phone (read more about the others in Chapter 1), so it's easy to get to. From the Home screen, press the Menu key and select Calendar. Voilà! — you have the Calendar app.

Choosing Your Calendar View

The first time you open Calendar, you'll likely see the Day view, which is a default setting on the Pearl, as shown in Figure 5-1. You can change the Calendar view, however, to a different one that works better for your needs:

- ✔ **Day:** This view gives you a summary of your appointments for the day.

  By default, it lists all your appointments from 9 a.m. to 5 p.m.

- ✔ **Week:** This view shows you a seven-day summary view of your appointments, so you can see how busy you are for the week.

- ✔ **Month:** The Month view shows you every day of the month. You can't tell how many appointments are in a day, but you can see on which days you have appointments.

- ✔ **Agenda:** The Agenda view is a time-based view like the others. Instead, this view lists your upcoming appointments, including details of the appointments, such as where and when.

Figure 5-1:
Day view in
Calendar.

4 Aug 2010 11:40 ‹M│T│W│T│F│S│S›
08:30 │ Rock of the Day △▷
│ (Over Skype)
08:45 │
09:00 │
10:00 │
11:00 │
12:00 │
13:00 │
14:00 │
15:00 │
16:00 │

Different views (like the ones shown in Figure 5-2) offer you a different focus on your schedule. Select the view you want based on your scheduling needs and preferences. If your life is a little more complicated, you can even switch between views to get a full grasp of your schedule.

To switch between different Calendar views, simply follow these steps:

1. **From the Home screen, press the Menu key and select Calendar.**

   Doing so calls up the Calendar app in its default view — more than likely the day view.

2. **Press the Menu key and select a view from the menu that appears (shown in Figure 5-3).**

   If you start from Day view, your choices are View Week, View Month, and View Agenda.

Figure 5-2:
Change your
Calendar
view to fit
your life.

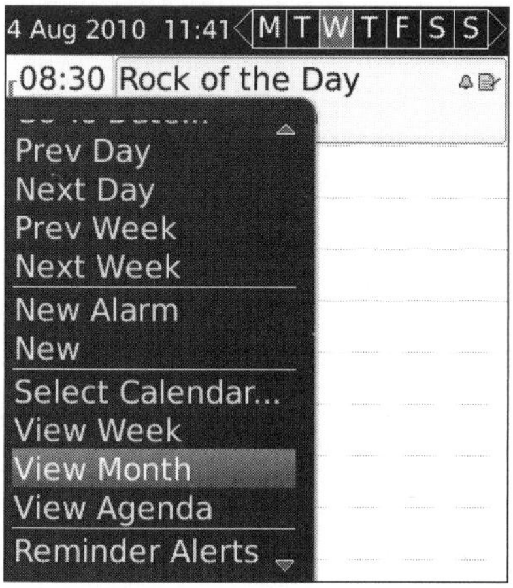

4 Aug 2010	Week 31	11:41

August

M	T	W	T	F	S	S
26	27	28	29	30	31	1
2	3	4	5	6	7	8
9	10	11	12	13	**14**	15
16	17	18	19	20	21	22
23	24	25	26	**27**	**28**	29
30	31	1	2	3	4	5

Figure 5-3:
The
Calendar
menu lets
you select
different
views.

4 Aug 2010 11:41 ⟨ M T W T F S S ⟩

08:30 Rock of the Day

Prev Day
Next Day
Prev Week
Next Week
New Alarm
New
Select Calendar...
View Week
View Month
View Agenda
Reminder Alerts

Moving between Time Frames

Depending on what view of Calendar you're in, you can easily move to the previous or the next day, week, month, or year. For example, if you're in the Month view, you can move to the next month, as shown in Figure 5-4. Likewise, you can also move to the previous month. Or if you like to look at things long term, you can jump ahead (or back) a year at a time.

4 Aug 2010	Week 31	11:42

Auqust

		F	S	S
Go To Date...				
Prev Month		30	31	1
Next Month				
Prev Year		6	7	8
Next Year		13	**14**	15
New Alarm				
New		20	21	22
Select Calendar...				
View Day		**27**	**28**	29
View Week		3	4	5
View Agenda				

Figure 5-4:
Move
between
months or
years in
Month view.

You have similar flexibility when it comes to the other Calendar views. See Table 5-1 for a summary of what's available.

Table 5-1	Moving between Views
Calendar View	*Move Between*
Day	Days and weeks
Week	Weeks
Month	Months and years
Agenda	Days

You can always go to today's date regardless of what Calendar view you're in. Just press the Menu key and select Today from the menu that appears.

Furthermore, you can jump to any date of your choosing by pressing the Menu key and selecting Go to Date from the menu that appears. Doing so calls up a handy little dialog box that lets you choose the date you want. To change the date, scroll the trackball to the desired day, month, and year, as shown in Figure 5-5.

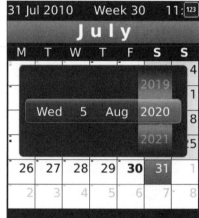

Figure 5-5:
Go to any date.

Customizing Your Calendar

To change the initial (default) view in your Calendar — from Day view to Month view, for example — Calendar Options is the answer.

To get to Calendar Options, open Calendar, press the Menu key, and select Options from the menu that appears. You see choices similar to the ones shown in Table 5-2.

Table 5-2	Calendar Options
Option	*Description*
Formatting	
First Day of Week	The day that first appears in your Week view.
Start of Day	The time that defines the start of a day in Day view. The default is 9 a.m. If you change this setting to 8 a.m., for example, your Day view starts at 8 a.m. instead of 9 a.m.
End of Day	The time that defines the end of a day in Day view. The default is 5 p.m. If you change this to 6 p.m., for example, your Day view ends at 6 p.m. instead of 5 p.m.

(continued)

Table 5-2 (continued)

Option	Description
Views	
Initial View	The Calendar view that appears when you open Calendar.
Show Free Time in Agenda View	If Yes, allows an appointment-free day's date to appear in Agenda view. If No, Agenda view doesn't show the date of days on which you don't have an appointment.
Show End Time in Agenda View	If Yes, shows the end time of each appointment in Agenda view. If No, Agenda view shows only the start time of each appointment.
Actions	
Snooze	The snooze time when a reminder appears. The default is 5 minutes.
Default Reminder	How far in advance your BlackBerry notifies you before your appointment time. The default is 15 minutes.
Enable Quick Entry	Available only in Day view. Allows you to make a new appointment by typing characters. This way, you don't need to press the trackpad and select New. ***Note:*** If you enable this option, Day view shortcuts described in this book's online Cheat Sheet don't apply.
Keep Appointments	The number of days your BlackBerry will save your Calendar item. We recommend that you keep this option set to Never.
Show Tasks	A scheduled task (a task with a due date) is displayed on your calendar just like a Calendar event.
Show Alarms	If Yes, you can see alarms in your Calendar.

All Things Appointments: Adding, Opening, and Deleting

After you master navigating the different Calendar views (which should take you all of about two minutes) and have Calendar customized to your heart's content (another three minutes, tops), it's time (pun intended) to set up, review, and delete appointments. We also show you how to set up a meeting with clients or colleagues.

Creating an appointment

Setting up a new appointment is easy. You need only one piece of information: when your appointment occurs. You can also add related information about the appointment, such as the meeting's purpose, its location, and whatever additional notes are helpful.

In addition to your standard one-time, limited-duration meeting, you can set all-day appointments. The BlackBerry Pearl can assist you in setting recurring meetings as well as reminders. Sweet!

Creating a one-time appointment

To add a new one-time appointment, follow these steps:

1. **Open Calendar.**

2. **Press the Menu key and select New.**

   The New Appointment screen appears, as shown in Figure 5-6.

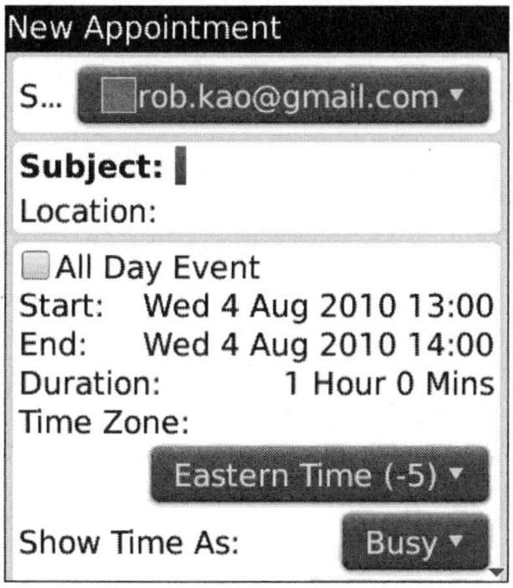

Figure 5-6:
Set an
appointment
here.

> New Appointment
> S... ☐rob.kao@gmail.com ▾
> **Subject:** |
> Location:
> ☐All Day Event
> Start: Wed 4 Aug 2010 13:00
> End: Wed 4 Aug 2010 14:00
> Duration: 1 Hour 0 Mins
> Time Zone:
> Eastern Time (-5) ▾
> Show Time As: Busy ▾

3. **Fill in the key appointment information.**

   Type all the information regarding your appointment in the appropriate spaces. You should at least enter the subject and time of your appointment. Note that the start and end time with duration are set automatically.

4. **Press the Menu key and select Save.**

   Your newly created appointment is saved.

Your new appointment is now in Calendar and viewable from any Calendar view. Also, keep in mind that you can have more than one appointment in the same time slot. Calendar allows conflicts in your schedule; you make the hard decision about which appointment you should forgo.

Creating an all-day appointment

If your appointment is an all-day event — for example, if you're in corporate training or have an all-day doctor's appointment — select the All Day Event check box in the New Appointment screen, as shown in Figure 5-7, by scrolling to the check box and pressing the trackball.

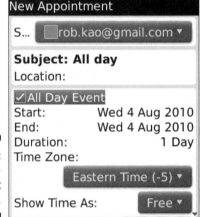

Figure 5-7: Set an all-day event here.

When you select the All Day Event check box, you specify just the start date and end date, not the time of your appointment (simply because it doesn't make sense to specify a time for an all-day event).

Setting your appointment reminder time

Any appointment you enter in Calendar can be associated with a reminder alert — either a vibration or a beep, depending on how you set things up in your profile. (For more on profiles, see Chapter 3.) You can also choose to have no reminder for an appointment. From the New Appointment screen, simply scroll to the Reminder field and select a reminder time anywhere from none to 1 week before your appointment time.

Profile is simply another useful BlackBerry Pearl feature that allows you to customize how your Pearl alerts you when an event occurs. Examples of events are an e-mail, a phone call, or a reminder for an appointment.

By default, whatever reminder alert you set goes off 15 minutes before the event. But you don't have to stick with the default. You can choose your own default reminder time. Here's how:

1. **Open Calendar.**

2. **Press the Menu key and select Options.**

   Doing so calls up the Calendar Options screen.

3. **Select Default Reminder.**

4. **Choose a default reminder time anywhere from none to 1 week before your appointment.**

So from now on, any new appointment has a default reminder time of what you just set up. Assuming that you have a reminder time other than none, the next time you have an appointment coming up, you see a dialog box like the one shown in Figure 5-8, reminding you of an upcoming appointment.

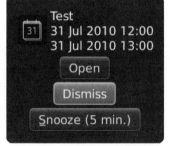

Figure 5-8:
You get a
reminder
dialog box if
you want.

Creating a recurring appointment

You can set up recurring appointments based on daily, weekly, monthly, or yearly recurrences. Everyone has some appointment that repeats, such as birthdays or anniversaries (or taking out the trash every Thursday at 7:30 a.m. — ugh).

For all recurrence types, you can define an Every field. For example, say you have an appointment that recurs every nine days. Just set the Recurrence

field to Daily and the Every field to 9, as shown in Figure 5-9.

Depending on what you select in the Recurrence field, you have the option to fill in other fields. If you enter Weekly in the Recurrence field, for example, you can fill in the Day of the Week field, so you can select the day of the week on which your appointment recurs.

If you enter Monthly or Yearly in the Recurrence field, the Relative Date check box is available. With this check box selected, you can ensure that your appointment recurs relative to today's date. For example, if you choose the following, your appointment occurs every two months on the third Thursday until July 15, 2011:

Start: Thursday, July, 15, 2010 at 12 p.m.

End: Thursday, July, 15, 2010 at 1 p.m.

Recurrence: Monthly

Every: 2

Relative Date: Selected

End: Saturday, July 15, 2011

On the other hand, if all options in the example remain the same except that Relative Date is not selected, your appointment occurs every two months, on the 15th of the month, until July 15, 2011.

If all this "relative" talk has you dizzy, don't worry: The majority of your appointments won't be as complicated as this one.

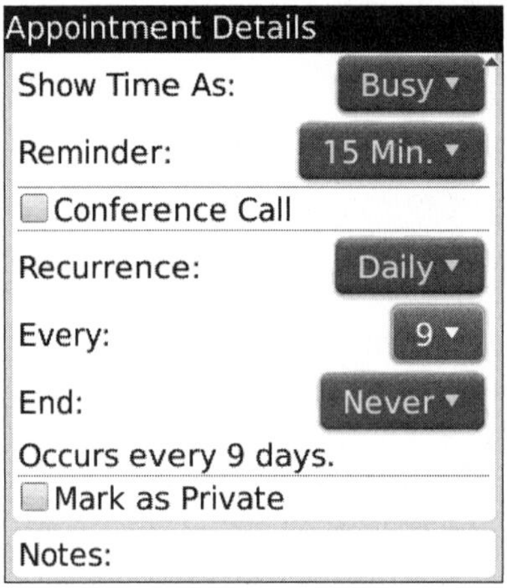

Figure 5-9:
An appointment recurring every 9 days.

Appointment Details	
Show Time As:	Busy ▼
Reminder:	15 Min. ▼
☐ Conference Call	
Recurrence:	Daily ▼
Every:	9 ▼
End:	Never ▼
Occurs every 9 days.	
☐ Mark as Private	
Notes:	

Opening an appointment

After you set an appointment, you can view it in a couple of ways. If you've set up reminders for your appointment and the little Reminder dialog box appears onscreen at the designated time before your appointment, you can view your appointment by clicking the Open button (refer to Figure 5-8). Or you can open the appointment from Calendar by going to the exact time of your appointment and viewing it there.

While looking at an appointment, you can change the appointment time and appointment location.

Deleting an appointment

Deleting an appointment is straightforward. In Day or Week view, simply scroll to the appointment that you want to delete, press the Menu key, and select Delete from the menu that appears.

If the appointment that you're deleting is part of a recurring appointment, a dialog box pops up asking whether you want to delete all occurrences of the appointment or just this particular one, as shown in Figure 5-10.

Figure 5-10:
Delete all occur-rences or just the single instance of a recurring appoint-ment.

Appointments versus Meetings

Technically, any event in your Calendar counts as an appointment, whether the event is a reminder of your best friend's birthday or a reminder of a doctor's appointment. However, when you invite people to an appointment or you are invited to one, regardless of whether it's a face-to-face meeting or a phone conference, that appointment becomes a *meeting*.

Sending a meeting request

Sending a meeting request to others is similar to creating a Calendar appointment. Follow these steps:

1. **Open Calendar.**

2. **Press the Menu key and then select New.**

3. **Fill in the key appointment information (subject, location, and time).**

4. **Press the Menu key and then select Invite Attendee.**

   You're taken to Contacts to select your meeting attendees.

5. **Select your contact via Contacts:**

   - If your contact is in Contacts: Highlight the contact you want and then press the trackpad.

   - If you don't yet have contacts or if the one you want isn't in Contacts: Select the Use Once option to enter the appropriate e-mail address and then press the Enter key to finish and return to Calendar.

   After returning from Contacts, you see the attendees in your Calendar meeting notice.

6. **Press the Menu key and then select Save.**

   An e-mail is sent to your meeting attendees, inviting them to your meeting.

Responding to a meeting request

Whether for work or a casual social event, you've likely received a meeting request by e-mail, asking you to respond to the meeting by choosing one of three options: Accept, Tentative, or Decline. (If the request is from your boss and it's so close to bonus time, that's an Accept.)

You can accept any meeting request from your managers or colleagues on your BlackBerry the way you would on your desktop PC. In the PC world, you respond to an e-mail request for a meeting by clicking the appropriate button in your e-mail client (Microsoft Outlook, for the vast majority of you). In the BlackBerry world, a meeting request also comes in the form of an e-mail; after reading the e-mail, just choose Accept, Tentative, or Decline in the Messages app. Your response is sent back in an e-mail. We go into more detail about the Messages app in Chapter 7.

Chapter 6

Setting Alarms and Keeping Your Passwords

*I*n this chapter, we introduce you to the Clock app, which not only tells you the time but also allows you to set alarms and a timer. Additionally, you can use the Clock app as a stopwatch. And, in keeping with one of the key themes of this book — making your life easier — the Clock app has a feature called bedside mode that turns your BlackBerry into a quiet bedside companion.

To add to the theme of making your life a little easier, we make sure that you get the scoop on keeping your passwords in a single location safely by using the Password Keeper app.

Accessing the Clock App

The Clock app is right on the Home screen, as you can see on the left side of Figure 6-1. Just look for the icon of an alarm clock. Once you find the Clock icon, simply select it, and you see a screen similar to the one on the right side of Figure 6-1.

If you've changed themes, you might see different icons (refer to Chapter 3 for more on themes). Just remember that the Clock app is always located on the Home screen.

Figure 6-1:
Launch
Clock (left)
and view
your clock
(right).

Customizing Your Clock

If the default analog clock doesn't fit your taste, you can change it. Customizing your clock is easy and doesn't take much time.

You customize the clock in the Options screen. Follow these steps:

1. **On the BlackBerry Home screen, select Clock.**

   The Clock app opens.

2. **Press the Menu key and select Options (the wrench icon).**

   The Clock Options screen appears. Figure 6-2 shows the first two pages of this screen.

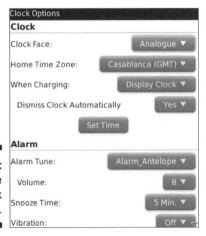

Figure 6-2:
Customize
your clock
here.

3. **Move to each field and select the option you want.**

   Each of these fields is described shortly.

4. **Press the Escape key and then select Save from the prompt.**

The Clock Options screen is divided into five sections, as follows:

✔ **Clock:** In this section, you choose the type of clock, time zone, and time.

- **Clock Face:** Set the type of clock. The options are Analog (the default; refer to the right side of Figure 6-1), Digital, Flip Clock, and LCD Digital. Digital is on the left side of Figure 6-3, and Flip Clock is on the right.

- **Home Time Zone:** Select your time zone from the list.

- **When Charging:** Control the behavior of the clock when you connect your BlackBerry to the charger. Possible choices are Do Nothing, Display Clock (the default), and Enter Bedside Mode.

- **Set Time:** Select this button to see a Date/Time screen that displays the time in edit mode, allowing you to change the time. You can also change the time zone and decide whether to synchronize your BlackBerry time to the network carriers' time.

✔ **Alarm:** Navigate here if you want to customize the behavior of the alarm:

- **Alarm Tune:** Choose from a list of ring tones you want to play. The default tone is Alarm_Antelope.

- **Snooze Time:** Hit snooze, just like with your ordinary alarm clock. You can choose 30, 15, 10, or 5 (the default) minutes, 1 minute, or None.

Figure 6-3:
Digital (left) and Flip (right) clocks.

- **Volume:** Set the volume of the tone to Silent, 1 to 10 (the default is 8), or Escalating.

- **Vibrations:** Enable or disable vibration. Choose Off, On (the default), or Custom. If you choose Custom, two new fields appear. In the first, Length, choose the duration of the vibration: Short, Medium (the default), or Long. The second field, Count, vibrates your BlackBerry as your alarm. Choices are 1, 2 (the default), 3, 5, and 10 repetitions.

- **Try It:** Check out the settings you just entered.

✔ **Bedside Mode:** This section allows you to set the behavior of your BlackBerry in bedside mode:

- **Disable LED:** Disable LED notifications during bedside mode. Choices are Yes (the default) and No.

- **Disable Radio:** Disable the radio during bedside mode. Choices are Yes and No (the default).

Disabling the radio means that no communication-related apps — e-mail, SMS, BlackBerry Messenger, instant messaging clients, and Phone — can receive incoming signals.

- **Dim Screen:** Control the dimming of the screen in bedside mode. Yes is the default.

- **Sound Profile:** Use for anything that requires sound notification. You can choose among several profiles: Active Profile (the default), Normal, Loud, Medium, Vibrate Only, Silent, Phone Calls Only, and All Alerts Off. You can always add a custom profile (see Chapter 3 for details).

✔ **Stopwatch:** Use this section changes the face of the stopwatch:

- **Stopwatch Face:** Choose between Analog (the default) and Digital.

✔ **Countdown Timer:** Navigate here if you want to customize the behavior of the timer:

- **Timer Face:** Choose between Analog (the default) and Digital.

- **Timer Tune:** Choose a ring tone to play when the timer reaches the time you set.

- **Volume:** Select Mute or set the volume of the tone to Low, Medium (the default), High, or Escalating. Escalating means that the tone starts Low and gradually goes to High.

- **Vibrate:** Choose Yes if you want the BlackBerry to vibrate when the timer reaches the time set; otherwise, choose No (the default).

Setting a Wake-Up Alarm

The Clock app is also your bedside alarm clock. You can set it to wake you up once or regularly.

Here's how you tell your wake-up buddy to do the work for you:

1. **On the BlackBerry Home screen, select Clock.**

   The Clock appears.

2. **Press the Menu key and select Set Alarm.**

   A time field appears, as shown in Figure 6-4. The time defaults to the previous Set Alarm time or, if you haven't used the alarm before, the current time. If the default time isn't your intended alarm time, proceed to Step 3 to change the time.

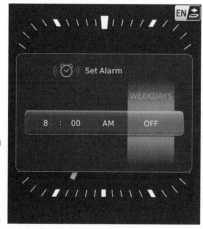

Figure 6-4: Set your alarm time here.

3. **Scroll sideways to select the specific portion of the time that you want to change, and enter the new values.**

   Any highlighted portion of the time is editable. You can change the hours; minutes; AM/PM; and whether the alarm is ON, OFF, or only WEEKDAYS. Setting a value doesn't create an entry in Calendar or Tasks. You can either enter the value or scroll up or down to choose among possible values.

4. **Press the trackpad to accept all your changes.**

Setting and Exiting Bedside Mode

You can use a setting in the Clock app called bedside mode to minimize disturbances by your BlackBerry. With bedside mode, you can dim the screen, disable the LED, and even turn off the radio, all of which pretty much makes your BlackBerry behave like a brick. Bear in mind that when you turn off the radio, you won't get incoming phone calls or any type of messaging. If you want a refresher on how to set these options, see the earlier "Customizing Your Clock" section.

If you are concerned about sleeping next to a "live" and connected smartphone, worry no more! You can have the network connection turn off automatically. To do this, see the earlier section "Customizing Your Clock," for details on disabling the radio in bedside mode.

To set your BlackBerry to bedside mode:

1. **On the BlackBerry Home screen, select Clock.**

2. **Press the Menu key and select Enter Bedside Mode (see Figure 6-5, left).**

   That's it. Your BlackBerry should now behave like a good bedside companion.

 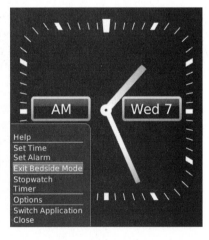

Figure 6-5: Enter and exit bedside mode here.

Buy a charging pod from shop.blackberry.com or shop.crackberry.com. Then you can put your BlackBerry on a bedside table in an upright position while the charging pod is adding juice to your device. Make sure that the Clock setting (not just the BlackBerry) is in bedside mode when charging. (To do so, select Clock from the Home screen. Press the Menu key and select Options. Under the Clock section, change When Charging to Enter Bedside Mode.)

To exit bedside mode, do the following:

1. **On the BlackBerry Home screen, select Clock.**

2. **Press the Menu key and select Exit Bedside Mode, as shown on the right side of Figure 6-5.**

Using Stopwatch

If you ever need a stopwatch, look no further than your BlackBerry. Here's how to run the stopwatch:

1. **On the BlackBerry Home screen, select Clock.**

2. **Press the Menu key and select Stopwatch.**

   You see a screen similar to Figure 6-6 with the following two buttons:

   • **Stopwatch:** Select this button to start and stop the stopwatch.

   • **Lap:** The image on this button looks like a circular arrow initially. After you start the stopwatch, the image changes to a connected arrow with an oval shape. This lap button is useful when someone is doing laps in a swimming pool or on a track field and you want to record how long each lap takes. Select the lap button to record the completion of a lap. The lap and the lap time will be listed onscreen, with Lap 1 for the first lap, Lap 2 for the second lap, and so on.

3. **To start the stopwatch, select the Stopwatch button.**

4. **To stop the stopwatch, select the Stopwatch button again.**

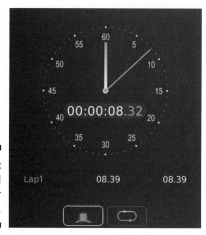

Figure 6-6:
Start and stop your stopwatch.

Using Timer

Have you overcooked something? Not if you have a good timer to warn you:

1. **On the BlackBerry Home screen, select Clock.**

2. **Press the Menu key and select Timer.**

   A screen similar to the left side of Figure 6-7 appears. The left button with the stopwatch image is the start and pause button. The right button with the circular arrow image stops and resets the timer. The default time for your timer is five minutes or the value you set when you last used Timer. If you want to change the time, proceed to the next step.

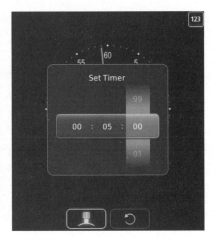

Figure 6-7:
Start and
set the time
of the timer.

3. **Press the Menu key and select Set Timer.**

   A screen similar to the right side of Figure 6-7 appears.

4. **Enter the time.**

   You can either enter the time with numeric keys or scroll up or down to choose from the provided values. From left to right, the time component is based on hours, minutes, and seconds. Scroll sideways to choose the time component.

5. **Select Start.**

   Your timer starts ticking. Once it reaches the time, it notifies you.

You can customize the timer notification to a tone, a vibration, or both. To do so, select Clock from the Home screen. Press the Menu key and select Options. In the Countdown Timer section, make your selections.

Using Password Keeper

Suppose that you're in front of an Internet browser, trying to access an online account. For the life of you, you just can't remember the account password. It's your third login attempt, and if you fail this time, your account will be locked. Then you have to call the customer hotline and wait hours before you can speak to a representative. Argghh! It's happened to all of us. Luckily, BlackBerry gives you an app to avoid this headache.

Password Keeper is the simple yet practical BlackBerry app that makes your life easier. Password Keeper is filed in Applications (as shown in Figure 6-8).

Figure 6-8: Password Keeper in the Applications folder.

Setting a password for Password Keeper

Every time you access Password Keeper, you're prompted to enter a password. *Be sure to remember the password you choose* because this is the password to all your passwords. You cannot retrieve a forgotten Password Keeper password.

Trust us — one password is much easier to remember than many passwords.

Creating new credentials

Okay, so you're ready to fire up your handy-dandy Password Keeper app. Now, what kinds of things does it expect you to do for it to work its magic? Obviously, you're going to need to collect pertinent info for all your various password-protected accounts so that you can store them in the protected environs of Password Keeper. So, when creating a new password entry, be sure you have the following information (see Figure 6-9):

  ✔ **Title:** Just come up with a name to describe the password-protected account — My Bank Account, for example.

  ✔ **Username:** Enter the user name for the account.

  ✔ **Password:** Enter the password for the account here.

  ✔ **Website:** Enter the Web site address (its URL).

  ✔ **Notes:** Add a comment or two.

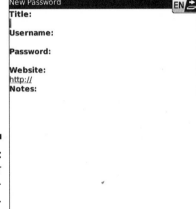

Figure 6-9:
Set your
new pass-
word here.

The only required field is Title, but a title alone usually isn't of much use. We suggest that you fill in as much other information here as possible, but at the same time *be discreet* about those locations where you use your user name and password — so don't put anything in the Website field or use My eBay Account as a title. That way, if someone *does* gain access to your password to Password Keeper, the intruder will have a hard time figuring out where exactly to use your credentials.

Generating random passwords

If you're the kind of person who uses one password for everything but knows deep in your heart that this is just plain wrong, wrong, wrong, random password generation is for you. When creating a new password for yet another online account (or when changing your password for an online account you already have), fire up Password Keeper, press the Menu key, and then select Random Password from the menu that appears. Voilà! A new password is automatically generated, as shown in Figure 6-10.

Figure 6-10:
A randomly
generated
password.

Using random password generation with Password Keeper makes sense because you don't have to remember the randomly generated password for any of your online accounts — that's Password Keeper's job.

Using your password

The point of Password Keeper is to let your BlackBerry's electronic brain do your password remembering for you. So, imagine this scenario: You can no longer live without owning a personal copy of the *A Chipmunk Christmas* CD, so you surf over to your favorite online music store and attempt to log in. You draw a blank on your password, but instead of seething, you take out your BlackBerry, open the Password Keeper app, highlight the online site in your list, and press the trackpad. The screen for your account appears, conveniently listing the password that was just on the tip of your tongue. All you have to do now is enter the password into the login screen for that online music store and Alvin, Simon, and Theodore will soon be wending their way to your address, ready to sing "Chipmunk Jingle Bells."

Yes, you *do* have the option of copying and pasting your password from Password Keeper to another app — your BlackBerry Browser, for instance. Just highlight the password name, press the Menu key, and select Copy to Clipboard. Then navigate to where you want to enter the password, press the trackpad and select Paste from the menu. However, for the copy/paste function to work for passwords from Password Keeper, you need to enable the Allow Clipboard Copy option in the Password Keeper options (see the upcoming Table 6-1). You can copy and paste only one password at a time.

After you paste your password in another app, clear the Clipboard by pressing the Menu key and selecting Clear Clipboard. The Clipboard keeps your last copied password until you clear it.

Changing Password Keeper options

The Options screen allows you to control how Password Keeper behaves. For example, you can set what characters can make up a randomly generated password. See Table 6-1 for a description of all options. To get to the Options screen, open Password Keeper, press the Menu key, and select Options.

Table 6-1	Password Keeper Options
Option	*Description*
Random Password Length	Select between 4 and 16 for the length of your randomly generated password.
Random Includes Alpha	If Yes, a randomly generated password includes alphabetic characters.
Random Includes Numbers	If Yes, a randomly generated password includes numbers.
Random Includes Symbols	If Yes, a randomly generated password includes symbols.
Confirm Delete	If Yes, all deletions are prompted with a Confirmation screen.
Password Attempts	Select between 1 and 20 attempts to successfully enter the password to Password Keeper.
Allow Clipboard Copy	If Yes, you can copy and paste passwords from Password Keeper.
Show Password	If Yes, the password displays; otherwise, asterisks take the place of password characters.

Changing your password to Password Keeper

If you want to change your password to Password Keeper — that is, the master password for opening Password Keeper — follow these steps:

1. **Select Password Keeper.**

   The initial login screen for Password Keeper appears.

2. **Enter your old password to access Password Keeper.**

3. **Press the Menu key and select Change Password.**

   You see the Password Keeper screen that allows you to enter your new password, as shown in Figure 6-11.

4. **Enter a new password, confirm it by entering it again, and then use your trackpad to click OK.**

Figure 6-11:
Change your
Password
Keeper
password
here.

Chapter 7

Calling Your Favorite Person

. . . .

In This Chapter

▶ Accessing the BlackBerry Phone app

▶ Making and receiving calls

▶ Managing your calls with call forwarding and more

▶ Customizing your BlackBerry Phone setup

▶ Conferencing

▶ Talking hands-free on your BlackBerry phone

▶ Multitasking with your BlackBerry phone

. . . .

*T*he BlackBerry smartphone operates no differently than any other phone you've used. So why bother with this chapter? Although your BlackBerry smartphone operates like any other phone, it has capabilities that far out-reach those of your run-of-the-mill cell phone. For example, when was the last time your phone was connected to your to-do list? Have you ever received an e-mail and placed a call directly from that e-mail? We didn't think so. But with your BlackBerry Pearl, you can do all these things and more.

In this chapter, we first cover phone basics and then show you some of the neat ways BlackBerry Phone app intertwines with other BlackBerry apps and functions.

Using the BlackBerry Phone App

Accessing the Phone app from the Pearl is a snap. From the Home screen, pressing any of the numeric keys brings you right into the BlackBerry Phone app. Or, if you prefer, you can press the green Send button located right below the display screen to get into the Phone app.

Making and Receiving Calls

The folks at RIM have created an intuitive user interface to all the essential Phone features, including making and receiving calls.

Making a call

To make a call, start from the Home screen and type the number you want to dial. As soon as you start typing numbers, the Phone app opens. When you've finished typing the destination number, press the green Send key.

Calling from Contacts

Because you can't possibly remember the phone numbers of all your friends and colleagues, call them from the Contacts app instead.

To call from Contacts, follow these steps:

1. **Open the Phone app.**

2. **Press the Menu key.**

   The Phone menu appears, as shown in Figure 7-1.

3. **Select Call from Contacts.**

   Contacts opens. From here, you can search as usual for the contact you'd like to call.

4. **From Contacts, highlight your call recipient and press the trackpad to select Call.**

   The call is made.

Figure 7-1:
The Phone
menu.

Dialing letters

One of the nice features of BlackBerry Phone is that you can dial letters, and BlackBerry will figure out the corresponding number. For example, to dial 1-800-11-LEARN, do the following on your BlackBerry:

1. **From the Phone app (or the Home screen), dial 1-8-0-0-1-1.**

   As you type the first number, the Phone app opens (if it isn't open already) and displays the numbers you dialed.

2. **Press and hold the Alt key and then dial (press) L-E-A-R-N.**

   The letters appear onscreen as you type.

3. **Press the green Send key.**

   This call is initiated.

Receiving a call

Receiving a call on your BlackBerry is even easier than making a call. You can receive calls a couple ways. One is by using your BlackBerry's automated answering feature; the other is by answering manually.

Automated answering is triggered when you take your BlackBerry out of your holster; in other words, just taking out the BlackBerry forces it to pick up any call, so you can start talking right away. However, you don't have time to see who is calling you (on your Caller ID). *Note:* To disable autoanswer, be sure that your BlackBerry isn't in its holster when an incoming call arrives.

What's the advantage of disabling autoanswer? Manual answering prompts you to answer or ignore an incoming call (see Figure 7-2). This way, you can see on caller ID who is calling before you decide to pick up or ignore the call.

Here's how to turn on autoanswer:

1. **Open the Phone app.**
2. **Press the Menu key.**

   The Phone menu appears (refer to Figure 7-1).

3. **Select Options.**

   The Phone Options screen appears, listing the categories of options.

4. **Select General Options.**

   The General Options screen appears.

5. **In the Auto Answer Calls field, select Out of Holster.**
6. **Press the Menu key and select Save.**

Figure 7-2:
Ignore or
answer
with manual
answering.

Selecting a ring tone

From the Phone app, you can quickly set the general ring tone for the current sound profile.

To set how you want your phone to ring, follow these steps:

1. **Open the Phone app.**

2. **Press the Menu key and select Set Ring Tone.**

   The Phone settings in the current Sound Profile appear. (Chapter 2 shows you how to set the sound profile for e-mails and other alerts.)

3. **In the Ring Tone field, select a ring.**

   You can also set the volume level ranging from 10 (the loudest) to 1 to silent.

4. **Press Escape to save your settings.**

You can also set personal ring tones for each of your contacts. Chapter 4 shows you how.

Handling missed calls

You missed a call from an important client. Worse, you didn't notice the missed call because you didn't see the little Missed Call icon; you pay attention only to what is in your e-mail message box. What can you do to make sure that you return that call?

You can have missed calls appear in your e-mail message box so that you are sure to return them (if you choose to, that is).

To have your missed calls appear in your inbox, follow these steps:

1. **Open the Phone app.**

2. **Press the Menu key and select Options.**

   The Phone Options screen appears, listing the different categories of options.

3. **Select Call Logging.**

   The Call Logging screen appears.

4. **Highlight the Missed Calls option and then click the trackpad.**

   You can also select All Calls, which means that incoming and outgoing calls are displayed in your e-mail inbox.

5. **Press the Menu key and select Save.**

You can find out the total call time and the last call time in the Phone Status screen. From the Phone menu, select Status to display the Phone Status screen.

Phone Options While on a Call

When you're on the phone, situations may arise where you'd want to mute your conversation or change the call volume. No problem. BlackBerry Pearl makes such adjustments easy.

Muting your call

While on a conference call (see the upcoming section, "Arranging Conference Calls"), you might want to use the mute feature when you don't need to speak but do need to hear what is being discussed. Maybe you're on the bus or have kids in the background, making your surroundings noisy. By using mute, all the background noises are filtered out from the conference call.

To mute your call, follow these steps:

1. **While in a conversation, press the Menu key.**

   The Phone menu appears in all its glory.

2. **Select Mute.**

   You hear a tone sound, indicating that your call is on mute.

To un-mute your call:

1. **While a call is on mute, press the Menu key.**

   The Phone menu makes another appearance.

2. **Select Turn Mute Off.**

   You hear a tone sound, indicating that your call is now unmuted.

Adjusting the call volume

Adjusting the call volume, a simple yet important action on your BlackBerry phone, can be performed by simply pressing the volume up or volume down key on the side of your Pearl.

Customizing the BlackBerry Phone

For your BlackBerry Phone to work the way you like, you have to first set it up the way you want it. In this section, we go through some settings that can make you the master of your BlackBerry Phone.

Setting up your voice mail number

This section shows you how to set up your voice mail access number. Unfortunately, the instructions for setting up your voice mailbox vary, depending on your service provider. Fortunately, however, most service providers are more than happy to walk you through the steps to get your mailbox set up in a jiffy.

To set up your voice mail number:

1. **Open the Phone app.**
2. **Press the Menu key and select Options.**

   The Phone Options screen appears, listing the different categories of options.

3. **Select Voice Mail.**

   The voice mail configuration screen appears.

4. **Scroll to the Access Number field and enter your voice mail access number.**

   If this field is empty and you don't know the voice mail access number, contact your service provider.

5. **Press the Menu key and select Save.**

Using call forwarding

On the BlackBerry, you have two types of call forwarding:

- ✔ **Forward All Calls:** Any calls to your BlackBerry are forwarded to the number you designate. Another name for this feature is *unconditional forwarding*.

- ✔ **Forward Unanswered Calls:** Calls that meet different types of conditions are forwarded to different numbers.

For the unanswered calls type of forwarding, three conditions determine what number to forward to:

- ✔ **If Busy:** You don't have call waiting turned on and are on the phone.

- ✔ **If No Answer:** You don't hear your phone ring or somehow are unable to pick up your phone (perhaps you're in a meeting).

- ✔ **If Unreachable:** You're out of network coverage and cannot receive any signals.

Out of the box, your BlackBerry Pearl forwards any unanswered calls, regardless of conditions, to your voice mail number by default. However, you can add new numbers to forward a call to.

You need to be within network coverage before can you change your call forwarding option. After you're within network coverage, change your call forwarding settings as follows:

1. **Open the Phone app.**

2. **Press the Menu key and select Options.**

   A list of phone options appears.

3. **Select Call Forwarding.**

   Your BlackBerry now attempts to connect with the server. If successful, you see the Call Forwarding screen.

   If you don't see the Call Forwarding screen, wait until you have network coverage and try again.

4. **From the Call Forwarding screen, press the Menu key and select Edit Numbers.**

   A list of number(s) appears. If this is the first time you're setting call forwarding, most likely only your voice mail number is on this list.

5. **To add a new forwarding number:**

   a. **Press the Menu key and select New Number.**

      A pop-up menu appears, prompting you to enter the new forwarding number.

   b. **Enter the number you want to forward to and then press the trackpad.**

      The number you entered appears on the call forward number list. You can add this new number to any call forwarding types or conditions.

   c. **Press the Escape key.**

      You return to the Call Forwarding screen.

6. **Scroll to the If Unreachable field and press the trackpad.**

   A drop-down menu appears and lists numbers from the call forwarding number list, including the one you just added.

7. **Select the number you want to forward to and then press the trackpad.**

   The selected number is placed in the If Unreachable field.

8. **Confirm your changes by pressing the Menu key and selecting Save.**

Configuring speed dial

Speed dial is a convenient feature on any phone. And after you get used to having it on one phone system, it's hard not to use it on other phones, including your BlackBerry phone.

Viewing your speed dial list

To view your speed dial list, do the following:

1. **Open the Phone app.**

2. **Press the Menu key and select View Speed Dial List.**

   You see a list of speed dial entries, as shown in Figure 7-3. If you haven't set up any speed dials, the list will be empty.

Speed Dial Numbers

> [1] Voice Mail +12013103747
> [2]
> [3]
> [4]
> [5]
> [6]
> [7]
> [8]
> [9]
> [!]
> [?]
> [@]
> [.]

Figure 7-3:
The speed
dial list.

Adding a new number to speed dial

It takes a few seconds to set up a speed dial number, but you benefit every time you use this feature.

To assign a number to a speed dial slot, follow these steps:

1. **Open the Phone app.**

2. **Press the Menu key, select Options, and then select View Speed Dial List.**

   You see a list of speed dial numbers.

3. **Scroll to an empty speed dial slot, press the Menu key, and select New Speed Dial.**

   BlackBerry Address Book appears so you can select a contact's phone number.

4. **Select a contact, and then press the trackpad.**

   The number appears in the speed dial list.

   If more than one number is associated with the selected contact in Address Book, you're prompted to select which number to add to the speed dial list.

Using speed dial

After you have a speed dial entry set up, you can start using it. While at the Home screen or Phone app, press a speed dial key. The call is initiated to the number associated with that particular speed dial key.

Arranging Conference Calls

To have two or more people on the phone with you — the infamous conference call — do the following:

1. **Use the Phone app to place a call to the first participant.**

2. **While the first participant is on the phone with you, press the Menu key and select Add Participant.**

   The first call is placed on hold, and a new call screen is displayed, as shown in Figure 7-4, prompting you to place another call.

Figure 7-4: The New Call screen, with a meeting participant on hold.

3. **Place a call to the second participant by dialing a number, pressing the trackpad, and then selecting Call.**

   You can dial the number using the number pad or select a frequently dialed number from your call log. You can place a call also from Address Book by pressing the trackpad from the New Call screen and choosing Call from Address Book. Your BlackBerry then prompts you to select a contact to dial to from the Address Book.

   Adding a second participant is just like any other phone call (except that the first participant is still on the other line).

4. **While the second participant is on the phone with you, press the Menu key and select Join Conference, as shown in Figure 7-5.**

   The first participant is reconnected, along with the second participant. Now you can discuss away with both participants at the same time.

Another name for having two people on the phone with you is *three-way calling,* which is not a new concept. If you want to chat with four people or even ten people on the phone at the same time, you certainly can. Simply repeat

Steps 2–4 in the preceding list until you have all the participants on the phone conference.

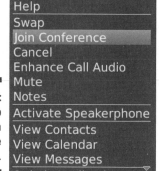

Figure 7-5:
Join two
people in a
conference
call.

Talking privately to a conference participant

During a conference call, you might want to talk to one participant privately. This is called *splitting* your conference call. Here's how you do it:

1. **While on a conference call, press the Menu key and select Split.**

   A pop-up screen appears, listing all the participants of the conference call, as shown in Figure 7-6.

Figure 7-6:
All partici-
pants in the
conference
call.

2. **From the pop-up screen, select the participant with whom you want to speak privately.**

   This action places all other participants on hold and connects you to the participant that you selected. On the display screen, you can see to whom you are connected — this display confirms that you selected the right person to privately chat with.

3. **To talk to all participants again, press the Menu key and select Join Conference.**

   You are brought back to the conference call with everyone.

Alternate between phone conversations

Whether you are in a private conversation during a conference call or are talking to someone while you have someone else on hold, you can switch between the two conversations by swapping them. Follow these steps:

1. **While talking to someone with another person on hold, press the Menu key and select Swap.**

   Doing so switches you from the person with whom you're currently talking to the person who was on hold.

2. **Repeat Step 1 to go back to the original conversation.**

Dropping that meeting hugger

If you've been on conference calls, you can identify those chatty "meeting huggers" who have to say something about everything. Don't you wish that you could drop them off the call? Well, with your Pearl, you can (as long as you are the meeting moderator or the person who initiates the call). Do the following:

1. **While on a conference call, press the Menu key and select Drop Call.**

   You see a pop-up screen, listing all the participants of the conference call.

2. **Select the meeting hugger you want to drop.**

   Doing so disconnects the meeting hugger.

3. **Continue the conversation as usual.**

Communicating Hands-Free

Because more and more places prohibit the use of mobile phones without a hands-free headset, we thought we'd go through the hands-free options you have on your BlackBerry.

Using the speakerphone

The speakerphone function is useful under certain situations, such as when you're in a room full of people who want to join in on your phone conversation. Or you might be all by your lonesome in your office but are stuck rooting through your files — hard to do with a BlackBerry scrunched up against your ear. (We call such moments *multitasking* — a concept so important we devote an entire upcoming section to it.)

To switch to the speakerphone while you're on a phone call, press the OP key or press the Menu key and select Activate Speaker Phone.

Pairing your BlackBerry with a Bluetooth headset

Your BlackBerry comes with a wired hands-free headset, and you can start using it by simply plugging it into the headset jack on the left side of your BlackBerry. You adjust the volume of the headset using the volume keys (on the side of the Pearl).

Using the wired hands-free headset can help you avoid being a police target, but if you're multitasking on your BlackBerry, the wired headset can get in the way and become inconvenient.

In this situation, the Bluetooth wireless thing comes in. You can purchase a BlackBerry Bluetooth headset to go with your Bluetooth-enabled BlackBerry. For a list of BlackBerry-compatible Bluetooth headsets, see Chapter 16.

After you purchase a BlackBerry-compatible Bluetooth headset, you can pair it with your BlackBerry. Think of *pairing* a Bluetooth headset with your BlackBerry as registering the headset with your BlackBerry so that it recognizes the headset.

First things first: You need to prep your headset for pairing. Each headset manufacturer has a different take on this, so you'll need to consult your headset documentation for details. When that is out of the way, you can continue with the pairing as follows:

1. **From the Home screen, press the Menu key and select Bluetooth.**

2. **Press the Menu key to display the Bluetooth menu.**

   You see the Enable Bluetooth option. If you see the Disable Bluetooth option instead, you can skip to Step 4.

3. **From the menu, scroll to Enable Bluetooth and press the trackpad.**

   Bluetooth is enabled on your BlackBerry.

4. **Press the Menu key to display the Bluetooth menu and select Add Device.**

   You see the Searching for Devices progress bar, um, progressing, as shown in Figure 7-7 (left). When your BlackBerry discovers the headset, a Select Device dialog box appears with the name of the headset, as shown in Figure 7-7 (right).

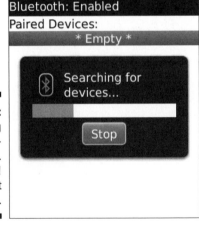

Figure 7-7: Searching for a headset (left). Success! A headset (right).

5. **From the Select Device dialog box, select the Bluetooth headset.**

   A dialog box appears to prompt you for a passkey code to the headset.

6. **Enter the passkey and press the trackpad.**

   Normally, the passkey is 0000, but refer to your headset documentation. After you successfully enter the passkey, you see your headset listed in the Bluetooth setting screen.

7. **Press the Menu key to display the Bluetooth menu and select Connect.**

   Your BlackBerry now attempts to connect to the Bluetooth headset.

8. **When you see a screen like Figure 7-8, you can start using your Bluetooth headset.**

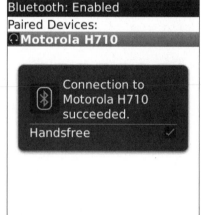

Figure 7-8:
You can
begin
using your
Bluetooth
headset.

Using voice dialing

With your headset and the Voice Dialing app, you can truly be hands-free from your BlackBerry. You may be thinking, "How do I activate the Voice Dialing app without touching my BlackBerry?" Good question. The majority of hands-free headsets (Bluetooth or not) come with a multipurpose button.

Usually, a multipurpose button on a hands-free headset can mute, end, and initiate a call. Refer to the operating manual of your hands-free headset for more info.

After your headset is active (see the preceding section), press its multipurpose button to activate the Voice Dialing app. You will be greeted with a voice stating, "Say a command." At this point, simply say, "Call," and state the name of a person or say the number. (For example, say, "Call President Obama" or "Call 555-2468.") The Voice Dialing app is good at recognizing the name of the person and the numbers you dictate. However, we strongly suggest that you try the Voice Dialing feature before you need it.

Multitasking While on the Phone

One of the great things about the BlackBerry is that you can use it for other tasks while you're on the phone. For example, you can take notes or make a to-do list. Or you can look up a phone number in BlackBerry Contacts that your caller is requesting. You can even compose an e-mail and receive e-mails while on a call!

When multitasking, you really need to be using a hands-free headset or a speakerphone. Otherwise, your face is stuck to your BlackBerry, and you can't engage in your conversation and multitask.

Accessing apps while on the phone

After you don your hands-free headset or turn on the speakerphone (by pressing the Speaker key; the same as the $ key), you can multitask after performing the following steps:

1. **While in a conversation, from the Phone app, press the Menu key and then select the Home screen.**

   This returns you to the Home screen without terminating your phone conversation.

   Alternatively, you can simply press the Escape key while in the Phone app to return to the Home screen.

2. **From the Home screen, you can now multitask.**

While on the phone and multitasking, you can still access the Phone menu from other apps. For example, you can end a call or put a call on hold from your to-do list.

Taking notes while on the phone

To take notes of your call, follow these steps:

1. **During a phone conversation, press the Menu key and then select Notes.**

   The Notes screen appears.

2. **Type notes for the conversation, as shown in Figure 7-9.**

   When the call ends, the notes are saved automatically.

Accessing phone notes

From the Call History list (see Figure 7-10), you can access notes you made during a regular call or a conference call. Additionally, you can edit notes and add new notes.

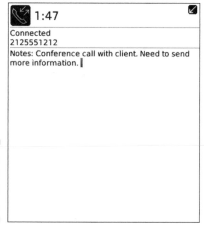

Figure 7-9:
Take notes
while on a
phone call.

Figure 7-10:
Call history,
where you
can see
conversa-
tion notes.

Forwarding phone notes

You can forward your phone notes the way you forward an e-mail. While on the Call History screen (refer to Figure 7-10), press the Menu key and then select Forward.

You can add notes while you're on the phone or later. While you're viewing a call history, press the Menu key. Then select Add Notes if you have no notes for the call or select Edit Notes if you already have notes for the call.

Part III
Getting Online

The 5th Wave   By Rich Tennant

"My spam filter checks the recipient address, http links, and any writing that panders to postmodern English romanticism with conceits to 20th-century graphic narrative."

In this part . . .

Here's the good stuff. You find out how to use your BlackBerry Pearl for e-mail in Chapter 8. But e-mail is old school; don't miss the texting and instant messaging with your buddies described in Chapter 9. However, nothing beats BlackBerry Messenger, as you find out in Chapter 10. Finally, in Chapter 11, you see how to go online and surf the Web.

Chapter 8

You've Got (Lots of) E-Mail

*Y*our BlackBerry Pearl brings a fresh new face to the convenience and ease-of-use that we associate with e-mail. You can direct mail to your Pearl from up to ten e-mail accounts from the likes of AOL and Yahoo!. You can set up an e-mail signature, configure e-mail filters, and search for e-mails.

In this chapter, we show you how to use and manage the mail capabilities of your Pearl to their full potential. From setup to sorts, we've got you covered.

Getting Up and Running with E-Mail

Regardless of your network service provider (such as T-Mobile or Rogers or Vodafone), you can set up your BlackBerry Pearl to receive mail from at least one of your current e-mail accounts. Thus, with whatever address you use to send and receive e-mail from your PC (Yahoo!, Gmail, and so on), you can hook up your Pearl to use that same e-mail address. Instead of checking your Gmail at the Google site, for example, you can now get it on your BlackBerry Pearl.

Most network service providers allow you to connect up to ten e-mail accounts to your BlackBerry. You get the convenience of one central point from which you get all your e-mail, without having to log in to multiple e-mail accounts.

Using the BlackBerry Internet Service client

You can pull together all your e-mail accounts into one by using the *BlackBerry Internet Service client* (former known as BlackBerry Web client). The BlackBerry Internet Service client allows you to

- **Manage up to ten e-mail accounts.** You can combine up to ten of your e-mail accounts onto your BlackBerry. See the upcoming section, "Combining your e-mail accounts."

- **Use wireless e-mail reconciliation.** No more trying to match your BlackBerry e-mail against e-mail in your combined account(s). Just turn on wireless e-mail reconciliation and you're good to go. For more on this topic, see the upcoming section, "Enabling wireless reconciliation."

- **Create e-mail filters.** You can filter e-mails so that you get only those e-mail messages that you truly care about on your BlackBerry. See the section "Filtering your e-mail," near the end of this chapter.

Think of the BlackBerry Internet Service client (Service client) as an online e-mail account manager. Unlike other online e-mail accounts, Service client doesn't keep your e-mails. Instead, it routes the e-mails from your other accounts to your BlackBerry Pearl (because it's directly connected to your Pearl).

Combining your e-mail accounts

To start herding e-mail accounts onto your BlackBerry, you must first run a setup program from the BIS client.

You can access the BIS client from your BlackBerry or from your desktop computer. To do so on the PC, you need the URL specific to your network service. Contact your network service provider (such as Verizon or Telus) directly to get that information.

We cover accessing the BIS client from your BlackBerry, but just remember that you can do all these functions from a Web browser as well.

To get started with BIS client from your BlackBerry, do the following:

1. **From the BlackBerry Home screen, select the Setup folder.**

2. **Select the Email Settings icon.**

   You're prompted with a screen similar to Figure 8-1.

3. **If you haven't created your BIS account, select the Create button and follow the onscreen instruction to create a username and password.**

   You'll use the user name and password to log in later.

Figure 8-1:
The BIS client login screen on the BlackBerry.

After you've logged in, you see a list of e-mail accounts that have been set up. If you haven't set up any e-mail accounts yet, you see an Add button. We show you how to add accounts in the next section.

Adding an e-mail account

You can set up your BIS account directly from your BlackBerry. (As mentioned, you can have up to ten e-mail accounts on your BlackBerry.) To add an e-mail account to your BlackBerry account, follow these steps:

1. **From your BlackBerry Home screen, select the Setup folder.**

2. **Select the Person E-mail Setup icon.**

   You're prompted with a login screen similar to Figure 8-1.

3. **If you haven't created your BIS account, select the Create button and follow the onscreen instruction to create a user name and password.**

4. **Log in by entering your user name and password.**

5. **Select Add.**

   A screen with different e-mail domains (Yahoo!, Gmail, and so on) appears, as shown in Figure 8-2.

Figure 8-2:
Select
an e-mail
domain.

6. **Select an e-mail domain.**

7. **Enter the e-mail address and password, and then select Next.**

   If you entered your e-mail credentials correctly, you see the setup confirmation screen.

As mentioned, you can also add an e-mail account to your BlackBerry from your desktop PC or Mac via a Web browser. Just follow these steps.

1. **From the BIS client, click Setup Account.**

   Contact your network carrier for the URL to access the BIS client on your PC or Mac Web browser.

2. **Enter the address and login credentials for that e-mail address.**

   The e-mail address is the address from which you want to receive e-mail, for example, myid@yahoo.com. The account login is the one you use to log in to this particular e-mail account. And the password is the one you use with the login.

3. **Click the Next button.**

   You're finished. It's that easy!

To find the URL to access the BIS client for your network carrier, simply go to Google and enter **carrier-name BIS login.** The first result returned is almost always the BIS login page for your carrier.

Configuring your e-mail signature

By default, your e-mail signature is something like *Sent via My BlackBerry* which can be cool in the first week, showing off to people that you are a la mode with your BlackBerry Pearl. But sooner or later, you may not want people to know you are out and about while answering e-mail. Or you may want something more personal.

Follow these steps to configure your e-mail signature by using the BIS client on your BlackBerry:

1. **From your BlackBerry Home screen, select the Setup folder.**
2. **Select the Email Setting icon.**

   You see a login screen similar to the one in Figure 8-1.
3. **If you haven't created your BIS account, select the Create button and follow the onscreen instruction to create a user name and password.**
4. **Log in to the BIS client on the BlackBerry.**

   You see the BIS main screen.
5. **Select the e-mail account for which you want to set up an e-mail signature.**
6. **In the Signature field, type the text for your e-mail signature.**
7. **Select Save.**

Enabling wireless reconciliation

With wireless reconciliation, you don't need to delete the same e-mail in two places. The two e-mail inboxes reconcile with each other, hence the term *wireless reconciliation.* Convenient, huh?

Enabling wireless e-mail synchronization

You can start wireless e-mail synchronization by configuring your BlackBerry:

1. **From the Home screen, press the Menu key and then select Messages.**

   The Messages app appears, and you see the message list.
2. **Press the Menu key and select Options.**

   The Options screen appears, with two option types: General Options and Email Reconciliation.

3. **Select Email Reconciliation.**

   The Email Reconciliation screen appears with the following options:

   - **Delete On:** This option configures how BlackBerry handles your e-mail deletion.

   - **Wireless Reconciliation:** This option turns on or off the wireless sync function.

   - **On Conflict:** This option controls how BlackBerry handles inconsistency between e-mail on your BlackBerry versus BlackBerry Internet Service client.

      You can choose who "wins" via this option: your BlackBerry or the BlackBerry Internet Service client.

4. **Select Delete On, and then select one of the following from the drop-down list:**

   - **Handheld:** A deletion on your BlackBerry takes effect on your BlackBerry only.

   - **Mailbox & Handheld:** A deletion on your BlackBerry takes effect on both your BlackBerry and your inbox on BlackBerry Internet Service client.

   - **Prompt:** Your BlackBerry asks you whether you want to delete.

5. **Select Wireless Reconciliation, and then select On from the drop-down list.**

6. **Select On Conflict, and make a selection from the drop-down list.**

   If you choose Handheld Wins, the e-mail in your e-mail account will match the ones on the handheld.

Next, you need to enable Synchronize Deleted Item on the BIS client:

1. **From the BlackBerry Home screen, select the Setup folder.**

2. **Select the Email Setting icon.**

   You see a login screen similar to Figure 8-1.

3. **If you haven't created your BIS account, select the Create button and follow the instructions to create a user name and password.**

4. **Log in to the BIS client on the BlackBerry.**

   The BIS main screen appears.

5. **Select an e-mail account for which you want to enable Synchronize Deleted Item.**

6. **Select Synchronization Options to expand the options, and make sure that the Deleted Items check box is selected.**

7. **Select Save.**

Unfortunately, some e-mail accounts may not work well with the e-mail reconciliation feature of the BlackBerry Pearl, so you may have to delete an e-mail twice.

Permanently deleting e-mail from your BlackBerry

When deleting e-mail on your BlackBerry, the same message in that e-mail account is placed in the Deleted folder. You can set up your BlackBerry to permanently delete e-mail, but use this option with caution — after that e-mail is gone, it's gone.

To permanently delete e-mail on your Service client from your BlackBerry, follow these steps:

1. **Open the Messages app.**

2. **In the message list, press the Menu key and select Options.**

3. **Select Email Reconciliation.**

4. **Press the Menu key and select Purge Deleted Items.**

   A pop-up appears listing all your e-mail accounts.

5. **Select the e-mail account from which you want to purge deleted items.**

   Another pop-up appears confirming that you are about to purge deleted e-mails on your Service client.

6. **Select Yes.**

   Deleted e-mails in the selected e-mail account are purged.

Unfortunately, some e-mail accounts may not work with the purge deleted items feature.

Accessing Messages

From Messages, you send and receive your e-mails and also configure wireless e-mail reconciliation with your e-mail accounts.

To access Messages from the Home screen, press the Menu key and select Messages. The first thing you see after opening Messages is the message list. Your message list can contain e-mail, voice mail messages, missed phone call notices, Short Messaging Service (SMS) messages, and even saved Web pages.

Receiving e-mails

Whether you're concerned about security or speed of delivery, you're in good hands when receiving e-mail on your BlackBerry Pearl.

And whether you've aggregated accounts or use the plain-vanilla BlackBerry Pearl e-mail account, you receive your e-mail the same way. When an e-mail arrives, your BlackBerry Pearl notifies you by displaying a numeral next to a mail icon (an envelope) at the top of the screen, as shown in Figure 8-3. This number represents how many new (unread) e-mails you have. The asterisk next to the envelope indicates that there is new mail and you haven't opened the Messages app yet.

Figure 8-3:
You've got
(79) e-mails!

Your BlackBerry Pearl can also notify you of new e-mail by vibration or a sound alert or both. You can customize this from Profile, as we detail in Chapter 3.

Retrieving e-mail

Retrieving your e-mail is simple:

1. **From the Home screen, press the Menu key and select Messages.**

   Your message list appears.

2. **In the message list, scroll to any e-mail and press the trackpad.**

   You can tell whether an e-mail is unopened by the small unopened envelope icon on the left side of the e-mail. A read e-mail bears an opened envelope icon, a sent e-mail has a check mark as its icon, and a draft e-mail is represented by a document icon.

3. **After you finish reading the message, press the Escape key to return to the message list.**

Saving a message to the saved folder

You can save any important e-mail into a folder so that you can find it without sorting through tons of e-mail. To do so, simply scroll to the e-mail you want to save, press the Menu key, and select Save from the menu. A pop-up message confirms that your e-mail has been saved. *Note:* Your saved e-mail still remains in the message list.

To retrieve or view a saved e-mail, follow these steps:

1. **Open the Messages app.**

2. **In the message list, press the Menu key and select View Saved Messages.**

   You see the list of all the messages you saved.

3. **Select the message you want and press the trackpad to open it.**

Viewing attachments

Your BlackBerry Pearl is so versatile that you can view most e-mail attachments just like you can on a desktop PC. And we're talking sizeable attachments, too, such as JPEGs (photos), Word docs, PowerPoint slides, and Excel spreadsheets. Table 8-1 lists the attachments you can view from your BlackBerry Pearl.

Table 8-1	BlackBerry-Supported Attachments
Supported Attachment Extension	*Description*
.bmp	BMP image file format
.doc/.docx	MS Word document
.dot	MS Word document template
.gif	GIF image file format
.htm	HTML Web page
.html	HTML Web page
.jpg	JPEG image file format
.pdf	Adobe PDF document
.png	PNG image file format
.ppt/.pptx	MS PowerPoint document
.tif	TIFF image file format
.txt	Text file
.wpd	Corel WordPerfect document
.xls/.xlsx	MS Excel document
.zip	Compressed file format

To tell whether an e-mail has an attachment, look for the standard paperclip icon next to your e-mail in the message list.

You retrieve all the different types of attachments the same way. To open an attachment, follow along:

1. **While reading an e-mail, press the Menu key and select Open Attachment.**

   You see a screen containing the name of the file. And for all supported file types, you see a Table of Contents option and a Full Contents option. For MS Word documents, you can see different headings in outline form in the Table of Contents option. For picture files, such as a JPEG, go straight to the Full Contents option to see the graphic.

2. **Scroll to Full Contents, press the Menu key, and then select Retrieve.**

   Your BlackBerry Pearl attempts to contact the BlackBerry server to retrieve your attachment. As you scroll through the document, BlackBerry Pearl retrieves more as the attachment. When you're retrieving a picture, all parts of the attachment appear.

Editing attachments

Your BlackBerry comes with Documents to Go, which means that out of the box, you can not only view but also edit Word and PowerPoint documents. You can even save the documents to your BlackBerry and transfer them later to your PC.

For example, suppose that you want to edit a Word document that you received as an e-mail attachment:

1. **In the message list, open an e-mail with a Word document attached.**

   A little paper clip indicates that that e-mail has an attachment.

2. **Press the Menu key and select Open Attachment.**

   A pop-up asks whether you want to view the Word document or edit with Documents to Go.

3. **Select Edit with Documents to Go.**

4. **Press the Menu key and select Edit Mode.**

5. **Edit the document.**

6. **Save the document on your BlackBerry and then e-mail it:**

   • **To save the document:** Press the menu key and select Save.

   To save the attachment to your BlackBerry, you have to navigate its folder structure. For documents, the default save location is usually the Documents folder.

- **To e-mail the edited document:** Press the Menu key and select Send via E-mail.

  You see an e-mail message with the Word document. Follow the steps described in the next section to send this e-mail attachment as you would any other e-mail.

Sending e-mail

The first thing you probably want to do when you get your BlackBerry Pearl is to write an e-mail to let your friends know that you've just received a BlackBerry Pearl. Follow these steps:

1. **Open the Messages app.**

2. **In the message list, press the Menu key and select Compose Email.**

   You are prompted with a blank e-mail that you just need to fill out as you would do on you PC.

3. **In the To field, type your recipient's name or e-mail address.**

   As you type, you see a list of contacts from your Address Book matching the name or address that you're typing.

4. **Type your message subject and body.**

5. **When you're finished, press the Menu key and select Send.**

   Your message has wings.

Forwarding e-mail

When you need to share an important e-mail with a colleague or a friend, you can forward that e-mail. Simply do the following:

1. **Open the e-mail.**

   For information on opening e-mail, see the previous section, "Retrieving e-mail."

2. **Press the Menu key and select Forward.**

3. **Type the recipient's name or e-mail address in the appropriate space, then add a message if needed.**

   When you start typing your recipient's name, you see a drop-down list of your contacts from which you can choose.

4. **Press the Menu key and select Send.**

   Your message is on its way to your recipient.

Saving a draft e-mail

Sometimes the most skillful wordsmiths find themselves lost for words to express the message they want. Don't fret, fellow wordsmith, you can save that e-mail composition as a draft until your words come back to you. Simply press the Menu key and select Save Draft.

This saves your e-mail as a draft. When you're ready to send your message, choose the draft from the message list. You can tell which messages are drafts because they sport a tiny document icon; finished messages have an envelope icon.

Attaching a file to your e-mail

Many people are surprised that you can attach any document on your BlackBerry or on the microSD card. You can attach Word, Excel, and PowerPoint documents as well as pictures, music, and videos. To send an e-mail with a file attached, follow these steps:

1. **Open the Messages app.**

2. **In the message list, press the Menu key and then select Compose E-mail.**

    You are prompted with a blank e-mail that you can fill out as you would on your PC. Enter the recipient's name in the To field and then enter the subject and body of the message.

3. **Press the Menu key and select Attach File.**

    You're prompted with a list of your folders. Think of these as the folders on your PC.

4. **Navigate to the file of your choice, and press the trackpad.**

    After you select a file, you see the file in the e-mail message.

5. **Press the Menu key and select Send.**

    Your message and attached file wing their way to the recipient.

Spell-checking your outgoing messages

Whether you're composing an e-mail message or an SMS text message, you can always check your spelling with the built-in spell checker. Simply press the Menu key and select Check Spelling. When your BlackBerry finds an error, the spell checker makes a suggestion, as shown in Figure 8-4. To skip the spell check for that word and go on to the next word, press the Escape key. If you want to skip spell-checking for an e-mail, simply press and hold the Escape key.

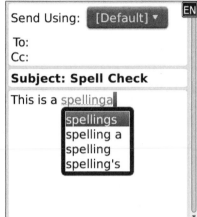

Figure 8-4:
The
BlackBerry
spell
checker in
action.

By default, the spell checker doesn't kick in before you send your message. However, you can configure the spell checker to always check spelling before you send an e-mail. Follow these steps:

1. **Open the Messages app.**
2. **Press the Menu key and select Options.**
3. **Select the Spell Check option.**
4. **Select the Spell Check E-mail before Sending check box.**
5. **Press the Menu key and select Save.**

Your BlackBerry, like Microsoft Word, underlines a word it thinks is misspelled. The underline feature is a default setting called Check Spelling as You Type. To turn off this feature, deselect the Spell Check option in Message Options.

Filtering your e-mail

Most of us get e-mail that either isn't urgent or doesn't concern us. Instead of receiving those messages on your BlackBerry Pearl — and wasting both time and effort to check them — you can filter them. While in the BlackBerry Pearl Internet Service client, set up filters to make your BlackBerry Pearl mailbox receive only those e-mails that you care about. (Don't worry; you'll still receive them on your main computer.)

The following example creates a simple filter that treats work-related messages as urgent and forwards them to your BlackBerry:

1. **From the BlackBerry Home screen, select the Setup folder.**

2. **Select the Email Settings icon.**

   You are prompted with a login screen similar to Figure 8-1, earlier in this chapter. If you haven't created your account, select the Create button and create your BIS account.

3. **Log in to the BIS client on the BlackBerry.**

   The BIS main screen appears.

4. **Select the e-mail account for which you want to set up filters.**

5. **Press the Menu key and select Filters.**

   You see a list of filters, if any, and an Add Filter button, as shown in Figure 8-5.

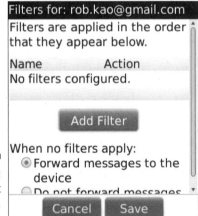

Figure 8-5:
Filter list
screen.

6. **Select the Add Filter button.**

   The Add Filter screen appears, as shown in Figure 8-6.

7. **Enter a filter name.**

   The filter name can be anything you want. We entered *To me*.

8. **In the Filter On drop-down list, select the condition to place on the filter:**

   • **High-Priority Mail Email:** The filter applies only to urgent e-mail.

   • **Subject:** The Contains field becomes enabled so you can type text in it. Specify what keywords the filter will look for in the Subject field, separating each entry with a semicolon (;).

   • **From Address:** The Contains field becomes enabled so you can type text in it. Type a full from-address or part of an address. For example, you can type *rob@robkao.com* or just *kao*. Separate each entry with a semicolon (;).

- **To Address:** The Contains field becomes enabled so you can type text in it. Type a full to-address or part of an address.

- **CC Address:** The Contains field becomes enabled so you can type text in it. Type a full cc-address or part of an address.

9. **In the Contains field, specify the text.**

    See details in the preceding step for what to enter in the Contains field. We selected From Address in the preceding step, and then typed the domain of our work e-mail address. For example, if your work e-mail address is `myName@XYZCo.com`, enter **XYZCo.com**.

10. **Select one of the following options for the Action field:**

    Forward Messages to the Device: You can select either or both of the following two check boxes:

    - **Header Only:** Choose this if you want only the header of the e-mails that meets the condition(s) you set in Steps 7–9 to be sent to you. (A *header* doesn't contain the message — just who sent it, the subject, and the time it was sent.) Choose this if you get automated alerts, for which receiving only the subject is sufficient.

    - **Level1 Notification:** Level1 notification is another way of saying *urgent e-mail.* A Level1 e-mail is bold in Messages.

    Do Not Forward Message to the Device: Any message that meets the conditions set in Steps 7–9 doesn't go to your BlackBerry.

11. **Confirm your filter by selecting the Save button.**

    You return to the Filter screen, where you can see your newly created filter in the list.

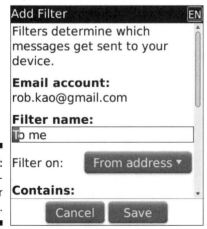

Figure 8-6: Create a filter for your e-mail.

If you have a hard time setting the criteria for a filter, guesstimate and then check how you did by having a friend send you a test e-mail. If the test e-mail isn't filtered correctly, re-do the conditions until you get them right.

Searching Messages Like a Pro

Searching is one of those functions you probably won't use every day — but when you do run a search, you usually need the information fast. Take a few minutes here to familiarize yourself with general searching.

The BlackBerry Messages app provides three ways to search through your messages. Two of the ways are specific, and one is a broad search:

- ✔ **Search by sender or recipient:** Specific. This method assumes that you already know the sender or recipient.
- ✔ **Search by subject:** Specific. This approach assumes that you already know the subject.
- ✔ **General search:** Broad. You don't have a specific assumption.

You can search through anything listed in the messages list, so you can search through SMS and voice mail as well as e-mail.

Searching by sender or recipient

Search by sender or recipient when you're looking for a specific message from a specific person. For example, suppose that your brother constantly sends you e-mail (which means your message list has many entries from him). You're trying to locate a message he sent you approximately two weeks ago regarding a fishing-trip location. You scrolled down the message list, but you just can't seem to find that message. Or maybe you want to find a message you sent to Sue but can't lay your hands on it.

To find a message when you know the sender or recipient, follow these steps:

1. **Open the Messages app.**

2. **In the message list, highlight a message that you sent to or received from that particular person.**

   The choice you get in the next step depends on whether you highlighted a sent message or a received message.

3. **Press the Menu key and select one of the following options:**

   • To search for a message *from* someone specific: Because that certain someone sent you the message, choose Search Sender.

• To search for a message *to* someone specific: Because you sent that certain someone the message, choose Search Recipient.

This starts the search. Any results appear onscreen.

Searching by subject

Search by subject when you're looking for an e-mail titled by a specific subject that you already know. As is the case when running a search by sender or recipient, first scroll to an e-mail that bears the same subject you're searching for. Then follow these steps:

1. **Open the Messages app.**

2. **In the message list, highlight an e-mail titled by the specific subject you're searching for.**

3. **Press the Menu key and select Search Subject.**

   The search starts, and the results appear onscreen.

Running a general search

A general search is a broad search from which you can perform keyword searches of your messages. To run a general search, follow these steps:

1. **Open the Messages app.**

2. **In the message list, press the Menu key and then select Search.**

3. **In the Search screen that appears, fill in your search criteria (see Figure 8-7).**

Figure 8-7:
The Search
screen in
Messages.

The search criteria for a general search follow:

- **Name:** Enter the name of the sender or recipient to search by.

- **In:** Related to the Name criterion. Use this drop-down list to indicate where the name may appear. Your choices are From, To, Cc, Bcc, and any address field.

- **Subject:** Type some or all keywords that appear in the subject.

- **Message:** Enter keywords that appear in the message.

- **Service:** Specify which e-mail account to search if you set up your BlackBerry to receive e-mail from more than one e-mail account.

- **Folder:** Select the folder in which you want to perform the search. Generally, you should select All Folders.

- **Show:** Specify whether you want to see only e-mails that you sent or e-mails that you received. From the drop-down list, your choices are Sent and Received, Received Only, Sent Only, Saved Only, Draft Only, and Unopened Only.

- **Type:** Specify the type of message you're trying to search for: e-mail, SMS, or voice mail. From the drop-down list, your choices are All, E-mail, E-mail with Attachments, PIN, SMS, Phone, and Voice Mail.

From the Search screen shown in Figure 8-9, you can have multiple search criteria or just a single criterion. It's up to you.

4. **Press the Menu key and select Search to launch your search.**

The search results appear onscreen.

You can narrow the search results by performing a second search on the initial results. For example, you can search by sender and then narrow those results by performing a second search by subject.

You can also search by sender or recipient when you're looking for a specific message from a specific person. Scroll to an e-mail that bears the sender or recipient. Press the Menu key and then select Search Sender or Search Recipient. If the e-mail that you highlighted is an incoming e-mail, you'll see Search Sender. If the e-mail is outgoing, you'll see Search Recipient.

Saving search results

If you find yourself searching with the same criteria over and over, you may want to save the search and then reuse it. Here's how:

1. **Follow Steps 1–3 in the preceding section for an outgoing e-mail search.**

2. **Press the Menu key and select Save.**

The Save Search screen appears, from which you can name your search and assign it a shortcut key (see Figure 8-8).

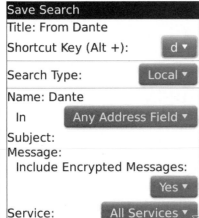

Figure 8-8:
Name your
search, and
assign it a
shortcut
key.

3. **In the Title field, enter a name.**

   The title is the name of your search, which appears on the Search
   Results screen.

4. **Scroll to the Shortcut Key field, press the trackpad and select a letter
   from the drop-down list.**

   You can choose among ten letters.

5. **Confirm your saved search by pressing the Menu key and selecting Save.**

Reusing saved searches

Right out of the box, your BlackBerry comes with five saved search results.
Any new saved result will make your search that much more robust.

Follow these steps to see all saved search results:

1. **Open the Messages app.**

2. **In the message list, press the Menu key and then select Search.**

3. **Press the Menu key and select Recall.**

   The recall screen opens, and you can see the five preloaded search
   shortcuts, as well as any searches you saved, as shown in Figure 8-9.

To reuse one of the saved search results, simply select a desired search from
the list, press the Menu key, and select Search.

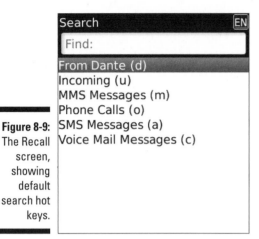

Figure 8-9:
The Recall
screen,
showing
default
search hot
keys.

If you have multiple e-mail accounts set up, you can set up a search shortcut so that you view only one specific account. For example, say you have both your personal e-mail and your small-business e-mail accounts set up on your BlackBerry. In the Message app, you see e-mails from both, which can be over-whelming at times. From the general Search screen (refer to Figure 8-8), set the Service drop-down list to the one you want, and follow the preceding steps to save the search and assign a shortcut key. The next time you want to see only a certain account, you can get to it in an instant!

Follow Up Your E-Mail

Do you get lots of e-mails? Do you sometimes forget to reply to e-mail? No worries. With your BlackBerry, you can automatically add reminders to any e-mail that you want to follow up, a feature similar to the follow-up flag in Microsoft Outlook.

The next time you get a flurry of e-mails, mark the ones you want to revisit later by using the follow-up flag:

1. **Open the Messages app.**

2. **Highlight the e-mail in need of a follow up, and press the Menu key.**

3. **Select Flag for Follow Up.**

   You see a red flag next to your message.

4. **While the flagged e-mail is still highlighted, press the Menu key and select Flag Properties.**

5. **Select any of the following:**

   • **Request:** The type of follow up. You can choose from Call, Review, Forward, and more.

- **Color:** The color of the flag.

- **Status:** Whether the status is completed or not.

- **Due:** The due date for this follow up. When the due date arrives, you get a pop-up reminder, similar to a Calendar reminder.

Long Live E-Mail

No closet has unlimited space, and your BlackBerry Pearl e-mail storage has limits, too. You've likely pondered how long your e-mails are kept in your BlackBerry Pearl. (The default is 30 days.) You can choose several options: from 15 days to as long as your BlackBerry Pearl has enough space for them.

Because any message you save is kept for as long as you want, a good way to make sure you don't lose an important message is to save it.

To change how long your e-mails live on your BlackBerry Pearl, follow these steps:

1. **Open Messages app.**

2. **Press the Menu key and select Options.**

3. **Select General Options.**

4. **Scroll to the Keep Messages option and press the trackpad.**

5. **From the drop-down list that appears, choose the time frame that you want and then press the trackpad.**

   - **Forever:** If you choose Forever, you'll seldom need to worry about your e-mails being automatically deleted. On the downside, though, you'll eventually run out of memory on your BlackBerry Pearl. At that point, you must manually delete some e-mail so that you have space to accept new e-mail.

     A good way to archive your e-mail is to back up your e-mail messages using BlackBerry Desktop Manager. See Chapter 16 for more on backing up your Pearl on your PC.

   - **Time option:** If you choose a set-time option, any message older than that time frame is automatically deleted from your BlackBerry Pearl the next time you reboot your Pearl. However, the message will be deleted only on your Pearl — even if you turn on e-mail reconciliation — because these deletions are not completed manually by you.

6. **Confirm your changes by pressing the Menu key and selecting Save.**

Chapter 9

Too Cool for E-Mail

*Y*our BlackBerry Pearl is primarily a communication tool, typically through e-mail messages and phone conversations. It's a wonderful technology, but sometimes another means of communication is more appropriate. For instance, e-mail isn't the tool of choice for instant messaging — most people would find that method slow and cumbersome. Nor is e-mail the best tool to use when you want to alert someone to something.

Your BlackBerry offers some less-obvious ways to communicate — ways that may serve as the perfect fit for a special situation. In this chapter, you get the scoop on PIN-to-PIN messaging and text messaging (also known as *Short Messaging Service,* or *SMS*). We also give you tips on how to turn your BlackBerry into a lean (and not-so-mean) instant messaging (IM) machine.

Sending and Receiving PIN-to-PIN Messages

What actually happens when you use PIN-to-PIN messaging? First and foremost, get the acronym out of the way. *PIN* stands for personal identification number (familiar to anyone who's ever used an ATM) and refers to a system for uniquely identifying your device. *PIN-to-PIN,* then, is another way of saying *one BlackBerry to another BlackBerry.*

As for the other details, they're straightforward. PIN-to-PIN messaging is based on the technology underpinning two-way pager systems, which is fast. When you send a PIN-to-PIN message, unlike a standard e-mail message, the message doesn't venture outside RIM's infrastructure in search of an e-mail server and (eventually) an e-mail inbox. Instead, the message stays solidly within the RIM world, where it is shunted through the recipient's network provider until it ends up on the recipient's BlackBerry. Trust us when we say it's fast. You have to try it to see the difference.

Getting a BlackBerry PIN

When you try to call someone on the telephone, you can't get far without a telephone number. As you might expect, the same principle applies to PIN-to-PIN messaging: no PIN, no PIN-to-PIN messaging.

In practical terms, you need the individual PIN of any BlackBerry device owned by whomever you want to send a PIN message to. (You also need to find out your own PIN so you can hand it out to those folks who want to PIN-message you.)

The cautious side of you may wonder why on earth you'd give your PIN to someone. Here's the difference: Unlike a PIN for an ATM account, this PIN isn't your password. In fact, this PIN doesn't give anyone access to your BlackBerry or do anything to compromise security. It's simply an ID, like a phone number.

Following are three quick paths to PIN enlightenment:

✔ **From the Message screen:** RIM makes it easy for you to send your PIN from the Message screen with the help of a keyword. A *keyword* is a neat feature with which you type a preset word, and your BlackBerry replaces what you type with a bit of information specific to your device.

It's easier than it sounds. To see what we mean, just compose a new e-mail in the Message app. In the subject or body of your message, type **mypin** and add a space. As soon as you type the space, mypin is miraculously transformed into your PIN in the format pin:*your-pin-number* (see Figure 9-1). Isn't that neat?

mypin isn't the only keyword that RIM predefines for you. mynumber and myver give you the phone number and OS version, respectively, of your BlackBerry.

✔ **From the Status screen:** You can also find your PIN on the Status screen. Display the Status screen by choosing the following links in succession, starting from the Home screen: Settings, Options, and Status. Use the trackpad to highlight and select each link. Figure 9-2 shows a typical Status screen.

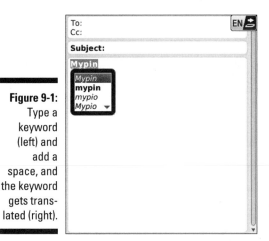 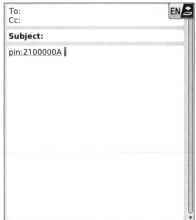

Figure 9-1:
Type a
keyword
(left) and
add a
space, and
the keyword
gets trans-
lated (right).

Figure 9-2:
Find your
PIN on
the Status
screen.

Assigning PINs to names

So, you convince your BlackBerry-wielding buddies to go to the trouble of
finding out their PINs and passing said PINs to you. Now, the trick is finding
a convenient place to store your PINs so you can use them. Luckily for you,
you have an obvious choice: BlackBerry Contacts. And RIM, in its infinite
wisdom, makes storing such info a snap. To add a PIN to someone's contact
info in Contacts, do the following:

1. **From the BlackBerry Home screen, select Contacts.**

   Contacts opens.

2. **Highlight a contact name, press the Menu key, and then select Edit.**

   The Edit Contact screen for the contact name you selected makes an appearance.

3. **On the Edit Contact screen, scroll down to the PIN field (as shown in Figure 9-3).**

Figure 9-3:
Add a contact's PIN info here.

4. **Type the PIN.**

5. **Press the Menu key and select Save.**

   The edit you made for this contact is saved.

It's that simple. And it's even easier if you think ahead and enter the PIN information you have when you set up your initial contact info (by using the New Contact screen), but we understand that a PIN isn't the kind of information people carry around.

If all this talk about New Contact screens and Edit Contact screens doesn't sound familiar, check out Chapter 4, which covers the Contacts app in more detail.

Sending a PIN-to-PIN message

Sending a PIN-to-PIN message is no different than sending an e-mail. Here's how:

1. **From the Home screen, press the Menu key and select Contacts.**

   The Address Book opens.

2. **Highlight a contact name, press the Menu key, and then select PIN <*contact name*>.**

   Say, for example, that you have a contact named Dante Sarigumba. When you highlight Dante Sarigumba in the list and press the Menu key, the menu item *PIN Dante Sarigumba* appears as an option, as shown in Figure 9-4.

Find:

New Contact:

Help
Filter
New Contact
New Group
View
Edit
Delete
Activity Log
Email Dante Sarigumba
PIN Dante Sarigumba
Call Dante Sarigumba
SMS Dante Sarigumba
SIM Phone Book
Send As Attachment
Add Picture
Options
Switch Application

Figure 9-4: Send a PIN message via Contacts.

3. **Select PIN <*contact name*> from the menu.**

   You see the ever-familiar New Message screen, with the PIN of your buddy already entered as an address.

4. **Enter the rest of the text fields — subject, message, and signature text — just as you would with an e-mail.**

Alternatively, if you know the PIN, you can type it directly. Here's how:

1. **From the BlackBerry Home screen, select Messages.**

   The Messages app opens.

2. **Press the Menu key and select Compose PIN.**

   The New Message screen makes an appearance.

3. **In the To field, enter the PIN and then press the trackpad.**

   You just added a recipient in the To field.

4. **Add a subject line, the message, and then the signature text, just like you would in an e-mail.**

Unlike sending an e-mail message, when you send a PIN-to-PIN message, you can tell almost instantly whether the recipient received your message. Viewing the Message list, you see the letter *D* — which means *delivered* — on top of the check mark next to the PIN-to-PIN message you sent.

Because of the nature of PIN-to-PIN messaging (the conspicuous lack of a paper trail, as it were), RIM has set it up so that companies can disable PIN-to-PIN messaging on your BlackBerry device. (No paper trail can mean legal problems down the road — can you say *Sarbanes-Oxley*?)

Receiving a PIN-to-PIN message

Receiving a PIN-to-PIN message is no different than receiving a standard e-mail. You get the same entry into your Messages list for the PIN-to-PIN message that you receive, and the same message screen displays when you open the message.

By default, your BlackBerry vibrates to alert you, but you can change this in Profiles. (Check out Chapter 3 for more details on changing your profile.) When you reply to the message, the reply is a PIN-to-PIN message as well.

Keeping in Touch, the SMS/MMS Way

Short Messaging Service (also known as *SMS*, or simply *text messaging*) is so popular that you've probably seen TV shows asking for your feedback via SMS. Multimedia Messaging Service (MMS) is a much later evolution of SMS. Rather than sending a simple text message, you can also send someone an audio or a video clip.

How short is *short?* The maximum size per message is about 160 characters. If you send more than that, your message gets broken down into multiple messages.

Text messaging does pose a challenge for beginners. Typing the letters on a small keyboard and keeping up with a conversation can be hard. Also, you need to know the trends and options for text messaging. In addition, in-the-know folks use abbreviations that may be difficult for you to understand in the beginning.

A quick preparation goes a long way toward avoiding being labeled uncool when it comes to your SMS syntax. The upcoming sections help smooth your path a bit by filling you in on the basics of SMS-speak.

Using shorthand for speedy replies

On a regular cell phone, three letters share a single key. Typing even a single paragraph can be a real pain.

Human ingenuity prevails. Abbreviations cut down the amount of text you need to enter. *Texting* (short for *text messaging)* language is fashionable, especially among the 14–18-year-old set. Veteran text messagers (the hip ones, at least) can easily spot someone who's new to SMS technology by how that person doesn't use the right lingo — or uses such lingo incorrectly.

AWHFY?

In text messaging, the challenge lies in using abbreviations to craft a sentence with as few letters as possible. Because text messaging has been around for a number of years, plenty of folks have risen to this challenge by coming up with a considerable pool of useful abbreviations. Don't feel that you have to rush out and memorize the entire shorthand dictionary at once, though.

As with mastering a new language, start with the most commonly used words or sentences. When you become familiar with those, slowly gather in more and more terms. In time, the language will be second nature.

Table 9-1 gives you our take on the most common abbreviations, which are enough to get you started. With these under your belt, you can at least follow the most important parts of an SMS conversation.

Table 9-1	SMS Shorthand and Its Meanings		
Shorthand	*Meaning*	*Shorthand*	*Meaning*
2D4	To die for	CUL8R	See you later
2G4U	Too good for you	CUS	See you soon
2L8	Too late	F2F	Face to face
4E	Forever	FC	Fingers crossed
4YEO	For your eyes only	FCFS	First come, first served
A3	Anytime, any-where, anyplace	FOAF	Friend of a friend

(continued)

Table 9-1 *(continued)*

Shorthand	Meaning	Shorthand	Meaning
AFAIK	As far as I know	FWIW	For what it's worth
ASAP	As soon as possible	GAL	Get a life
ASL	Age, sex, location	GG	Good game
ATM	At the moment	GR8	Great
ATW	At the weekend	GSOH	Good sense of humor
AWHFY	Are we having fun yet?	H2CUS	Hope to see you soon
B4	Before	IC	I see
BBFN	Bye-bye for now	IDK	I don't know
BBL	Be back later	IMHO	In my honest opinion
BBS	Be back soon	IMO	In my opinion
BCNU	Be seeing you	IOU	I owe you
BG	Big grin	IOW	In other words
BION	Believe it or not	KISS	Keep it simple, stupid
BOL	Best of luck	LOL	Laughing out loud
BOT	Back on topic	OIC	Oh, I see
BRB	Be right back	RUOK	Are you okay?
BRT	Be right there	W4U	Waiting for you
BTW	By the way	W8	Wait
CMON	Come on	WTG	Way to go
CU	See you	TOM	Tomorrow

Showing some emotion

Written words can get folks into trouble every now and then; the same words can mean different things to different people. A simple example is the phrase "You're clueless." When you speak such a phrase (with the appropriate facial and hand gestures), your friend knows (you hope) that you're teasing and that it's all a bit of fun. Write that same phrase in a text message, and, well, you may get a nasty reply — which you then have to respond to, which prompts another response, and soon enough, you've just ended a seven-year friendship.

SMS is akin to chatting, so *emoticons* show what you mean when you write "You're clueless." (I'm joking! I'm happy! I'm mad!) These cutesy codes help you telegraph your meaning in sledgehammer-to-the-forehead fashion.

We're talking smileys here — those combinations of keyboard characters that, when artfully combined, resemble a human face. The most popular example — one that you've probably encountered in e-mails from especially chirpy individuals — is the happy face, which (usually at the end of a statement) conveys good intentions or happy context, like this :). (Tilt your head to the left to see the face.)

Table 9-2 shows you the range of smiley choices. Just remember that smileys are supposed to be fun. They could be the one thing you need to make sure that your "gently teasing remark" isn't seen as a hateful comment. Smileys help, but if you aren't sure if what you're about to send can be misconstrued even with the help of the smileys, just don't send it.

Table 9-2	Smileys and Their Meanings		
Smiley	*Meaning*	*Smiley*	*Meaning*
:)	Happy, smiling	:(	Sad, frown
:-)	Happy, smiling, with nose	:-(	Sad, frown, with nose
:D	Laughing	:-<	Super sad
:-D	Laughing, with nose	:'-(	Crying
:'-)	Tears due to laughter	:-0	Yell, gasped
:-)8	Smiling with bow tie	:-@	Scream, what?
;)	Winking	:-(o)	Shouting
;-)	Winking, with nose	|-0	Yawn
0:-)	I'm an angel (male)	:----(	Liar, long nose
0*-)	I'm an angel (female)	%-(	Confused
8-)	Cool, with sunglasses	:-|	Determined
:-!	Foot in mouth	:-()	Talking
>-)	Evil grin	:-ozz	Bored
:-x	Kiss on the lips	@@	Eyes
(((H)))	Hugs	%-)	Cross-eyed

(continued)

Table 9-2 *(continued)*

Smiley	Meaning	Smiley	Meaning
@>-- ;--	Rose	|@@|	Face
:b	Tongue out	#:-)	Hair is a mess
;b	Tongue out with a wink	&:-)	Hair is curly
:-&	Tongue tied	$-)	Yuppie
-!-	Sleepy	:-($)	Put your money where your mouth is
<3	Heart, or love	<(^(oo)^)>	Pig

Shorthand and smileys may not be appreciated in business. Use them appropriately.

Sending a text message

After you have the shorthand stuff and smileys under control, get your fingers pumped up and ready for action: It's message-sending time! Whether it's SMS or MMS, here's how to do it:

1. **From the Home screen, select Contacts.**

2. **Highlight a contact with a cell phone number, press the Menu key, and then select SMS *<contact name>* or MMS *<contact name>*.**

   SMS works only on mobile phones.

   The menu item for SMS or MMS is intelligent enough to display the name of the contact, as shown in Figure 9-5. For example, if you choose John Doe, the menu item reads SMS John Doe or MMS John Doe. If you chose SMS, skip Step 3 and proceed directly to Step 4.

3. **If you chose MMS, browse from your multimedia folders and select the audio or video file you want to send.**

   This extra step allows you to choose the multimedia file and is the only difference between SMS and MMS with regards to sending a message.

4. **Type your message.**

5. **Press the trackpad and then select Send from the menu that appears.**

   Your SMS/MMS message is sent on its merry way.

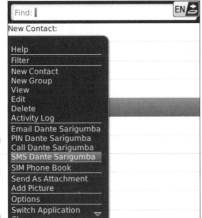

Figure 9-5:
Start your
text mes-
sage here.

Messaging etiquette and a few words of caution

Here are some commonsense messaging rules as well as a few words of caution. Even if you're new to messaging, being a neophyte doesn't give you license to act like a jerk. Play nice and take the following pointers to heart:

- ✔ **Use smileys to avoid misunderstandings.** Read more about emoticons and smileys earlier in this chapter.

- ✔ **Don't ever forward chain letters.** We mean it. Never.

- ✔ **If you need to forward a message, check the entire message content first.** Make sure nothing offends the recipient.

- ✔ **Some things in this world need to be said face to face, so don't even think of using messaging for it.** Ever try dumping your girl-friend or boyfriend over the phone? Guess what? Using messaging is far worse.

- ✔ **Keep your tone gender neutral.** Some messages that are forwarded through e-mails are inappropriate to the opposite sex.

- ✔ **Capital letters are as rude as shouting.** *DON'T USE THEM.*

- ✔ **Know your recipient.** A newbie might not easily grasp smileys and shorthand at first, so act accordingly. (Read more about shorthand earlier in this chapter.)

- ✔ **Don't reply to any message when you're angry.** You can't unsend a sent message. It's better to be prudent than sorry.

- ✔ **Don't gossip or be rude.** Beware! Your messages can end up in the wrong hands and haunt you in the future.

- ✔ **Easy does it.** No documented evidence reveals the deleterious effects (physi-cal or psychological) of too much tex-ting. However, don't text as if you want to enter the books as the first recorded case of Instantmessagingitis. As your great-grandma would tell you, too much of any-thing is bad for you. It's easy to lose track of time when IMing.

- ✔ **Drive safely.** Tuck away your BlackBerry when you're in the driver's seat.

Viewing a message you receive

If you have an incoming SMS or MMS message, you get notification just like you do when you receive an e-mail. Also, like e-mail, the e-mail icon on the top of the Home screen indicates the arrival of a new message. In fact, everything about viewing SMS/MMS messages is pretty much the same as what you do when reading e-mail messages; so if you have Chapter 8 loaded into *your* memory, you know how to read SMS/MMS messages.

Customize how your BlackBerry notifies you when you receive an SMS message. (In Chapter 3, see the section on customizing your profile.)

Always Online Using Instant Messaging

Real-time (as they happen) conversations with your friends or buddies over the Internet are easier with IM (instant messaging). IM enables two or more people to send and receive messages over the Internet. Instant messaging started with pure text messages and evolved into a rich medium involving voice and even video conversations in real-time.

IM may not be available on your BlackBerry Pearl because service providers choose whether to include it. (Most providers, however, do support it for the BlackBerry.) You can add IM to your BlackBerry even if it didn't come with it:

1. **Open your browser.**

2. **Go to `http://mobile.blackberry.com`.**

3. **Navigate to IM and Social Networking.**

   Here, you'll find download links for all the free apps for the popular IM networks and also a download link for BlackBerry Messenger. (Chapter 10 covers BlackBerry Messenger.)

Chatting using IM rules

When you're IMing — that's right; it's a verb — you can tell lots of things:

✔ When someone's typing a message to you

✔ Whether your buddies are online

✔ When your buddies are away from their computers

✔ When your buddies are simply too busy to be interrupted at the moment

IM adds a different slant on long-distance communication, opening a wide array of possibilities — possibilities that can be used for good (team collaboration) or ill (mindless gossip), depending on the situation.

As you may expect, IM is great for both personal and business apps. Whether you're maintaining friendships or working to create new ones, IM is definitely one powerful tool to consider adding to your social-skills toolbox.

 If your employer provides your BlackBerry Pearl, IM might not work on your device. Companies have the option of telling their network administrators to block all IM network addresses, effectively shutting you out of the IM system. If that's the case, your chances of being able to use IM on your BlackBerry Pearl are zero. (You can always get your own personal BlackBerry Pearl, though.)

Instant messaging on your BlackBerry

Most network providers dish out the three most popular IM services to their BlackBerry customers:

- Google Talk
- Yahoo! Messenger
- Windows Live Messenger

Those three IM programs aren't the only popular ones. Here are a few more:

- AOL Instant Messenger (AIM)
- ICQ Instant Messenger
- iChat AV (on the Macintosh)
- Jabber (open source)

If you're using an IM network that isn't preloaded, you can always check the RIM Web site to download the apps: `mobile.blackberry.com`. On this page, go to IM and Social Networking. The list of IM apps is listed on the next page with a link for downloading.

IM basics: What you need

Assuming that you have the IM app available on your BlackBerry, you need just two things to start using the standard five IM programs: a user ID and a password.

Getting a user ID/password combo is a breeze. Just go to the appropriate registration Web page (from the following list) for the IM app(s) you want to use. Note that it's easier and faster to use your desktop or laptop to sign up:

✔ **Google Talk**

> `www.google.com/accounts/NewAccount`

✔ **AOL Instant Messenger (AIM)**

> `www.aim.com/aimnew/register.adp`

✔ **ICQ Instant Messenger**

> `www.icq.com/register`

✔ **Windows Live Messenger**

> `http://messenger.msn.com/download/getstarted.aspx`

✔ **Yahoo! Messenger**

> `http://edit.yahoo.com/registration`

Given the many IM network choices available, your friends are probably signed up to a bunch of different networks. You may end up having to sign up for multiple networks if you want to reach them all through IM.

Going online with IM

After you obtain a user ID/password combo for one or more IM services, you can start chatting with your buddies by following these steps:

1. **From the Home screen, press the Menu key and select Instant Messaging.**

   A screen displaying the available IM services appears. You can choose from any of the four IM app icons, based on where your ID is valid.

2. **Highlight the IM app icon of your choice and press the trackpad.**

   We highlighted Google Talk. An application-specific login screen appears so you can sign on, similar to the one shown in Figure 9-6. It's straightforward, with the standard user name and password fields. (In some apps, the user name is called a screen name or ID.)

3. **Enter your user name and password.**

4. **(Optional) Select the Remember Password check box. Also if you want, select the Automatically Sign Me In check box.**

   When the Remember Password check box is enabled, the ID/password information is pre-entered the next time you come back to this screen. (Um, that is, you don't have to type this stuff every time you want to IM.)

We recommend that you select this check box to save time but also set your handheld password to Enabled so that security isn't compromised. Refer to Chapter 3 if you need a refresher on how to enable passwords on your BlackBerry.

The Automatically Sign Me In check box turns on and off sign-in when your BlackBerry is powered up. This is helpful if you have a habit of turning off your BlackBerry periodically.

5. **Press the trackpad and select Sign On.**

   At this point, IM tries to log you in. This can take a few seconds. After you're logged in, a simple listing of your contacts (AIM refers to contacts as *buddies*) appears.

6. **Select the person you want to chat with.**

   A menu appears, listing various things you can do. Features can differ a little bit for each IM app, but for Google Talk, here's a sample of what you can do: Start Chat, Send File, Add a Friend, Rename, Remove, and Block.

7. **Select the action you want.**

Google Talk

talk

User name:

Password:

Sign In

☑ Remember password

☑ Automatically sign me in

Need an account?
Go to google.com/accounts on your computer.

Forgot your password?

Figure 9-6:
Log in to
Google Talk
here.

Adding a contact/buddy

Before you can start chatting with your buddies, you need to know their user IDs (see Table 9-3).

Table 9-3	Obtaining Your Friend's Credentials
Provider	*Where You Get Someone's User ID*
AOL Instant Messenger	Your friend or by searching AOL's directory
Google Talk	The text before the @ sign in his Google e-mail address
ICQ Instant Messenger	Your friend's e-mail or the ICQ Global Directory
MSN Live Messenger	MSN passport ID or Hotmail ID
Yahoo! Messenger	The text before the @ sign in her Yahoo! e-mail address

Luckily for you, you don't need to search for IDs every time you want to IM someone. You can store IDs as part of a contacts list. Follow these steps:

1. **Starting in the IM service of your choice, press the Menu key.**

2. **Select Add a Friend, as shown in Figure 9-7.**

   The Add a Friend screen appears.

3. **Enter the user ID of your contact.**

4. **Press the trackpad.**

   IM is smart enough to figure out whether this contact has a valid user ID. If the ID is valid, the app adds the ID to your list of contacts. The buddy goes either to the Online or Offline section of your list, depending on whether he or she is logged in. You'll be warned if the ID you entered isn't valid.

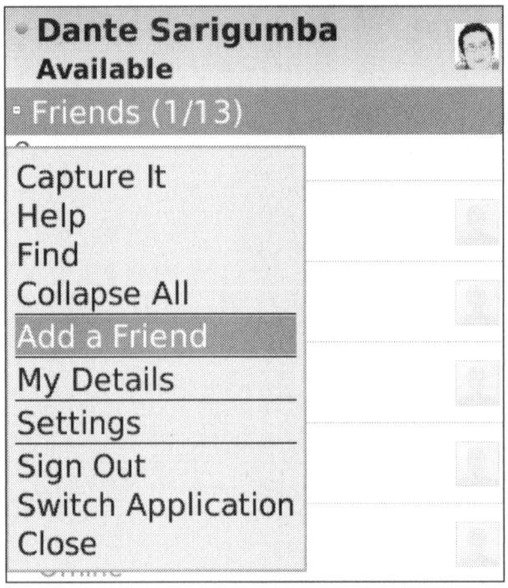

Dante Sarigumba
Available

Friends (1/13)

Capture It
Help
Find
Collapse All
Add a Friend
My Details
Settings
Sign Out
Switch Application
Close

Figure 9-7:
Adding a
friend.

Doing the chat thing

Suppose you want to start a conversation with one of your contacts (a safe assumption, we think). When you send a message within the IM app, you're initiating a conversation. Here's how:

1. **Log in to the IM app of your choice.**

2. **Select the person you want to contact.**

   A typical online chat screen shows up. The top portion lists old messages sent to and received from this contact. You type your message in the bottom part of the screen.

3. **Type your message.**

4. **Press the Enter key.**

   Your user ID and the message you just sent show up in the topmost (history) section of the chat screen. When you get a message, it's added to the history section so that both sides of your conversation stay in view.

Sending your smile

You can quickly add emoticons to your message (without having to remember all the character equivalents in Table 9-1). Follow these steps:

1. **While you're typing your message, press the Menu key.**

2. **From the menu that appears, select Show Symbols.**

   All the icons appear, as shown in Figure 9-8.

3. **Select the emoticon you want.**

   The emoticon is added to your message.

Figure 9-8:
You can choose among many smileys.

Taking control of your IM app

If you use IM frequently — and you tend to chat with many contacts at the same time — your BlackBerry's physical limitations may cramp your IM style. No matter whether you use AIM, Yahoo! Messenger, ICQ Instant Messenger, MSN Live Messenger, or BlackBerry Messenger (see Chapter 10), it's still slower to type words on the tiny keypad than it is to type on your PC.

Do you just give up on the dream of IMing on the go? Not necessarily. The following sections show how you can power up your BlackBerry IM technique.

Jive on

If you want to make sure that you won't have text-messaging fees for using an IM client, check out these IM programs:

- **BeejiveIM** (www.beejive.com/download/blackberry.htm): This one-time-fee program connects directly to the Web instead of using SMS. It works with multiple IM networks and multiple accounts per network: AIM, Windows Live Messenger, Yahoo! Messenger, Google Talk, ICQ Instant Messenger, Jabber, and MySpace IM. BeejiveIM is one of the best options. On their Web site, they have versions to support old BlackBerry devices, BlackBerry Storm, and high-resolution screens. Download the version for high-resolution screens.

- **Nimbuzz** (www.nimbuzz.com): Nimbuzz supports many of the popular IM networks. It even supports calls using the Skype network. And best of all, it's free and doesn't use SMS.

- **IM+** (www.shapeservices.com/eng/im/blackberry): If you don't want to pay annually, consider this service. IM+ asks for a one-time fee and also supports Yahoo!, MSN, AOL, ICQ, Google Talk, and Jabber networks. The best thing about IM+ is that it sends messages by using the Internet rather than SMS, so it's best suited for people who have the unlimited data plan. You have to choose a version: The Regular version connects to BlackBerry Enterprise Server, which is used by companies as a way of connecting the BlackBerry platform to a corporate network and e-mail server. The WAP version allows a personal BlackBerry to use the network provider's WAP gateway to connect to the Internet. The Shape Services Web site has a comprehensive FAQ list for details about the software.

Less is more

If you can't keep up with all your buddies, your best bet is to limit your exposure. Take a whack at your contacts list so that only your true buddies remain as contacts whom you want to IM from your BlackBerry. Trimming your list is easy. To delete a contact from your IM app, highlight the contact from the main screen of the IM app, press the Menu key, and select Delete.

Deleting a contact or buddy from an IM app on your BlackBerry also deletes it from the desktop or laptop computer version of the app. That's because the list of contacts is maintained at a central location — an IM server, to be precise — and not on your BlackBerry.

Set up two accounts of your favorite IM app: one for your BlackBerry and one for your desktop PC. By using these accounts separately, you can limit the number of contacts you have on your BlackBerry and still maintain a full-blown list of contacts on your desktop.

Although Twitter is a message broadcast and doesn't fall under the umbrella of instant messaging in the traditional sense, it's becoming the communication medium of choice for millions of people. On the BlackBerry, we recommend that you check out ÜberTwitter, TweetGenius, or SocialScope for your Twitter needs. Be sure to send us a tweet at @danters and @robertkao.

Less typing — use shorthand

Cut down your typing time. Don't forget the shorthand described earlier in this chapter. It's widely used in IM as well as texting, so refer to Table 9-1 whenever you can so that you can respond quickly. Before you know it, you will have the abbreviations memorized and will be using them with ease. Emoticons also make your conversation interesting, so make sure you take them out of your toolbox. Refer to Table 9-2 earlier in this chapter for a list of the most common ones.

SMS versus connecting via the Web

SMS messages are short messages designed for cell phones. IM is a step up, evolving from the Internet, where bandwidth is no longer a concern. It provides a better real-time conversation experience across distances. These two technologies evolved in parallel. As more people used IM, it became apparent that the technology had a place in handheld devices, where mobility is an advantage. Some of the IM programs developed and used in the BlackBerry in the past use SMS behind the scenes. And because your BlackBerry can connect to the Internet, other programs use the Internet directly. These differences can affect your monthly bill as well as your messaging experience. Read on.

If you don't have unlimited SMS but have an unlimited data plan, be careful with any third-party IM software. Make sure that it uses the Internet instead of SMS. If it uses SMS, you'll incur charges for every message sent and received, and most network providers charge 20 cents for every SMS message, which can add up quickly and lead to a nasty surprise on your monthly bill.

Chapter 10

Instant Messaging

- -

- -

*I*n Chapter 9, you find a slew of ways to send messages on your BlackBerry Pearl. In this chapter, you get the scoop on another way to send messages, using a special app known and loved by BlackBerry users.

Research in Motion provides IM (instant messaging) in the form of BlackBerry Messenger. This app is based on the PIN-to-PIN messaging technology (refer to Chapter 9), which means that it is mucho fast and quite reliable.

Note that with BlackBerry Messenger, you can chat with only those buddies who have a BlackBerry and have PIN-to-PIN messaging enabled. The app supports IM features common to many other apps, such as group chatting and the capability to monitor the availability of other IM buddies.

Using BlackBerry Messenger

You can access BlackBerry Messenger in the Instant Messaging folder from the Home screen, as shown in Figure 10-1. The first time you run BlackBerry Messenger, a welcome screen asks you to enter your display name. This display name is the one you want someone else to see on his or her BlackBerry Messenger when you send a message.

The next time you open Messenger, you see a contacts list, as shown on the left in Figure 10-2. (Okay, this figure displays some contacts, but your list should be empty; we'll show you how to populate the list in a minute.)

Figure 10-1:
Launch
BlackBerry
Messenger
here.

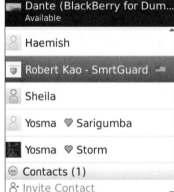

Figure 10-2:
The con-
tacts list
(left) and
menu (right).

Pressing the menu key lets you do the following, as shown on the right side
of Figure 10-2:

- ✔ **Broadcast Message:** Send a message to multiple contacts in BlackBerry
  Messenger. The messages appear as conversations in the recipients'
  BlackBerry Messenger.

- ✔ **Start Chat:** Initiate a conversation with the highlighted contact.

- ✔ **Invite to Conference:** Initiate a group conversation. See "Starting a
  group conversation," later in this chapter, for details.

- ✔ **Forward to Messenger Contact:** Send the highlighted contact information to your other BlackBerry Messenger contacts.

- ✔ **Invite Contact:** Add a new contact to BlackBerry Messenger (see the
  next section).

- ✔ **Add Category:** Create custom groupings in BlackBerry Messenger.

- ✔ **Contact Profile:** Display a screen showing the information of the highlighted contact.

✔ **Delete Contact:** Delete the highlighted contact.

✔ **Move Contact:** Move the highlighted contact to a different category.

✔ **My Profile:** Customize your personal information and control how you want others to see you from their BlackBerry Messenger contacts list. You can do the following (see Figure 10-3):

• Change your picture. Select the default image, navigate to your picture, scroll the picture to center your face in the square, press the Menu key, and then select Crop and Save.

• Change your display name.

• Allow others to see the title of the song you're listening to.

• Allow others to see that you're using the phone.

• Enter a personal message that others can see.

• Set your time zone.

• Allow others to see your location and time zone information.

• Display your barcode.

The menu has more items. Scroll down the menu screen to see the following:

✔ **Options:** Customize the behavior of BlackBerry Messenger.

✔ **Create New Group:** Create custom groupings for your contacts.

This option is helpful if you have several contacts in BlackBerry Messenger. Simply select this menu item, and an Add Group screen appears so you can enter a group name.

✔ **Scan a Group Barcode:** Add members to the open group by scanning your friend's BlackBerry barcode.

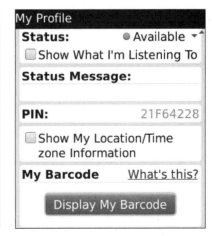

Figure 10-3: Set your personal information (left). The rest of the My Profile screen (right).

Adding a Contact

With no one in your contacts list, BlackBerry Messenger is pretty useless. Your first order of business is to add a contact to your list — someone you know who

- ✔ Has a BlackBerry
- ✔ Is entered in your contacts
- ✔ Has PIN-to-PIN messaging enabled
- ✔ Has a copy of BlackBerry Messenger installed on his or her device

If you know someone who fits these criteria, you can add that person to your list by doing the following:

1. In BlackBerry Messenger, press the Menu key and select Add a Contact.

The Add Contact screen appears, listing actions related to adding a contact, as shown on the left side of Figure 10-4. The top two options are the ones you use to add a contact to BlackBerry Messenger.

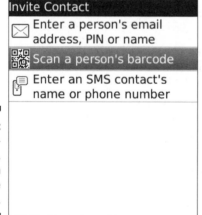

Figure 10-4:
Add a contact (left). An invitation barcode (right).

2. If you want to *scan* your friend's BlackBerry barcode:

a. On the same screen (Figure 10-4, left), but using your friend's BlackBerry, select the third option, which reads Show Your Invitation Barcode to Another BlackBerry.

A barcode image similar to Figure 10-4, right, appears on your friend's BlackBerry.

b. **On your BlackBerry, select the second option, Scan Invitation Barcode from Another BlackBerry.**

The Camera app appears to allow you to capture the barcode. Once captured, the contact information is added to your BlackBerry Messenger contacts list.

That's it. You're finished.

The following steps show you how to enter your contact directly from the Add Contact screen. To enter the contact's e-mail address or BlackBerry PIN:

1. **On the Add Contact screen, select the first option, Add a Contact by Entering Their Email Address or PIN.**

The Invite Contact screen appears.

2. **Start typing the name of the contact, and when a list of possible contacts appears, select the name you want to add.**

3. **Type your message.**

A default message is provided, but you can edit this message. This is the message that the contact will receive after you finish Step 4.

4. **Select OK and then select OK again in the screen that follows.**

The app sends your request. As long as the person hasn't responded to your request, his or her name appears as part of the Pending group, as shown in Figure 10-5. When your contact responds positively to your request, that name goes to the official contacts list.

Figure 10-5:
To-be-approved contacts are in the Pending group.

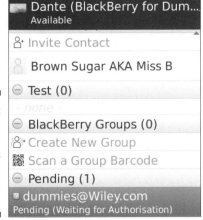

Having Conversations

What you really want to do is use Blackberry Messenger to chat with your friends. The short sections here give you a quick rundown on starting individual or group conversations. We also throw in some steps on sharing files and saving your conversation history.

Starting a conversation

You can easily start a conversation with any of your contacts. Follow these steps:

1. **On the BlackBerry Messenger main menu, select the name in your contacts list.**

   A traditional chat interface opens, with a list of old messages at the top and a text box for typing messages at the bottom.

2. **Type your message.**

3. **Press the Enter key.**

   Any messages you send (as well as any responses you get) are appended to the history list at the top.

Starting a group conversation

You can easily invite others to your BlackBerry Messenger conversation. Follow these steps:

1. **During a conversation, press the Menu key.**

   The BlackBerry Messenger main menu appears. This time, an Invite option has been added.

2. **Select Invite to Group Chat.**

   The Select Contacts screen opens, listing your BlackBerry Messenger contacts who are available, as shown in Figure 10-6.

3. **Invite people by selecting the corresponding check boxes.**

   You can choose any number of people.

4. **Select OK.**

   You're back to the preceding conversation screen, but this time, the history list shows the contacts you added to the conversation. The newly selected contact(s) can now join the conversation.

Figure 10-6:
See your available contacts here.

You can set a subject for your message. This feature is especially useful for group conversations. To add a subject to a conversation, follow these simple steps:

1. **Press the Menu key while you're on the conversation screen and then select Set Subject.**

   On the screen that follows, the cursor is in the subject line, waiting for you to enter a subject. This works for an individual conversation and a conference, as shown in Figure 10-7.

2. **On the screen that follows, enter the subject and then select OK.**

   The conversation screen is updated with the subject.

Figure 10-7:
Add a subject to your conversation here.

You can make your name appear snazzy by adding symbols, such as Dante☺ and Yosma♨ (see Figure 10-8 for symbols to choose from):

1. **On the BlackBerry Messenger screen, press the Menu key.**

2. **Select My Profile.**

3. **Press the Menu key and select Add Smiley to choose the symbol you want.**

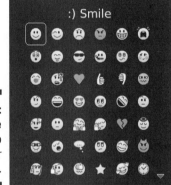

Figure 10-8:
Choose
symbols to
add to your
name here.

Sending a file

BlackBerry Messenger, like any other IM app, can send files. During a conversation, just press the Menu key, and you'll see several menu items allowing you to share a file:

- ✔ **Send Picture:** Selecting this option shows a screen similar to the left side of Figure 10-9, where you can either launch the Camera app to take a picture to send or select the picture file you want to send (navigate to a specific folder if necessary). The default location for picture files is the Media Card pictures folder. Just select Camera to launch the Camera app.

  Before sending the picture, BlackBerry Messenger displays a prompt so that you can resize your picture. The options are Original (the default), Large (1024x768), Medium (800x600), and Small (640x480). Make your picture smaller if you are concerned with bandwidth. Sending large images uses a lot of bandwidth and can cost you money in excess bandwidth charges by the carrier if you don't have an unlimited data plan.

- ✔ **Send Voice Note:** Selecting this option gives you the Voice Note screen (refer to Figure 10-9, right), where you can record the voice message you want to send. When you're ready to record, follow these steps:

Figure 10-9: Send a picture (left) or start recording a voice message (right).

a. **Select Start.**

BlackBerry is ready to record your voice message. A recording screen appears with a Stop button, as shown on the left side of Figure 10-10.

b. **When you finish speaking your message, select Stop.**

A screen similar to the right side of Figure 10-10 appears. You can play the message to review what you said, send the message if you're satisfied, or cancel sending a voice note.

c. **Select Send.**

A prompt asks you to add a description of your voice message. Selecting No sends the message right away.

d. **Select Yes.**

e. **Enter a description and then select OK.**

A request to transfer the file is sent, and your friend needs to accept it in his or her BlackBerry Messenger for the transmission to begin.

✔ **Send File:** This option displays a screen that lists which file types you can send. Aside from giving you a different way of sending picture and voice message, the screen lists the following options:

• **File:** Send any type of file. You see an Explorer-type screen so that you can navigate to the file you want to send. The default folders shown are Media Card and Device Memory.

• **BlackBerry Contact:** Send a vCard (see Chapter 4 for details on the vCard). When selected, you see the Contacts screen, allowing you to select the contact to whom you want to send a vCard.

• **Messenger Contact:** Choose a contact from your list of BlackBerry Messenger contacts and send the contact info as a file.

Figure 10-10:
Record and
send your
voice mes-
sage here.

Saving the conversation history

While you're on the conversation screen, you can save your chat history in two ways. Both methods are accessible by a simple press of the Menu key:

- ✔ **Copy Chat:** Copies the existing chat history to the Clipboard. You then paste the history into the app where you want it saved, such as Calendar or MemoPad.

- ✔ **Email Chat:** Displays the Compose Message dialog screen, shown in Figure 10-11, with the Subject field prepopulated with `Chat with <Contact> on <Date>` and the body of the message prepopulated with the chat history.

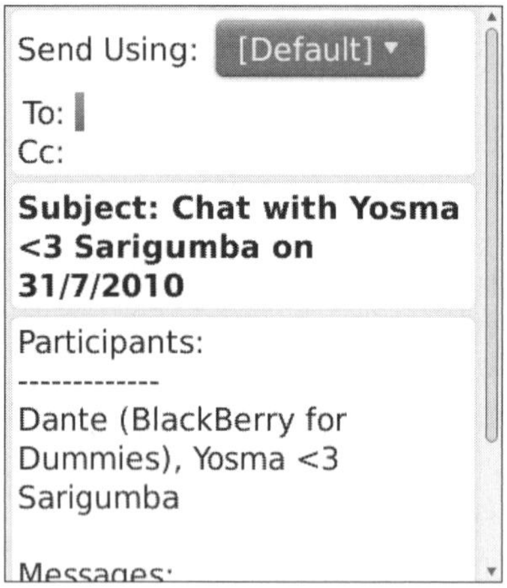

Figure 10-11:
E-mail your
chat history
here.

Send Using: [Default] ▾

To:

Cc:

**Subject: Chat with Yosma
<3 Sarigumba on
31/7/2010**

Participants:

Dante (BlackBerry for
Dummies), Yosma <3
Sarigumba

Messages:

Broadcasting a Message

Do you feel the need to start a conversation on the same subject with *several* people? You can start with a group chat, but what if you want to get a per-sonal opinion from each individual, something that each person isn't comfortable saying in front of the crowd? The best way to do this is to broad-cast a message to multiple recipients:

1. **On the BlackBerry Messenger screen, press the Menu key and select Broadcast Message.**

   The Broadcast Message screen appears, as shown in Figure 10-12, allow-ing you to enter your message and select the recipients.

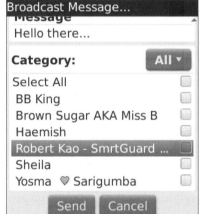

Figure 10-12:
Broadcast
a message
here.

2. **Enter your message.**
3. **Select the recipients.**
4. **Select Send.**

Customizing BlackBerry Messenger

Like any other BlackBerry apps, BlackBerry Messenger can be customized. To begin, press the Menu key on the BlackBerry Messenger screen and select Options (the wrench icon) to display the screen shown in Figure 10-13.

Customizing chats

Starting at the top of the Options screen and below the Chats section, you can finesse the following options:

✔ **Press Enter Key to Send:** Make pressing the Enter key while in the conversation screen equivalent to pressing the Menu key and selecting Send. This option is selected by default.

 ✔ **Show Chats in Messages App:** List every transmitted and received conversation on the Messages screen. This option is selected by default.

 ✔ **Group Sequential Messages in Chat:** If a series of messages are received or transmitted before the other party responds, group the messages. This option is selected by default.

 ✔ **Show Display Names in Chat:** Decide whether you want to include the display name on every message in the chat history. The default is not selected.

 ✔ **Conversation Style:** Decide how you want to display the chat history. Standard is a plain-vanilla listing of messages, Bubbles (the default) displays messages in oval boxes, and Stripes divides the messages using lines.

 ✔ **Sort Chats By:** Determine how recent conversations are listed in the chat folder of the main screen. Alphabet (the default) sorts by name, and Activity sorts by the latest conversation.

Going down the Options screen, under Display Pictures, one useful option is Replace Caller ID Pictures with Display Pictures. This option overrides the caller ID picture with the contact's picture on your BlackBerry Messenger. This saves you the effort of adding photos of your contacts in Contacts. The option is deselected by default.

Figure 10-13: Customize BlackBerry Messenger here.

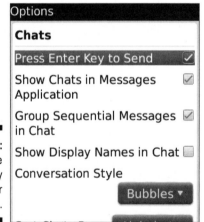

Backing up, restoring, and deleting contacts

BlackBerry Messenger stores your contacts on RIM's servers so you can restore them if you change BlackBerry smartphones. You also have the option of backing up contacts to your microSD card. Each backup operation creates a single file in your microSD, which you use for the restore process.

The following features appear on the Options screen, below the Contact List section:

✔ **Save a copy of your contact list:** Select the Backup button to launch a Back Up Contact List screen. This screen displays the following options:

- **Back Up Files Remotely:** Display the Remote Backup screen, with e-mail addresses that you use when registering BlackBerry Messenger.

- **Back Up Files Locally:** Display the Local Backup screen, so you can manually back up your contacts to BlackBerry's memory or the microSD card.

✔ **Restore a Previously Saved Copy of Your Contact List:** Navigate to the backup file of your contact list and restore it to BlackBerry Messenger.

✔ **Delete Backup Files:** Navigate to and delete your contact list backup files.

Dealing with recent updates

Toward the bottom of the Options screen, below the Recent Updates section, are features you can customize if you want to see status updates or the music your contacts are currently listening to:

✔ **Show Recent Updates:** Display in chronological order your contacts' recent status updates (what the users are currently doing, such as listening to a specific music track). Updates are in the Recent Updates folder on the main BlackBerry Messenger screen. Your choices are None, 25 (the default), 50, or 100 recent updates.

✔ **Group Recent Updates from Same Contact/Group:** The default is checked, which means recent updates for the same contact or group of contacts are grouped together.

✔ **Display Music Updates from Contacts:** Display in the Recent Updates folder the songs your contacts are currently listening to on their Blackberry. The option is unselected by default.

Miscellaneous options

At the bottom of Options screen are the following miscellaneous options that you can customize:

✔ **Vibrate When receiving a Ping:** If selected (the default), your BlackBerry Pearl will vibrate whenever a *ping* (a short message) is received. If you deselect this, a ping will be treated like any BlackBerry Messenger message.

✔ **Display Security Question on Invitation:** Include a question with any invitation you send. You also have to enter the answer to the question, which will be included in the invite message but hidden to the receiving person. The person receiving the invitation must answer the question and match the hidden answer before your BlackBerry Messenger contact is added to his or her contact list. This feature verifies the identify of the other person. The option is unselected by default.

✔ **Save Message History:** Save conversations you have in BlackBerry Messenger. Your choices are Off (the default), saving the messages in Device, or saving the messages in Media Card. If you choose Device or Media Card, you see a message that it is illegal to record chats in certain areas.

✔ **Auto Accept Voice Notes:** Display a confirmation for accepting a voice note file. The default is to automatically accept the voice note file and do away with the confirmation screen.

We recommend that you don't automatically accept voice notes if your BlackBerry Pearl was issued by your company. Most companies have policies on offensive media, and you don't want to inadvertently receive voice notes that violate that policy.

Chapter 11

Surfing the Internet Wave

∙ ∙

In This Chapter

▶ Using BlackBerry Browser to surf the Web

▶ Creating and organizing bookmarks

▶ Customizing and optimizing Browser

▶ Downloading and installing apps from the Web

▶ Using browsers in business

∙ ∙

*W*eb surfing has become a necessity and part of our daily existence. Nearly everyone can surf the Web anytime and anywhere from a desktop computer, a netbook, or even a tiny mobile device such as a PDA or smartphone. Having said that, it should be no surprise that your BlackBerry Pearl has a Web browser of its own.

In this chapter, we show you how to use BlackBerry Browser. We give you shortcuts and timesaving tips, including the coolest ways to make pages load faster, as well as a complete neat freak's guide to managing your bookmarks.

And, because network service providers may also have browsers for you to use, we compare these proprietary browsers with the default BlackBerry Browser so that you can decide which of them best suits your needs.

Kicking Up Browser

BlackBerry Browser comes loaded on your Pearl and accesses the Web with a cell phone connection. Browser can be named differently, depending on how the service provider customizes it. Sometimes Browser is named *BlackBerry Browser, Internet Browser, Hotspot Browser,* or most likely, just *Browser.* We call it *Browser* to make things easier.

Browser has multiple personalities:

✔ **One that's connected to your company's BlackBerry Enterprise Server**

BlackBerry Enterprise Server is a software app from RIM that companies can use to control and manage BlackBerry devices. The software also allows your device to see your company's network and connect to your company's databases. If you're a corporate BlackBerry user, your company administrator may turn off or not install all browsers except for the one that connects through the company's BlackBerry Enterprise Server.

✔ **One that goes directly to your service provider's network**

This browser might be called by the network service provider's brand name.

✔ **One that uses a Wi-Fi connection**

The Browser accesses the Internet through a Wi-Fi connection and retrieves page content without having to go through BlackBerry Enterprise Server or BlackBerry Internet Service. Therefore, page content and images are not processed, compressed, or encrypted before they are retrieved

✔ **A WAP browser**

Wireless application protocol, or WAP, was popular in the 1990s, when mobile device displays were limited and could display only five or six rows of text. WAP lost its appeal with the advent of high-resolution screens.

The following sections get you started using Browser. After you get your feet wet, we promise that you'll be chomping at the bit to find out more!

Although Browser is a decent app, it isn't the strongest BlackBerry feature compared to browsers in other smartphones. If you'd like to try another browser, we recommend that you check out third-party browsers such as Bolt Browser (`http://Boltbrowser.com`) and Opera Mini 5 (`m.opera.com`).

Getting to Browser

Browser is a main app on your device, with its globe icon visible right on the Home screen, as shown in Figure 11-1. In most cases, you open Browser by scrolling to this icon and then pressing the trackpad.

If Browser is your default browser, you can access it from any app that distinguishes a Web address. For example, from Contacts, you can open Browser by opening a link in the Web Page field. If you get an e-mail message that contains a Web address, just scroll to that link. The link is highlighted, and you can open the page by pressing the trackpad and selecting Open Link, as shown in Figure 11-2.

Figure 11-1:
You can open Browser from the Home screen.

Figure 11-2:
Open Browser from Messages.

When you access Browser from another app, you don't have to close that app to jump to Browser. Just press the Alt key (to the left of the Z key) and the Escape key at the same time to open a pop-up screen with application icons. Use your track-pad to highlight the Browser icon; then press the trackpad to launch Browser.

By default, accessing Browser by selecting a Web address or a Web link in another app opens the Web page associated with that address. (In Figure 11-2, we're opening Browser from the Messages app.)

Opening Browser by selecting its icon on the Home screen gives you a start page similar to Figure 11-3, which lists the latest Web sites you've visited. The page also displays a Bookmarks link. You find out more about adding book-marks later in this chapter, in the "Bookmarking Your Favorite Sites." section. Note that you can reconfigure the start page and the display of bookmarks, as explained in the "Configuring Browser" section, later in the chapter.

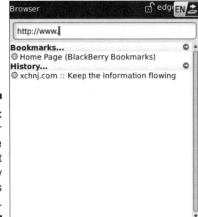

Figure 11-3:
Browser
with the
default
empty
Bookmarks
screen.

Hitting the (air)waves

After you open Browser, you're ready to surf the Web. Here's how:

1. **Open Browser.**

   Unless the BlackBerry Browser configuration is changed, BlackBerry displays a default start page when you open Browser (refer to Figure 11-3). This page lets you enter a Web address.

   If you haven't changed the start page (see "Configuring Browser," later in the chapter, to customize the start page), skip to Step 3.

2. **Press the Menu key and select Go To.**

3. **Type a Web address, as shown in Figure 11-4.**

4. **Select OK.**

   The progress of the loading page is indicated at the bottom of the screen.

If a Web page contains a phone number or an e-mail address, you can scroll to that information to highlight it. Then press the trackpad to initiate a phone call or open a new e-mail message, respectively.

Navigating Web pages

Using Browser to navigate a Web page is easy. Note that hyperlinks are highlighted onscreen. To jump to a particular hyperlink, scroll to the highlighted link and press the trackpad.

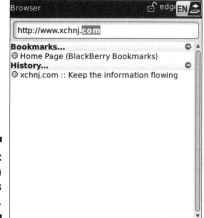

Figure 11-4:
Opening a
Web page is
simple.

Here are few shortcuts you can use while navigating a Web page:

- Quickly move up and down one full display page at a time by pressing 9 (down arrow) or 3 (up arrow).

- Move to the top of the page: ER key.

- Move to the bottom of the page: CV key.

- Move to the next page: M or Space key.

- Move to the previous page: UI key.

- Quickly switch between full-screen mode and normal mode by pressing the exclamation point (!) key. Think of full-screen mode simply as another way to view the same Web page on your BlackBerry, but the BlackBerry doesn't show anything extra (for example, signals level) on the top portion of the display screen. Normal mode is what you get by default.

- To stop loading a page, press the Escape key.

- After a page fully loads, you can go back to the previous page by pressing the Escape key.

And don't forget the Browser menu (press the Menu key). It has some useful shortcuts, as shown in Figure 11-5.

The Browser menu options follow:

- **Help:** Displays a quick guide. This option is always available on the menu screen.

- **Page View:** Displays the page as you would typically see it on a PC's Internet browser. The Web page takes up the entire screen, so you may have to zoom in and scroll to see a portion of the page clearly. This option appears only in Column view.

✔ **Column View:** Displays the Web page vertically (the default) — a wide Web page wraps down, and you can use the trackpad to scroll up and down the page. This option appears only in Page view.

✔ **Zoom In/Out:** Zooms in and out.

✔ **Find:** Locates and highlights text on the current page. Like any other basic Find tool, selecting this option displays a prompt to enter the text you want to find. Then a Find Next menu appears after the initial search so you can find the next matching text.

✔ **Select:** Highlights text onscreen for copying. This option appears only if the trackpad pointer is placed on text.

✔ **Stop:** Cancels a request. This option appears only if you're in the middle of requesting a page. Selecting the Stop option is the same as pressing the Escape key.

✔ **Copy:** Copies text you've highlighted to memory so that you can use it later for pasting elsewhere, such as in MemoPad. This option appears only if you've highlighted text.

✔ **Full Image:** Displays the image in full. This option appears only if you highlight an image and a portion of the image is displayed onscreen.

✔ **Save Image:** Saves the image in the BlackBerry's built-in memory or to a microSD card. This option appears only if you highlight an image.

✔ **Home:** Goes to your home page. The default home page can vary from carrier to carrier. To change the default home page, display the Browser menu, select Options, select Browser Configuration, and then change the Home Page Address field.

✔ **Get Link:** Opens the page represented by the link. This option appears only if you have a highlighted link.

Figure 11-5:
The Browser menu has lots of good stuff.

xchnj.com :: Keep the informatio...   edge

xchnj

Help
Column View
Zoom In
Find
Home
Go To...
Recent Pages
History
Refresh
Set Encoding
Add Bookmark
Bookmarks
Page Address
Send Address
Options
Save Page
Switch Application
Close

SmrtWebAlerts

application that can be
favorite RSS and twitter
ds. If enable it can also
sages of newly received
witter items.

d **EmailBuddy**

ewest BlackBerry utility
l help you view, sort and
ails using EmailBuddy's
ndly interface.

To open a link more quickly, press the Enter key.

✔ **Go To:** Opens a Web page when you type a Web address and press the trackpad. As you enter more addresses, they're listed in the History portion of the screen so that you don't have to retype them. To find out how to clear this list, see the "Cache operations" section, later in this chapter.

✔ **Back <Esc>:** Goes back to the previous page you viewed. Appears only if you have navigated to more than one Web page.

You can achieve the same function by pressing the Escape key.

✔ **Forward:** Progresses one page at a time. This option appears only if you have gone back at least one Web page.

✔ **Recent Pages:** Displays a list of pages you've viewed previously. This is a convenient way of revisiting pages.

✔ **History:** Tracks up to 20 pages of Web addresses you've visited, which you can view on the History screen. From there, you can go to any of those Web pages by highlighting the page name and pressing the trackpad.

✔ **Refresh:** Updates the current page. This option is helpful when you're viewing a page with data that changes frequently (such as stock quotes).

✔ **Set Encoding:** Specifies the encoding used in viewing a Web page. This option is useful when viewing foreign languages that use different characters, a situation most of us don't have to deal with. If you have to set encoding, make sure you know the appropriate encoding.

When you try to open a Web page, indicators that show the progress of your request appear at the bottom of the screen. The left side of Figure 11-6 shows Browser requesting a page; the right side of the figure shows that you've reached the page and the page is still loading.

Figure 11-6: Requesting a page (left) and then loading it (right).

The icons in the top-right corner of both screens in Figure 11-6 are described, from right to left, in the following list:

- ✔ Your **connection type** appears in the rightmost side, below the signal strength bars. In Figure 11-6, *WiFi* means that the connection is using a Wi-Fi network.

  If you aren't connected to Wi-Fi, an icon with vertical bars and an antenna appears to the right of the connection type, showing the strength of the network signals (the same signal indicators for phone and e-mail).

- ✔ The **lock icon** indicates whether you're at a secure Web page. Figure 11-6 shows a nonsecure page. If you're accessing your bank, you most likely see the secured icon (a closed lock). Most pages don't need to be secure, so you see the unsecured icon (an open lock). When this icon is selected, it displays the connection information screen, which tells you the amount of Web page data transferred between your BlackBerry and the network provider. In Browser, you should see a trackpad pointer in the screen, which is similar to a PC mouse pointer. Scroll the trackpad until the pointer hovers in the lock icon and then press the trackpad. The next screen displays the connection information.

If you lose patience waiting for a page to load and want to browse somewhere else, press the Escape key to stop the page from loading.

Saving a Web page address

Entering a Web address to view a page can get tedious. Fortunately, you can return to a page without manually entering the same address. While you're viewing a Web page, simply use the Browser menu (shown on the left in Figure 11-7) to save that page's address.

No place like Home

Changing your Home screen background is a neat trick. You can use an image you've saved in your Pictures list as the background on your Home screen. Here's how:

1. **From the Home screen, select the Media icon and then select Pictures.**

2. **Scroll to and select the image you want to set as your background.**

3. **Press the Menu key and then select Set As.**

4. **Select Wallpaper.**

Figure 11-7:
Use the
Browser
menu to
save a
Web page
address.

You can save a Web page address in several ways:

- ✔ **Page Address:** Views the Web address of the current page from a pop-up screen. This screen presents you with two options:

  - • **Copy Address:** Saves the page's address to your BlackBerry Clipboard and allows you to paste it somewhere else.

  - • **Send Address:** Sends the address in one of several ways, as described in the next bullet.

- ✔ **Send Address:** Presents a screen so that you can choose whether to send the address by e-mail (see Chapter 8), MMS (see Chapter 9), PIN (see Chapter 9), SMS (see Chapter 9), or Messenger Contact (see Chapter 10).

- ✔ **Options:** Displays a screen allowing you to customize the behavior of Browser. See the section "Exercising Options and Optimization Techniques," later in this chapter, for details.

- ✔ **Save Page:** Saves the Web address of the current page to Messages. A message appears with the Browser globe icon to indicate that the message is a Web link, as shown on the right in Figure 11-7. Highlighting that entry and pressing the trackpad launches Browser and opens the page for your viewing pleasure.

  Saving a page to your message list has a different purpose from bookmarking a page. The saved page is initially displayed as unread in Messages, to remind you to check back later.

Note: When you don't have network coverage and you try to access a Web page, you're prompted to save your request. When you do, your request is automatically saved in the message list. Then, when you do have coverage later, you can open the same Web page from the message list, with the content loaded already!

Pressing a letter key while you're in a menu selects the first menu item that starts with that letter. Pressing the same letter again selects the next menu item that starts with that letter.

Sending an address by e-mail

You can send a Web address to any recipient via e-mail using the Page Address option in the Browser menu. For a more direct way, simply select Send Address from the Browser menu while the Web page is displayed. If you know right away that you're going to send an address to someone, use the more direct method.

Saving Web images

You can view and save pictures or images in BMP, GIF, JPEG, or PNG format from a Web page. Any saved image can be accessed using the Picture app, which enables you to view it later, even when you're out of range. To save an image, just select the image and then select Save Image from the menu that appears.

Bookmarking Your Favorite Sites

You don't have to memorize the addresses of your favorite sites. Instead, use BlackBerry Browser to keep a list of sites you want to revisit. In other words, make a *bookmark* so you can come back to a site quickly.

Adding and visiting a bookmark

Add a bookmark this way:

1. **Open Browser and go to the Web page you want to bookmark.**

2. **Select Add Bookmark from the Browser menu.**

   The menu is always accessible by pressing the Menu key.

3. **(Optional) In the Add Bookmark dialog box, change the bookmark name.**

   The name of the bookmark defaults to the Web site title and, in most cases, is appropriate to use as the name. But you can always change this name; refer to the next section, "Modifying a bookmark."

4. In the Add Bookmark dialog box, navigate to the folder where you want to save the bookmark.

The dialog box is shown in Figure 11-8. The default saved-bookmark folder is BlackBerry Bookmarks, but you can save the bookmark in any folder you create. To see how to create a bookmark folder, skip to the later section "Adding a bookmark subfolder."

5. Scroll to the bottom of the dialog box and select Add.

Figure 11-8:
Name the
bookmark
and specify
where to
store it.

Here's how to open a bookmarked page:

1. In Browser, select Bookmarks from the Browser menu.

You see the Bookmarks screen. From there, you can find all the pages you've bookmarked.

2. Select the bookmark for the page you want to visit.

Available offline

The Add Bookmark dialog box contains the Available Offline check box. When you select this check box, you not only save a page as a bookmark but also *cache* it so that you can see it even when you're out of range (such as when you're stuck deep in a mountain cave). The next time you click the bookmark, that page opens quickly. We recommend making bookmarks available offline for pages that don't change from day to day, such as those from search engines (for example, Google).

Modifying a bookmark

You have the option to change the attributes of existing bookmarks. Why change them? Say you bookmarked a few pages from the same Web site but the author of the Web pages didn't bother to have a unique title for each page. Now you have several bookmarks with the same name.

Changing a bookmark is a snap:

1. **From the Browser menu, select Bookmarks.**

   The Bookmarks screen appears.

2. **Highlight the name of the bookmark you want to modify, press the Menu key, and then select Edit Bookmark.**

3. **On the screen that follows, edit the existing name, the address the bookmark is pointing to, or both.**

4. **Select Accept to save your changes.**

Organizing your bookmarks

Over time, the number of your bookmarks will grow, and trying to find a site from a tiny screen can be tough. A handy workaround is to organize your bookmarks in folders. For example, you can group related sites in a folder, and each folder can have one or more subfolders. Having a folder hierarchy narrows your search and allows you to easily find a site.

For example, your sites might fall into these categories:

- ✔ Reference

    New York Times

    Yahoo!

- ✔ Fun

    Flickr

    The Onion

- ✔ Shopping

    Etsy

    Gaiam

Adding a bookmark subfolder

You can add subfolders only to folders that are already listed on the Bookmarks page. That is, you can't create your own root folder. Your choices for adding your first subfolder are under WAP Bookmarks or BlackBerry Bookmarks.

Suppose that you want to add a subfolder in your BlackBerry Bookmarks folder. Simply follow these steps:

1. **On the Bookmarks screen, highlight BlackBerry Bookmarks.**

   The BlackBerry Bookmarks folder is the *parent* of the new subfolder. In this case, the BlackBerry Bookmarks folder will contain the Reference subfolder.

2. **Press the Menu key and select Add Subfolder, as shown in the left of Figure 11-9.**

   You see a dialog box where you can enter the name of the folder. (We're using Reference as the name.)

3. **Type the folder name and select OK.**

   The Reference folder now appears on the Bookmarks screen (as shown in the left of Figure 11-9), bearing a folder icon.

Figure 11-9:
Add a
folder (left).
The new
subfolder
(right).

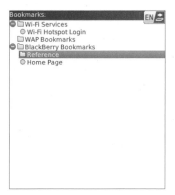

Renaming a bookmark folder

Although you can't rename the root bookmark folders (BlackBerry Bookmarks and WAP Bookmarks) the folders you create under them are fair game. Renaming a bookmark folder that you created is as easy as editing a bookmark. Follow these steps:

1. **On the Bookmarks screen, highlight the name of the folder you want to change.**

2. **Press the Menu key and then select Rename Folder.**

3. **Type the name of the folder.**

4. **Select OK to save your changes.**

Moving your bookmarks

If you keep going astray looking for a bookmark that you think exists in a particular folder but is instead in another, move that bookmark where it belongs:

1. **Highlight the bookmark, press the Menu key, and select Move Bookmark.**

2. **Use the trackpad to move the bookmark to the location on the list where you want it to appear.**

3. **After you find the right location, press the trackpad.**

   Your bookmark is in its new home.

Cleaning up your bookmarks

Maybe you like a site but eventually stop visiting it. Or, maybe a site disappears and every time you click the bookmark, you see a 404 Not Found error. It's time for a little spring cleaning. From the Bookmarks screen, highlight the name of the bookmark you want to delete, press the Menu key, and select Delete Bookmark. It's that easy.

You can — repeat, *can* — clean up bookmarks wholesale by deleting an entire folder. A word to the wise, though: All contents of that folder are deleted, so purge with caution.

Exercising Options and Optimization Techniques

Sure, Browser works out of the box, but folks have their own tastes, right? Look to Browser Options for attributes and features you can customize.

Press the Menu key and then select Options. The Browser Options screen that opens offers four main categories to choose from, as shown in Figure 11-10:

✔ **Browser Configuration:** A place to toggle Browser features

✔ **General Properties:** Settings for the general look and feel of Browser

✔ **Cache Operations:** Options for clearing file caches used by Browser

✔ **Gears Settings:** A place to enable certain Web sites that take advantage of Gears. For more on Gears, see the "Gears settings" section later in this chapter.

If you want to make Browser faster after adjusting the options, see the sidebar "Speeding up browsing," later in this chapter.

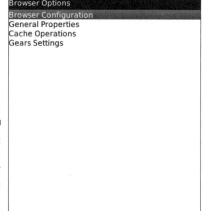

Figure 11-10:
The
Browser
Options
screen.

Configuring Browser

You can define browser-specific settings from the Browser Configuration screen, which you access from the Browser Options screen. You can amend the following customization items you can amend (shown in Figure 11-11):

✔ **Support JavaScript:** The JavaScript scripting language is used to make dynamic Web pages. A Web page might not behave normally when this option is turned off. It's on by default.

✔ **Allow JavaScript Popups:** Most ad pages are launched as JavaScript pop-ups, so having this check box deselected minimizes these ads. Be aware, though, that some important pages are also displayed as JavaScript pop-ups. *Note:* This option appears only if you select the Support JavaScript check box.

✔ **Prompt to Enable JavaScript:** This option appears and comes into play only if you haven't selected Support JavaScript. The default value for this option is selected.

✔ **Terminate Slow Running Scripts:** Sometimes you find Web pages with scripts that aren't written well. Leave this option selected to keep Browser from hanging. This option appears only if you select the Support JavaScript check box.

✔ **Show Images:** This option controls the display of images depending on the content mode of WML or HTML, or both. Think of WML pages as Web pages made just for mobile devices, such as the BlackBerry. We recommend leaving this option selected for both WML and HTML.

Turn on and off the display of image placeholders if you opt to not display images.

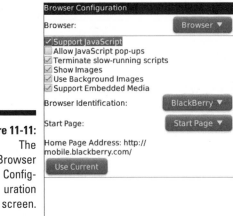

Figure 11-11:
The
Browser
Config-
uration
screen.

- ✔ **Use Background Images:** A Web page background image can make the page look pleasing, but if the image is big, downloading it can take time.

- ✔ **Support Embedded Media:** Select this option to support media such as scalable vector graphics (SVG). Think of SVG as Adobe Flash for mobile devices such as the BlackBerry. SVG can be a still image or an animated one.

- ✔ **Browser Identification:** This option specifies which browser type your browser emulates. The default is BlackBerry, but Browser can also emulate Microsoft Internet Explorer and Mozilla Firefox.

  Keep the default BlackBerry mode. We don't see much difference in emulating Microsoft Internet Explorer or Mozilla Firefox.

- ✔ **Start Page:** Use this option to specify a starting page to load when you open Browser.

- ✔ **Home Page Address:** Use this one to set your home page, which you can access from the Browser menu.

- ✔ **Use Current:** Clicking this button assigns the current Web page you're browsing as your default home page.

General Browser properties

The General Properties screen is similar to the Browser Configuration screen (see the preceding section) in that you can customize some Browser behaviors. General Properties, however, is geared more toward the features of the Browser content. As shown in Figure 11-12, you can configure features and also turn features off or on.

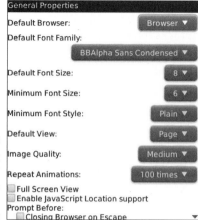

Figure 11-12:
The General
Properties
screen.

From this screen, use the Space key to change the value of a field. You can configure the following features:

- ✓ **Default Browser:** If you have multiple browsers available, use this option to specify which one you want to use when opening a Web link.

- ✓ **Default Font Family:** When a Web page doesn't specify the text font, Browser uses the one you selected here.

- ✓ **Default Font Size:** When a Web page doesn't specify the text font size, Browser uses the one you selected here. The smaller the size, the more text can fit onscreen.

- ✓ **Minimum Font Size:** A Web page might specify a font size too small to be legible. Specifying a legible font size overrides the Web page.

- ✓ **Minimum Font Style:** When Browser is using the minimum font size, you can choose which font to use. Some fonts are more legible, even in a small size, than others. If you aren't sure which one to use, leave this one set to the default.

- ✓ **Default View:** You can toggle the default view. Your options are

  - • **Column:** Wraps all Web page elements vertically, so you just scroll up and down by panning the page.

  - • **Page:** Displays the page as you normally see it in your PC's Internet browser. Pan the page to scroll left, right, up, and down.

- ✓ **Image Quality:** The higher the quality, the slower the page loads. You have three options: Low, Medium (the default), and High.

- ✓ **Repeat Animations:** Sets the number of times an animation repeats. This option pertains to animated images that most banner ads use. Your choices are Never, Once, 10 Times, 100 Times (the default), and As Many As the Image Specifies.

✔ **Full Screen View:** If this option is selected, Browser opens in full-screen view, which uses the entire screen to display the Web page and doesn't display the top and bottom indicators.

✔ **Enable JavaScript Location Support:** If you select this option, Web pages that have scripts that take advantage of your BlackBerry's location by GPS will work.

✔ **Prompt Before:** You can have BlackBerry Browser give you a second chance before you do the following:

- **Close Browser on Escape:** You're notified immediately before you exit BlackBerry Browser.

- **Close Modified Pages:** You're notified immediately before you close a modified Web page (for example, some type of online form you fill out).

- **Switch to WAP for Streaming Media:** You're prompted to switch to WAP when streaming media. This prompt appears only if you are using the network carrier wireless signal and aren't using a Wi-Fi hotspot. The WAP data formatting protocol is designed for mobile devices and generally translates to a faster response when viewing Web pages. However, the Web page format doesn't look as good as the normal Web page viewed in a non-WAP browser.

Some network carriers don't include WAP in their unlimited data plans, so you pay separately for data received using WAP. Be sure to check the terms of your data plan to avoid having to pay a ridiculous monthly bill from simply watching YouTube videos and using WAP. Remember that streaming media on the BlackBerry always uses WAP.

- **Run WML Scripts:** The WML script tells a wireless device how to display a page. This option was popular years ago, when resolutions of device screens were low, but few Web sites are using it now. We recommend leaving this field deselected.

Cache operations

At any given time, your BlackBerry uses a few cache mechanisms. A *cache* (pronounced "cash") temporarily stores information used by Browser so that the next time the information is needed, Browser doesn't have to go back to the source Web site. The cache can speed up displays when you want to view the Web page again and is also useful when you're suddenly out of network coverage. When you visit a site that uses cookies, Browser caches that cookie. (Think of a *cookie* as a piece of text that a Web site creates and places in your BlackBerry's memory to remember something about you, such as your user name.)

Some Web sites *push* (send) Web pages to BlackBerry devices. An icon appears on the Home screen, allowing you to quickly view the page. After the Web page is delivered to your BlackBerry, it becomes available even if you leave the coverage area. If you subscribe to this service, your device stores Web pages in the cache. Also, the addresses of the pages you visited (or the latest 20 sites in your history list) make up a cache.

The Cache Operations screen, shown in Figure 11-13, allows you to manually clear your cache. To view the Cache Operations screen, follow these steps:

1. **From the Browser screen, press the Menu key.**

2. **Select Options.**

3. **Select Cache Operations.**

Figure 11-13:
The Cache
Operations
screen.

Gears settings

Gears is a mechanism by which Browser sends your geographic location so that sites can provide features catered to your location. The Gears technology was developed by Google.

For Web site owners to take advantage of Gears, they have to incorporate the technology into their Web pages, record the user's location, and use location information in their app. At the end of 2009, Google announced that it was no longer working on making Gears available in Mac OS X, and word in the street is that Google will likely retire Gears and concentrate on HTML 5.0, which supports much of what Gears can do. By the time you read this, Gears will likely be a legacy technology that no one uses.

Speeding up browsing

On a wireless network, many factors can affect the speed with which Web pages are displayed. If you find that browsing the Web is extremely slow, you can make your pages load faster in exchange for not using a few features. Here are some of the speed-enhancing work-arounds you can use:

✔ **Don't display images.** You can achieve a big performance improvement by turning off the display of images. From the Browser menu, select Browser Options, and then select Browser Configuration. Scroll to Show Images, and change the value to No.

✔ **Check your BlackBerry memory.** When your BlackBerry's memory is depleted, its performance degrades. The BlackBerry low-memory manager calls each app every now and then, telling them to free resources.

Hint #1: Don't leave many e-mail messages unread. When the low-memory manager kicks in, Messages tries to delete old messages, but it can't delete unread messages.

Hint #2: Purge the BlackBerry event log to free needed space. Enter the letters **LGLG** while pressing down the Shift key. An event log opens. These codes are usually helpful for technical-minded folks trying to figure out what's going on in your BlackBerry, but you don't need the codes. You can clear the event log to free memory.

✔ **Turn off other features.** If you're interested mostly in viewing content, consider turning off features that pertain to processing the content, such as Support HTML Tables, Use Background Images, Support JavaScript, Allow JavaScript Popups, and Support Style Sheets. To turn off other Browser features, navigate to Browser Options and select General Properties.

Warning: We don't advise turning off features while performing an important task such as online banking. If you do, you may not be able to perform certain actions on the page. For example, the Submit button may not work, which is not good.

Some familiar Web applications such as Gmail, Picas, and YouTube use Gears, but as of this writing, few Web sites take advantage of it. You know whether a Web site uses Gears because Browser prompts you for authorization. After you authorize a Web site, it's listed on the Gears Settings screen. To see that screen, press the Menu key from the Browser screen, press Options, and then press Gear Settings.

The size of each type of cache is displayed on this screen. If the cache has content, you also see the Clear button, which you can use to clear the specified cache type. You can clear all cache types except history, which has its own Clear History button. You find these four cache types:

✔ **Content Cache:** Any offline content. You may want to clear this option whenever your BlackBerry is running out of space and you need to free some memory. Or, maybe you're tired of viewing old content or pressing the Refresh option.

✔ **Pushed Content:** Any content that was pushed to your BlackBerry from Push Services subscriptions. You may want to clear this option to free memory on your BlackBerry.

✔ **Cookie Cache:** Any cookies stored on your BlackBerry. You may want to clear this option for security's sake. Sometimes, you don't want a Web site to remember you.

✔ **History:** The list of sites you've visited by using the Go To function. You may want to clear this one for the sake of security if you don't want other people knowing which Web sites you're visiting on your BlackBerry.

From the Help Me! Screen, you can easily check how much memory your device has. To go to the Help Me! screen, press and hold Alt+Shift+H from the Home screen. Shift is the ↑ key, to the left of the 0 key.

Installing and Uninstalling Apps from the Web

You can download and install apps on your BlackBerry via Browser if the app has a link that lets you download and install the files. (See Chapter 20 for other installation options.) The downloading and installing parts are easy. Follow these steps:

1. **From Browser, click the app's link.**

   You see a simple prompt that looks like the screen shown in Figure 11-14. The screen displays what you're about to download. In the case of Figure 11-14, we're downloading SendMeLater (from xchnj.com), an app that lets you send form e-mails.

2. **Select the Download button.**

   The download starts, and you see a progress screen.

As long as you stay within network coverage while the download is progressing, your BlackBerry can finish the download *and* install the app for you. If the download finishes without any problems, you see the screen shown in Figure 11-15.

As with downloading on a desktop computer, the download may or may not work for a variety of reasons. Sometimes the app

✔ Requires you to install libraries

✔ Works on only a certain version of the BlackBerry OS

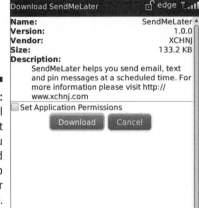

Figure 11-14:
A typical
page that
lets you
download
an app
on your
BlackBerry.

Figure 11-15:
The down-
load and
installation
were com-
pleted.

These issues have been resolved with most reputable sources, and successful downloading and installation are a snap.

Installing apps from a source that isn't reputable can make your BlackBerry
unstable. Before you download an app from the Web, be sure to read reviews
about the app. Don't be the first to write a bad review!

You can find app reviews at BlackBerry App World and on the Web sites of
BlackBerry enthusiasts. The top Web sites are `crackberry.com`, `blackberry
cool.com`, `berryreview.com`, and `blackberryforums.com`.

Your BlackBerry Enterprise Server administrator can disable the feature in your
BlackBerry to download and install an app (applies mostly to company-issued
devices). If you have problems downloading and installing an app, check your
company policy or contact the BlackBerry support person in your company.

If you download an app that turns out to be a dud, uninstall it. See Chapter 20
for more on uninstalling an app from your BlackBerry.

Browser's Behavior in Business

Getting a device from your employer has both a good side and an ugly side:

- ✔ **Good:** Your company foots the bill.
- ✔ **Ugly:** Your company foots the bill.

Because your company pays, it dictates what you can and cannot do with your BlackBerry, especially with respect to browsing the Web.

Two scenarios come into play when using your browser in business:

- ✔ **Your browser may be running under your company's BlackBerry Enterprise Server.** In this setup, your BlackBerry Browser is connecting to the Internet by using your company's Internet connection. The browser is connected to the Internet in the same way as your office desktop machine at work.
- ✔ **Your browser is connected through a network service provider.** Most of the time, this kind of browser is called by the company's name.

In most cases, your device fits in only one scenario. The following sections describe the major differences between the two scenarios and indicate what you can expect.

Using Browser on your company's BlackBerry Enterprise Server

In an enterprise setup, your BlackBerry Browser is connected through your company's BlackBerry Enterprise Server server. In this setup, the browser is named *BlackBerry Browser.* BlackBerry Enterprise Server is located in your company's intranet. This setup allows the company to better manage the privileges and functions you can use on your device.

For the BlackBerry Browser app, this setup lets the company use the existing Internet infrastructure, including the company's firewall. Because you're within the company's network, the boundaries that your network administrator set up on your account apply to your BlackBerry as well. For example, when browsing the Web, your BlackBerry doesn't display any Web sites that are blocked by your company's server.

The good thing, though, is that you can browse the company's intranet: That is, all Web pages you have access to inside your company on your company's PC are available also in your BlackBerry.

Know (and respect) your company's Web-browsing policy. Most companies keep logs of sites you view on your browser and may even have software to monitor usage. Also, your company may not allow downloading from the Web.

Using your network provider's browser

Any new device coming from a network service provider can come with its own, branded Web browser. It's the same BlackBerry Browser, but the behavior may differ in the following ways:

- ✔ **The name is different.**
- ✔ **The default home page usually points to the provider's Web site.** This behavior isn't necessarily a bad thing. Most of the time, the network provider's Web site is full of links that you may not find on BlackBerry Browser.
- ✔ **You can browse more sites.** You aren't limited by your company's policy.

Setting the default browser

If you have two Web browsers on your BlackBerry, you have the option to set the *default* browser. Setting the default browser comes into play when you view a Web address by using a link outside the Browser app. For example, when you view an e-mail with a Web link, selecting that link launches the default browser.

To set up the default browser, follow these steps:

1. **From the Home screen, select Options.**

2. **Select Advanced Options.**

2. **Select Browser.**

3. **Use the Space key to change the default browser configuration, as shown in Figure 11-16.**

Figure 11-16:
Change
the default
browser.

Part IV
Getting the Fun Stuff

By Rich Tennant

"He seemed nice, but I could never connect with someone who had a ring tone like his."

In this part . . .

You're in the midst of building an intimate relationship with your Pearl. In Chapter 12, discover how to navigate using GPS. Always be ready to take those silly poses and capture that YouTube moment with your Pearl's still and video camera, described in Chapter 13. And what better way to get entertained and have fun than with BlackBerry's media player, which we describe in Chapter 14. Finally, in Chapter 15, see how to manage your media files.

Chapter 12

Getting Around with Your BlackBerry GPS

A few years back, when some of the North American network carriers introduced GPS on their versions of the BlackBerry, we were quite impressed . . . until we tried it. The response time was slow, and it wasn't accurate. On top of that, the network carriers charged users an arm and a leg for this inferior service. As it turns out, those GPS functions were implemented by using the network — that is, GPS wasn't embedded in the BlackBerry. How low-tech!

Your BlackBerry Pearl comes with built-in GPS, which makes finding yourself easy. In this chapter, we show you how to use your BlackBerry's built-in GPS and show you two GPS apps you can use on your BlackBerry, both of which are free!

Putting Safety First

Some GPS features are useful while you're driving a car. However, even when tempted to use your BlackBerry GPS while driving, we *strongly* suggest that you *do not* adjust it while you're driving.

Before you start using BlackBerry GPS in your car, you need a BlackBerry car holder — preferably a car kit with a car charger. You can buy a car kit on the Internet; just search for *BlackBerry car kit.* Or, go to one of the following Web sites:

✔ www.shopblackberry.com

✔ http://shop.crackberry.com

Now that you have all you need to keep you safe, keep reading.

What You Need

For GPS to work on your BlackBerry, it needs navigation maps, which are usually downloaded in little pieces as required. And, because these maps are downloaded, you must subscribe to a data plan and have a radio signal to obtain them.

The more you use your GPS while you move about, the more data (map pieces) you'll download. If you don't subscribe to an unlimited data plan from your network carrier, you may incur overage charges.

In summary, for your BlackBerry GPS to work, you need

- **A data plan from your network carrier:** We recommend an unlimited data plan.
- **To be in an area where you have a radio signal:** That way, you can download the maps.

Your GPS App Choices

Two free GPS apps that you can use on your BlackBerry are

- **BlackBerry Maps** (comes with your BlackBerry)
- **Google Maps** (m.google.com/maps)

BlackBerry Maps

Your BlackBerry Pearl probably comes with the BlackBerry Maps app loaded (see Figure 12-1).

If you have a BlackBerry with AT&T as your network carrier, you may not have BlackBerry Maps installed out of the box. You can download it by going to www.blackberry.com/send/maps.

You can use BlackBerry Maps to do the following:

- Find a location by typing an address or by using Contacts.
- Get point-to-point directions.
- E-mail or SMS a location to colleagues and friends.

✔ Turn GPS on or off.

✔ Zoom in and out of the map.

Figure 12-1:
BlackBerry
GPS apps,
with the
Google Map
app high-
lighted.

With GPS turned on, you can track where you are and follow point-to-point directions, as shown in Figure 12-2.

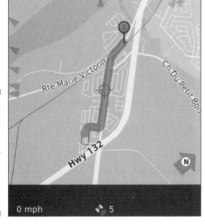

Figure 12-2:
BlackBerry
Maps on the
BlackBerry
smartphone
with GPS
on.

Google Maps

Google Maps on your BlackBerry has most of the features of the online version of Google Maps, including satellite imaging and traffic information. Having Google Maps on your BlackBerry is like having the desktop version of Google Maps in the palm of your hands. Best of all, it's free.

Because Google Maps doesn't come with your BlackBerry, you need to download it. To do so, go to `http://m.google.com/maps`. After the program downloads, its icon appears on your Home screen (refer to Figure 12-1).

With Google Maps loaded, press the 0 key to display your current location, shown in Figure 12-3, left. From the menu (see Figure 12-3, right), you can do the following:

Figure 12-3:
Google
Maps showing your
location
(left). The
Google
Maps menu
(right).

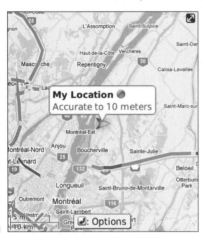

- ✔ **Search Map:** Find businesses and landmarks, including phone numbers, address information, and Web addresses and find and map exact addresses

- ✔ **Get Directions:** Get step-by-step directions from point A to point B

- ✔ **Join Latitude:** See where your friends are

- ✔ **Satellite View:** View a satellite image of the current map (see Figure 12-4, left)

- ✔ **Show Traffic:** Get traffic information for major highways (see Figure 12-4, right)

With GPS or Google's MyLocation on, you can see your current location as a blue blinking dot.

Here are some keyboard shortcuts for Google Maps:

- ✔ **Zoom in:** UI key

- ✔ **Zoom out:** ER key

- ✔ **Go to the current location:** 0 (zero) key

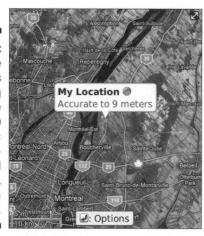 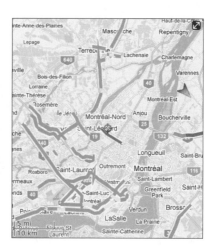

Figure 12-4: Google Maps showing a satellite photo (left) and traffic information around Montreal, Canada (right).

You need to have a radio signal to download maps to your BlackBerry. Additionally, we recommend that you have an unlimited data plan if you're a frequent user of the GPS feature on your BlackBerry.

TeleNav GPS Navigator

At the time of writing, TeleNav does not support the BlackBerry Pearl 9100. However, check www.telenav.com/products for TeleNav's availability on the BlackBerry Pearl 9100 in the future.

Garmin Mobile

At the time of writing, Garmin Mobile does not support the BlackBerry Pearl 9100. You can check www.garmin.com/mobile/blackberry/ for Garmin Mobile's availability on the BlackBerry Pearl 9100 in the future.

Chapter 13

Taking Great Pictures and Capturing Videos

*F*orget your camera? Don't worry! Your BlackBerry is there when you need to capture the unbelievable: Grandma doing a handstand, Grandpa doing a cartwheel, or your roommate doing her laundry. And, if pictures aren't enough, you can record your unbelievable scene in full motion.

Before you try taking pictures, read this chapter so you know what to expect and how to get the best shot. We walk you through the easy steps for capturing that funny pose and tell you how to store those photos and videos. Don't miss reading how to share the joy with your buddies, too.

 Just about every BlackBerry has a camera, but some companies have a no-camera policy. Yes, Research in Motion (RIM) makes versions of some of its models minus the camera. If you're holding that camera-less BlackBerry smartphone, you can skip this chapter.

Saying "Cheese"

Snapping shots with your BlackBerry couldn't be easier. Just turn on the Camera app, line up your shot, and snap away. Here's the bird's-eye view:

1. **Press the right convenience key (bottom key on the right side of your BlackBerry) to display the Camera app.**

   Figure 13-1 shows all you need to know about using your BlackBerry Pearl as a handy camera.

   The Camera key on the right side of your BlackBerry Pearl is really a convenience key, which you can program to open your favorite app. Most network carriers set the right convenience key on the BlackBerry to bring up the Camera app. However, if your network carrier has changed this setting, you can launch the Camera app by selecting the Camera icon on the Home screen.

   Make sure that your finger isn't blocking the lens on the back of your device.

Number of pictures you can capture
Zoom
Flash
Right convenience key
Low-light indicator

Figure 13-1: The camera screen ready to take pictures.

2. **When you see the image onscreen, press the Camera key to take the picture.**

   You should hear a funky shutterlike sound. Neat and easy, isn't it?

The Camera key (right convenience key) behaves like a button on your point-and shoot-camera. A halfway press auto-focuses, and a full press takes the picture. Most people mistake the Camera for being slow. But if the image is already in focus, you can take a picture quickly with a full press of the Camera key.

Keep reading to discover more about Camera's features.

The Screen Indicators

When you open the Camera app, the first thing you see is the screen shown in Figure 13-1. The top portion of this screen allows you to see the image you're about to capture. Immediately below the preview are icons that indicate the following (starting from the left):

- ✔ Number of pictures you can capture
- ✔ Zoom
- ✔ Flash
- ✔ Low-light indicator

Choosing picture quality

Your camera is capable of capturing up to 3.2 megapixels of resolution, but saving images at this resolution requires considerable room. Consider saving images at a lower quality to save some space on your BlackBerry.

To fit more pictures on your Pearl, buy a big microSD card. Nowadays, even a 32GB microSD card is inexpensive, and it holds thousands of pictures.

You can choose from the following three resolutions:

- ✔ **Normal:** The default setting. This is the lowest quality but lets you save the most pictures. The trade-off is that Normal picture quality won't be as smooth or as fine as the other resolution choices.

  If you're just taking pictures of your friends' faces so you can attach them as caller IDs, Normal is appropriate.

- ✔ **Fine:** A middle setting between Normal and SuperFine. This resolution is a compromise if you're concerned about space and want to capture more pictures. The option is good for electronic viewing but not for printing.

- ✔ **SuperFine:** The best quality your Camera can capture. Choose this option if you plan to print the images.

Changing picture quality is a snap. Here's how:

1. **Open the Camera app.**

   From the Home screen, press the Menu key and select Camera.

2. **Press the Menu key and select Options.**

3. **Highlight Picture Quality and press the trackpad.**

4. **Select the resolution you want.**

5. **Press the Menu key and select Save.**

The picture quality you've chosen is now active.

Zooming and focusing

You need to be steady to get a good focus while taking your shots. Although it's convenient to use one hand while taking pictures, most of the time you'll get a blurry image if you try that.

When taking pictures, hold your BlackBerry Pearl with both hands — one holding the smartphone steady and the other pressing the trackpad. If the right convenience key is set to Camera, you can press that instead of the trackpad.

Holding the smartphone with both hands is even more important if you're zooming in. Yes, your camera is capable of up to 3.0x digital zoom. Here's what you need to do to focus and zoom:

- ✔ **To focus:** Your camera has autofocus. Just hold it steady.
- ✔ **To zoom in:** Slide up with the trackpad.
- ✔ **To zoom out:** Slide down with the trackpad.

While zooming, the value in the indicator changes from 1.0x to 2.0x to 3.0x and vice versa, depending on the direction you scroll.

When zooming, your thumb is already on the trackpad. What a convenient way to take the picture — just press.

We don't recommend using the zoom. Digital zoom (which is what your camera has) gives poor results because its software degrades the quality of the picture. The higher the zoom factor, the more pixelated the picture becomes. To get a clearer picture, get closer to the object.

Setting the flash

The rightmost indicator on the Camera screen is the flash. The default is Automatic, which shows a lightning bolt with the letter A. Automatic means it detects the amount of light you have at the moment you capture the image. Where it's dark, the flash fires; otherwise it will not.

You can turn the flash to On, Off, or Automatic (the default). When set to Off, the lightning bolt is crossed with a diagonal line, the way you see on No

Smoking signs. You can toggle the settings in Camera's Options screen, which is accessible by pressing the Menu key and selecting Options.

Setting the white balance

In photography, filters are used to compensate for the dominant light. For instance, a fluorescent versus an incandescent light can affect how warm the picture appears. Instead of using filters, most digital cameras, including the BlackBerry, have a feature called *white balance* that corrects or compensates for many types of light settings.

You can choose Sunny, Cloudy, Night, Incandescent, Fluorescent, or Automatic (the default). *Automatic* means your camera determines what it thinks is the best setting to apply. You can change the white balance through the camera's Options screen, which is accessible by pressing the Menu key and then selecting Options.

Setting the picture size

You can adjust not only the picture quality but also the picture size. Your choices are as follows:

- **Large:** 1600 x 1200. This is the default setting.

  Large uses more memory.
- **Medium:** 1024 x 768
- **Small:** 640 x 480

Again, camera settings are accessible through Camera's Options screen — press the Menu key and then select Options from the menu that appears.

Geotagging

Because your BlackBerry has GPS capability, you can easily determine your location based on longitude and latitude. You can then add this information to your media files, including pictures taken from your camera, so you don't have to wonder where you took that crazy pose. Adding geographic information is called *geotagging*.

Geotagging is disabled by default. Enable it from Camera's Options screen: Press the Menu key and then select Options to get to the Options screen.

If you have longitude and latitude information from one of your photos, you can use one of the free sites on the Web to locate where you were when you took the photo. One such site is `www.travelgis.com/geocode/default.aspx`.

Working with Pictures

You've taken a bunch of pictures and now you want to see them. And maybe delete the unflattering ones. Or perhaps organize them. No problem.

Viewing

If you take a picture, you want to see it, right? You can see an image you just captured right then and there, as shown in Figure 13-2.

Figure 13-2:
The Camera screen after taking a picture.

IMG00001-20100925-2138

All the pictures you took on your Camera are filed directly to a folder in your system. The possible default folder location is based on where you opt to save the pictures:

- ✔ **Device Memory:** /Device Memory/home/user/pictures
- ✔ **Media Card:** /Media Card/BlackBerry/pictures

Let your device file the pictures in the media card (microSD). The first time you use Camera, it prompts you whether to save pictures to the media card. If you aren't sure what the current setting is, simply close the Camera app and then take out the microSD card and put it back in. The next time you open Camera, it displays the same prompt about letting you save pictures to the media card.

The format of the picture's filename is based on the current date and time and named as IMG<counter>-<yyyymmdd>-<hhmm>.jpg. So if you took the 21st picture at 9:30 a.m. on October 20, 2010, you end up with IMG00021-20101020-0930.jpg.

If you're browsing through your picture folders, view a picture by highlighting it and pressing the trackpad.

Creating a slide show

To see your pictures in a slide show, follow these steps:

1. **From the Camera screen, press the Menu key and then select View Pictures from the menu that appears.**

2. **Press the Menu key and select Slide Show.**

   Voilà! Your BlackBerry displays your pictures one at a time at a regular time interval. The default interval between each picture is two seconds. If you aren't happy with this interval, change it in the Options screen. (Press the Menu key and then select Options to get to the Options screen.)

Deleting

If you don't like the image you captured, you can delete it. Follow these steps:

1. **Highlight the picture you want to trash.**

2. **Press the Menu key and then select Delete from the menu that appears.**

   You can press the Del key instead. In either case, a confirmation screen appears.

3. **Select Delete.**

You can also delete an image right after taking the picture; just select the X icon when viewing the photo (refer to Figure 13-2).

Listing filenames versus thumbnails

When you open a folder packed with pictures, your BlackBerry automatically shows *thumbnails,* which are small previews of your pictures.

A preview is nice, but what if you want to search for a picture by filename? Here's how:

1. **Go to a picture folder.**

   To go to a picture folder, select Media from Home screen and then select Pictures.

2. **Press the Menu key and select View List.**

   You see a list of all the pictures in the folder. What's neat is that the option also displays the file size, which can give you a clue about what settings you used to take the picture. For example, a photo taken at a SuperFine quality produces a much bigger file size compared with one taken at Normal.

Checking picture properties

Curious about the amount of memory your picture is taking? Want to know the time you took the photo? Follow these steps:

1. **Highlight the picture in the list.**

   On the Camera screen, view the list of your pictures by pressing the Menu key and then selecting View Pictures.

2. **Press the Menu key and select Properties.**

   You see a screen similar to Figure 13-3, which displays the file's location in your BlackBerry, size, and last modification. The arrow with the *Removable* label indicates that the photograph is filed in the media card. The Hidden check box allows you to hide the file when navigating through your picture list. Once hidden, the file disappears from the list, and the only way to see the file in your BlackBerry again is to use Explore. Check Chapter 14 for details about Explore.

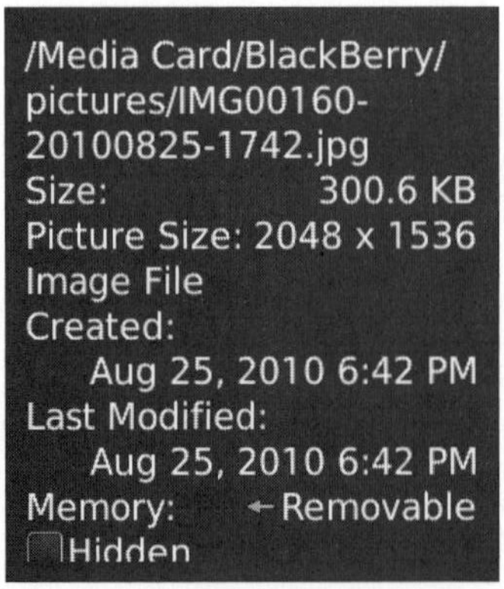

Figure 13-3: Your picture properties.

/Media Card/BlackBerry/
pictures/IMG00160-
20100825-1742.jpg
Size: 300.6 KB
Picture Size: 2048 x 1536
Image File
Created:
      Aug 25, 2010 6:42 PM
Last Modified:
      Aug 25, 2010 6:42 PM
Memory: ← Removable
☐ Hidden

Organizing your pictures

You may be interested in putting some order into where your pictures are stored and how they are named. Organization is all about time and the best use of it. After all, you want to enjoy looking *at* your pictures — not looking *for* them. BlackBerry enables you to rename and move pictures to different folders. Plus, you can create folders. With those capabilities, you should be on your way to organization nirvana.

Renaming a picture file

BlackBerry autonames a file when you capture a picture. The name of the picture is generic, something like IMG*xxxx-currentdate-time,* where *x* is a number. Not very helpful.

Make it a habit to rename photos as soon as you capture them. Using a name such as *Dean blows birthday candles* is much more helpful than *IMG0029-20101013-0029.*

Renaming a photo file is a snap. Here's how:

1. **Display the picture screen or highlight the photo file in the list.**

   Press the Menu key and select View Pictures to see the list.

2. **Press the Menu key and select Rename.**

   A Rename screen appears, as shown in Figure 13-4.

3. **Enter the name you want for this picture and then select Save.**

   Your picture is renamed.

Figure 13-4:
Rename your picture here.

Creating a new folder

Being the organized person you are, you must be wondering about folders. Don't fret; it's simple to create one. Here's how:

1. **In the Camera screen, press the Menu key and select View Pictures.**

   The screen displays the list of pictures in the folder where Camera saves the pictures.

   - If the current folder is still the default location, this folder will be the root of where you can create your subfolder. You can proceed to Step 3.

   - Otherwise, follow Step 2 to navigate to the folder above this folder.

2. **Select the Up icon to navigate to the main folder where you want your new folder to be created.**

   You should be within the folder where you want your new folder to be created. If you are not, repeat this step to navigate to that folder.

3. **Press the Menu key and select New Folder.**

4. **Enter the name of the folder and select OK.**

   Your folder is created.

Moving pictures

Here's how to move pictures to a different folder:

1. **From the Camera screen, press the Menu key and select View Pictures.**

   The screen displays the list of pictures in the current folder. If the picture you want to move isn't in this folder, click the Up icon to navigate to another folder.

2. **Highlight the picture you want to move, press the Menu key, and select Move.**

3. **Click the Up icon and use the trackpad to navigate to the folder where you want to move this picture.**

4. **Press the Menu key and select Move Here.**

   Your picture is moved.

You can easily transfer your pictures to your PC or copy pictures from your PC to your BlackBerry Pearl. See Chapter 15 for details.

Sharing your pictures

Where's the joy in taking great pictures if you're the only one seeing them? Your BlackBerry Pearl has several options for sharing your bundle of joy:

1. **From the Camera screen, press the Menu key and then select View Pictures.**

2. **Highlight a picture you want to share.**

3. **Press the Menu key and select one of the following choices:**

   - **Send As Email:** This option goes directly to the Message screen for composing an e-mail, with the currently selected picture as an attachment.

   - **Send as MMS:** Similar to Send as Email, this opens a Compose MMS screen with the selected picture as an attachment. MMS first displays Contacts, though, letting you select the person's phone number to receive the MMS before going to the Compose screen. Another difference is that in MMS, the BlackBerry sends a tiny version of the picture.

   - **Send to Messenger Contact:** This option is available if BlackBerry Messenger is installed. This function is similar to Send as MMS but displays only those contacts you have in BlackBerry Messenger. The option uses BlackBerry Messenger to send a tiny version of the picture file.

   - **Send Using Bluetooth:** This option allows you to send the picture to any device that is capable of communicating through Bluetooth. See Chapter 10 for details on how to enable and pair Bluetooth devices.

You may see other ways to send a picture file if you have other instant messaging (IM) clients installed. For example, if you have Google Talk installed, you will see a Send as Google Talk option.

Setting a picture as the caller ID

Wouldn't it be nice when your girlfriend calls if you also could see her beautiful face? You can. Start with a photo of her saved on your BlackBerry. Then follow these steps:

1. **From the Home screen, select the Media icon and then select Pictures.**

2. **Navigate to the location of the photo.**

3. **Highlight the photo that you want to see when the person calls.**

4. **Press the Menu key and select Set as Caller ID.**

   The photo is displayed onscreen, with a superimposed, portrait-size cropping rectangle. Inside the rectangle is a clear view of the photo; outside the rectangle, the photo is blurry. The clear view represents the portion of the photo that you want to display. To reposition the rectangle, move the trackpad.

5. **Crop the photo by pressing the trackpad and selecting Crop and Save.**

   Contacts appears.

6. **Select the contact you want this picture to represent.**

   You see a message indicating that a picture is set for that contact. You're set.

You can add a photo to your contacts also through the Contacts app. (For more on Contacts, refer to Chapter 4.)

Setting a Home screen image

Suppose you have a stunning picture that you want to use as the background image of your BlackBerry Pearl. Follow these steps to set the image:

1. **From the Home screen, select the Media icon and then select Pictures.**

2. **Navigate to the location of the picture you want to use.**

3. **Highlight the picture.**

4. **Press the Menu key and select Set as Wallpaper.**

You can always reset the screen image or go back to the default Home screen image by following the preceding steps but selecting Reset Wallpaper from the Menu screen in Step 4.

Say "Action"

Your BlackBerry Camera app can do more than take still photos. You can use it also to take videos.

Here are the quick and easy steps to use Video Camera mode:

1. **Open the Camera app.**

2. **Press the Menu key and then select Video Camera (see Figure 13-5).**

   The next screen looks like a viewfinder on a typical digital video camera. Press the trackpad to start recording. The onscreen controls are all context related. When you launch the video camera, all you see is the Record button with the big white dot at the bottom of the screen. When you use the trackpad to select the Record button, the video camera starts taking video, and the only available control is a Pause button.

The indicators on your screen, as shown in Figure 13-6, are as follows:

- ✔ **Available memory:** The more blue squares you see, the more free space you have for saving videos to the device memory or the media card.

- ✔ **Zoom:** Like your still camera, the video camera is capable of 3.0x digital zoom.

- ✔ **Video light:** A circle around the lightning icon, similar to what you see in Figure 13-6, indicates that the video light is off, which is the default setting. (The following section shows how to enable the video light.)

- ✔ **Recorded time:** This indicator tells you how long, in seconds, you've been recording.

Available memory   Zoom | Recorded time

Video light

To stop recording and save the captured video, press the Escape key. To pause recording, press the trackpad. When you pause the recording, the screen updates to show the rest of the controls, as you see in Figure 13-7.

Figure 13-7:
The video camera controls.

Record — Play — Delete

Stop — Rename — Send

The controls are the familiar buttons you see on a typical video recorder/ player. From left to right, they are as follows:

- ✔ **Record:** Continue recording.
- ✔ **Stop:** End the recording.
- ✔ **Play:** Play the video you just recorded.
- ✔ **Rename:** Rename the video file.
- ✔ **Delete:** Get rid of the video file of the recording.
- ✔ **Send:** Share your video recording. You have the option to send the recording as e-mail, as MMS, or through Bluetooth. If you have IM clients installed, such as Google Talk or Yahoo! Messenger, the IM client is listed as an option for sending the video file.

Customizing the Video Camera

Your BlackBerry has a few settings you can tweak to change the behavior of the video camera. And, as with every other BlackBerry app, to see what you can customize, simply look at the app's Options screen — in this case, the Video Camera Options screen.

Follow these steps to get to the Video Camera Options screen:

1. **Open the Camera app.**
2. **Press the Menu key and select Video Camera.**
3. **Press the Menu key and select Options.**

   The Video Camera Options screen appears, as shown in Figure 13-8.

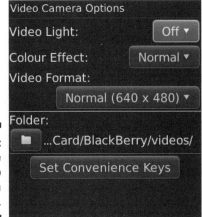

Video Camera Options

Video Light: Off ▾

Colour Effect: Normal ▾

Video Format:

Normal (640 x 480) ▾

Folder:

📁 ...Card/BlackBerry/videos/

Set Convenience Keys

Figure 13-8: Customize your video camera here.

The available options are easy to understand, but in case you need a little help, here's what you can tweak:

- ✔ **Video Light:** If the light level is a little dim, you can turn on the video camera's lights. This option is available only if your BlackBerry has a flash. While on the video camera screen, you can toggle this setting on or off by simply pressing the Space key.

  Dropped something in a dark alley? The video light is a good alternative to a flashlight.

  Video light is the flash you use when taking still pictures. It stays lit when you set the setting to On and open Video Camera. The default is Off.

  When you use video light, you create a drain on your battery.

- ✔ **Color Effect:** The default color effect is Normal, which is standard color. If you're in the mood for effects, you can opt for Black & White or Sepia.

- ✔ **Video Format:** This option is the screen resolution size. The default is Normal (640 x 480), which is set at the maximum size of your BlackBerry screen.

  If you're planning to send your video to friends through MMS, you can choose MMS mode, which has the smaller size of 176 x 144 and is optimal for MMS.

- ✔ **Folder:** Use this option to change the default location where your BlackBerry saves the video file.

Chapter 14

Satisfying All Your Senses with Media Player

*I*f one word describes today's phone market trends, it's *convergence.* Your BlackBerry Pearl is among the participants of the race to convergence. In addition to sending and receiving e-mail and being a phone, a camera, and a PDA, the Pearl is an excellent portable media player.

In this small package, you can

✔ Listen to music.

✔ Record and watch video clips.

✔ Sample ring tones.

✔ Snap and view pictures.

These capabilities are bundled into an app with a name you'd recognize even after sipping a couple of pints of strong ale — Media.

Accessing Media

To run Media, simply press the Menu key from the Home screen and select Media. Or if you've chosen Media as one of the five apps you display on the Home screen, you can select its icon there. The Media folder is easy to distinguish, as you can see in Figure 14-1, because it bears the image of a folder with a right arrow like the play button you typically see on a music player.

Figure 14-1:
Explore
Media here.

Media is a collection of the following apps:

✔ Music

✔ Pictures

✔ Ring Tones

✔ Video Camera

✔ Videos

✔ Voice Notes

✔ Voice Notes Recorder

When you open Media, each app is represented with an easily identifiable icon.

These apps can cooperate:

✔ The videos you capture in the Video Camera app are listed in Videos. You can even launch the Video Camera app inside the Videos app.

✔ You can launch Voice Notes Recorder from Voice Notes and play recorded notes from Voice Notes.

Ready to have some fun?

Let the Music Play

You don't need a quarter to play music in your BlackBerry Pearl. Just select the Music app from the Media folder (see Figure 14-2, left). The Music screen appears, listing several potential views of your music collection, as shown to the right of Figure 14-2:

- ✔ **All Songs:** Displays all your music files in alphabetical order.
- ✔ **Artists:** Lists your music files by artist so that you can play your John Mayer songs in one go.
- ✔ **Albums:** Displays your music collection one album at a time.
- ✔ **Genres:** Keeps your country music separate from your cutting-edge techno.
- ✔ **Playlists:** Organizes and plays songs as you prefer — the perfect mix tape!
- ✔ **Shuffle Songs:** Plays your tunes in random order. Select this option when you're tired of the song order in your playlist.

Figure 14-2: Launch Music from the Media screen (left), and choose how to view your music collection (right).

After you choose a view, select one of the songs to start playing it. After BlackBerry starts playing a song, it plays the rest of the music listed in the view you selected. The standard interface shown in Figure 14-3 doesn't require much explanation.

The two small icons at the bottom left indicate repeat and shuffle:

- ✔ If you want to hear the songs again after the last song in the list is played, just press the Menu key, select Repeat, and then select Album.
- ✔ Tired of hearing the same sequence of songs played? Press the Menu key and select Shuffle. Your songs will be played randomly.

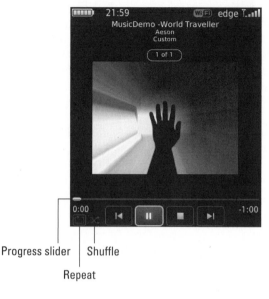

Figure 14-3:
The music
plays here.

Progress slider | Shuffle

Repeat

You can't fast-forward or rewind, but you can position where BlackBerry is playing by dragging the progress slider. Use the trackpad to select the progress slider and then slide the trackpad to change the slider's position. Select the trackpad again, and the music starts playing from that position.

BlackBerry Pearl supports the following music formats and file extensions:

- **AAC:** Advanced Audio Coding (`.aac`, `.m4a`); audio compression formats AAC, AAC+, EAAC+, and AAC-LC
- **AMR-NB:** Adaptive Multi-Rate– Narrow Band (`.mmr`, `.3gp`); speech coder standard
- **MIDI:** Musical Instrument Digital Interface (`.mid`, `.midi`, `.smf`); a popular audio format for musical instruments
- **MP3:** MPEG (Moving Pictures Expert Group)-1 and MPEG-2 Audio Layer 3 and 4 (`.mp3` and `.mp4`); digital audio encoding format
- **WMA:** Windows Media Audio 9, Pro, and 10 (`.wma` and `.asf`)

The earpiece combo mic that comes with BlackBerry Pearl is for one ear only, which is an issue when you're on a train. To improve your experience, you can buy a stereo (two-ear) headset. A Bluetooth headset is a good option.

Ever wonder what song you're hearing? We recommend that you get Shazam Encore, an app that listens to music playing nearby and tells you information about the song. After it identifies a song, you have the option to purchase it. You can buy Shazam Encore for $4.99 from BlackBerry App World.

Creating a playlist

We're sure that you have favorites in your song library. Wouldn't it be nice to have a playlist? On your BlackBerry, you can create two types of playlists:

- ✔ **Standard:** You can create a bare-bones playlist and manually add the music you want.

- ✔ **Automatic:** You can specify a combination by artist, by album, by genre, or any combination thereof.

Is a song playing that you want to add to your playlist? No problem. While you're playing the song, simply press the Menu key and select Add to Playlist. In the screen that appears, select the playlist to which you want to add the song.

Standard playlists

To create a standard playlist, follow these steps:

1. **On the Music screen, select Playlists.**

   To get to the Music screen, select Music in Media or from the Home screen.

2. **Select [New Playlist].**

3. **Select Standard Playlist.**

4. **Press the Menu key and then select Add Songs.**

   Your music library listing appears.

5. **Scroll to your music list, and select a song you want to add to your playlist.**

   You return to the preceding screen, and the selected song is added to your playlist.

6. **Repeat Step 5 to add additional songs.**

7. **When you've finished adding songs, press the Menu key and select Save.**

Automatic playlists

To create an automatic playlist, follow these steps:

1. **On the Music screen, select Playlists.**

   To get to the Music screen, select Music in Media or from the Home screen.

2. **Select [New Playlist].**

3. **Select Automatic Playlist.**

4. **Select the + button to the right of the music type criteria, and then select one of the listed combinations.**

   You can select by Artist, by Albums, by Genres, or a combination of any of the three options. If you select by Artist, you'll be presented with a list of artists. Select by Albums, and you see a list of albums.

5. **Repeat Step 3 to add more values to your criteria.**

6. **After you add all the criteria you want in Automatic Playlist, press the Menu key and select Save.**

Playing from your playlist

Playing your playlist is a no-brainer:

1. **From the Music screen, select Playlists.**

   To get to the Music screen, select Music in Media or from the Home screen.

2. **Scroll to highlight the playlist you want to start playing.**

3. **Press the Menu key and then select Play.**

Listening to music from the Web

In general, most Web sites provide music either streamed or cached. We describe both methods in this section.

Streaming music

Listening to *streaming* music on your BlackBerry smartphone is similar to listening to a radio. The music is not stored on your device but is constantly received from a remote source. Unlike a radio, which uses radio frequencies, your BlackBerry smartphone receives music over the data channel. This is the same channel that you use to check your e-mail or browse the Web. As long as you've purchased a data plan for your BlackBerry, you can listen to streaming music.

Streaming music over a non–Wi-Fi connection is data intensive. Unless your plan includes unlimited data transfers, you may have heart palpitations when you get your first bill. Check the fine print on your contract before you stream audio or video.

A good popular BlackBerry app that streams music is Pandora, which you can download for free from BlackBerry App World.

Caching music

The second way to listen to music is by caching. *Caching* means the app fully downloads music files into your smartphone. The major advantages of caching versus streaming are that you can listen when you have a poor signal or no signal and can save up to five times your battery life because caching, unlike streaming, doesn't require a constant connection to play songs. The downside of caching is that it eats up memory space on your smartphone.

Slacker Radio is one of the most popular BlackBerry apps that employ caching. You can download Slacker Radio for free in BlackBerry App World.

Now Showing

Playing or recording a video is similar to playing music. Follow these steps:

1. **From the Media screen, select Videos.**

   You can launch Media by selecting the Media icon from the Home screen. The screen shows Video Camera, and a list of video files appears at the bottom. If you want to watch a video, skip to Step 5.

2. **To start video recording, select Video Camera.**

   A screen shows the image in front of the camera.

3. **Select the screen again to start recording.**

   Don't wait for "Cut!" You can pause the camera by clicking the trackpad. You see the familiar video and audio controls: from left to right, they are continue recording, stop, and play. The other buttons are rename (for renaming the filename), delete, and send via e-mail.

4. **Select the stop button when you're ready to wrap up your home video.**

   You wind up at the previous screen, with the video clip file listed. We know you're itching to watch it.

5. **Select the file to play it onscreen.**

To record a video from the Videos app, do the following:

1. **From the Media screen, select Videos.**

   The screen displays your videos and a link to the video camera, as shown in Figure 14-4.

2. **Select Video Camera and press the trackpad to start recording.**

3. **Press the Escape key to wrap up your home video.**

Figure 14-4:
Record your
home video
here.

You can access the Video Camera app through the Camera app, too. In fact, Video Camera and Camera were one app in older BlackBerry models. Check out Chapter 13 for more about Video Camera, including how to customize its behavior.

Your Pearl has a small screen, and when it comes to loading feature films to watch on your next plane ride, the easiest thing to do is to have the source video on your PC and encode it for your Pearl. You can then copy the encoded video to your Pearl. (See Chapter 15 for more on managing media files.) Ultra Mobile 3GP Converter is a good choice for an encoder; you can purchase it for $29.99 from the AONE SOFTWARE Web site at `www.aone-soft.com/mobile_3gp_video_converter.htm`.

Lord of the Ring Tones

Nothing beats hearing a loud funky ring tone while you're sleeping on a bus or a train. You, too, can wake other passengers, whether you want to use the Top 40, old-fashioned digital beats, or something you recorded.

To hear ring tones that come with your BlackBerry, do the following:

1. **From the Media screen, select Ring Tones.**

   You see two views: All Ring Tones and My Ring Tones.

2. **Select All Ring Tones.**

   You see all ring tones, including the preloaded ones, as shown in Figure 14-5.

Figure 14-5:
Stumble on
a default
ring tone
here.

3. **Select a ring tone and enjoy.**

   While playing a ring tone, select the right arrow to go to the next tone; select the left arrow to go the previous one.

4. **Select a ring tone you like.**

5. **Press the Menu key and select Set as Ring Tone.**

   You see a screen allowing you to choose the profile to which this ring tone applies. (Check out Chapter 3 for a quick refresher on profiles.) You can choose All Profiles, Normal Profile Only, or Cancel.

Downloading sounds

RIM offers a Web site from which you can sample and download new ring tones, alarms, notifiers, and tunes. On your BlackBerry, go to http://mobile.blackberry.com. Scroll down to the Personalize section, and click the Ringtones link. A list of available ring tones is displayed. Did we mention that they're free?

Clicking the ring tone link gives you an option to either play the ring tone or download it to your BlackBerry. Downloaded ring tones are filed in the My Ring Tones section when you open Ring Tones in the Media application.

RIM isn't the only site where you can find ring tones. The Web is a treasure trove. Ring tones and other media files are safe to download, so go hunting. The best place to find BlackBerry-related software — including ring tones — is the ever-growing BlackBerry community on the Web. Check out http://crackberry.com, http://blackberrycool.com, and http://blackberryreview.com, to name a few.

A ring tone is similar to a music file and includes many of the same music formats:

- ✔ **AAC:** Advanced Auto Coding format, used by iTunes
- ✔ **AMR:** Adaptive Multi-Rate, a popular audio format for mobile transmission and mobile apps
- ✔ **M4A:** A subset of AAC for audio only
- ✔ **MIDI:** Musical Instrument Digital Interface, a popular audio format for musical instruments
- ✔ **MP3:** MPEG Audio Layer 3, the most popular music format
- ✔ **WMA:** Windows Media Audio, a Microsoft audio file format

If you're familiar with any audio-editing software, you can make your own ring tones. Save the file in one of the formats in the preceding list and copy it to your BlackBerry. (See Chapter 15 for details on copying files from your PC to your BlackBerry.) The Internet has a plethora of ring tones, and many are free. The only possible harm from downloading one is being annoyed with how it sounds. The Fun and Pages link on Browser's Home page (`http://mobile.blackberry.com`) has links to sources of ring tones as well.

Picture This

If you upgraded from an older BlackBerry, you may already know about Pictures, which you use to view and zoom into images. To display a picture, follow these steps:

1. **From the Media screen, select Pictures.**

2. **Select one of the listed views (see Figure 14-6) to navigate to your pictures.**

   You can choose among the following views:

   - **All Pictures:** Displays pictures filed in device memory and on the microSD card.

   - **Picture Folders:** Displays only pictures filed in the current location of images captured by the Camera app. The default folder is the Picture folder on the microSD card.

   - **Sample Pictures:** Displays sample pictures that come with your smartphone.

3. **Scroll to find the picture and then select the file.**

   Pretty easy, right? At this point, your photo file is displayed on the screen.

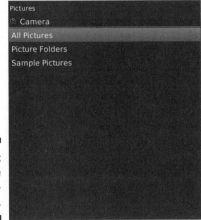

Figure 14-6:
Navigate
to your pic-
tures here.

Check out Sample Pictures. Your BlackBerry comes with a collection of pictures that you can use as the Home screen background. You can also assign a
cartoon to a contact as a caller ID until you get a chance to take the person's
picture (a topic we describe in Chapter 13).

Your BlackBerry supports the following standard picture formats:

- **BMP:** Bitmap (`.bmp`) file format
- **JPEG:** Developed by the Joint Photographic Experts Group committee
  (`.jpg`); typically compresses the image file to a tenth of its size with
  little perceptible loss of image quality
- **PNG:** Portable Network Graphics (`.png`), a bitmapped image format that
  employs a lossless data transmission
- **TIFF:** Tagged Image File Format (`.tif`), mostly used in scanners and
  under the control of Adobe Systems
- **WBMP:** Wireless Bitmap (`.wbmp`) file format, which is optimized for
  mobile devices

Viewing in Pictures

When you're navigating a folder in the Pictures app, the default view displays
thumbnails, which enable you to quickly view many pictures at the same time
before deciding which one to open.

Want to view all the pictures instead? Run a slide show by pressing the Menu
key and selecting View Slide Show.

A convenient way to view pictures is to scroll sideways using the trackpad. Scrolling right transitions the view to the next picture, and you see a smooth sideways movement of the picture on the screen. Scrolling left transitions in the opposite direction until the preceding picture is displayed.

Zooming to see details

To zoom in a photo, open the photo and click the trackpad. The picture zooms in. You can repeat the trackpad-clicking to increase the degree of zoom. To zoom out, press the Escape key.

An image normally defaults to fit the screen, but you can change this setting by pressing the Menu key and selecting the View Actual Size option. To switch back, select the Fit to Screen option.

Recording and Playing Your Voice

A feature-packed smartphone like your BlackBerry Pearl *should* come with a voice recorder, and it does. Within Media, you can find Voice Notes Recorder, a neat recording app. Now you can record your billion-dollar ideas without having to type every detail:

1. **From the Media screen, select Voice Notes Recorder (the icon of a little microphone beside the waves).**

   The Voice Notes Recorder app launches, sporting the simple and clean screen shown in Figure 14-7.

   You can access Voice Notes Recorder also through Voice Notes. In fact, Voice Notes and Voice Notes Recorder were one app in older BlackBerry models.

Figure 14-7:
Record your
voice here.

2. **When you're ready, click the trackpad.**

   Your BlackBerry's microphone is designed to be close to your mouth, like any mobile phone's mic should be.

   You can pause at any time by clicking the trackpad. Familiar video/audio controls appear. From left to right, they are continue recording, stop, and play. Other buttons are rename (for renaming the file), delete, and send via e-mail.

3. **To wrap it up, click the trackpad and then select the stop button.**

   You return to Voice Notes screen, and your recent voice recording appears in the list.

After you record your billion-dollar idea, recalling it or playing it back is a snap:

1. **From the Media screen, select Voice Notes.**

   The Voice Notes app launches, with your voice notes listed.

2. **Select your voice recording to hear your idea.**

Viewing and Controlling Media Files

The previous sections show what types of files you can record or play on your BlackBerry Pearl. In this section, we give you the lowdown on controlling those files when you're playing or viewing them.

Media shortcuts

Master the following media shortcuts now, and you'll save time later. Following are the must-know Media shortcuts:

- **Mute key:** Toggles between pausing and playing of music and video

- **6:** Moves to the next item

- **4:** Moves to the previous item

- **3:** Zooms in on a picture

- **9:** Zooms out on a picture

- **5:** Zooms back to the original picture size

- **, (comma):** Rotates a picture counterclockwise

- **Space key:** Toggles between pausing and resuming a slide show

---

Turning it up or down

Whether you're listening to music or watching a video, adjusting the volume is easy.

Your BlackBerry Pearl comes with dedicated volume keys. They're located on the top-right side of the device. The top key (with the plus sign) turns up the volume, and the one below it (with the minus sign) turns down the volume. The onscreen volume slider reflects anything you do with the volume keys.

Navigating the menu

All Media apps except the Pictures app have a common menu. The menu items are mostly self-explanatory, but the following sections highlight what you'll see.

Navigating the Pictures menu

When using Pictures to view your photos, most of the navigation options are accessible only through the menu. Press the Menu key while you're viewing an image. In the menu that appears, you see the following items:

- **Next:** Jumps to the next image in the list. This option appears only if an image is after the currently viewed image file in the current folder. Alternatively, while viewing an image, you can jump to the next image by scrolling to the right using the trackpad.

- **Previous:** Jumps to the preceding image. This option appears only if a previous image is in the current folder. Alternatively, while viewing an image, you can jump to the next image by scrolling to the right using the trackpad.

- **Delete:** Deletes the image file.

- **Move:** Moves the image file to a different folder.

- **Copy:** Copies the image file to a different folder.

- **Rename:** Renames the image file.

- **Properties:** Displays a screen that shows the location of the image file, its size, and the time it was last modified.

Navigating the Music, Videos, Ring Tones, and Voice Notes menus

Whether you're watching a video, playing music, hearing a ring tone, or listening to a voice note, you see the following after pressing the Menu key:

✔ **Media Home:** Displays the Media screen.

✔ **<Media App> Home:** This menu item depends on the Media app you're using. For example, if you're in the Music app, the menu item displays Music Home, and selecting this menu item displays the Home screen of the Music app.

✔ **Activate Handset:** Mutes the device's speaker. Select this item if you want to use the earpiece. This menu item appears only if you've activated the speakerphone.

✔ **Activate Speakerphone:** Uses the device's speaker and mutes the earpiece. This menu item appears only if the handset is activated.

Using Explore

You can navigate to your media file in many ways, but Explore is probably the quickest way to find a file. It's easy to use because it has some similarities to Windows Explorer, and it also has a search facility similar to Find in other BlackBerry apps such as Contacts, MemoPad, and Tasks.

To launch Explore, simply select Media from the Home screen, press the Menu key, and select Explore. The Explore screen, as shown in Figure 14-8, starts with the device root folders: Media Card and Device Memory.

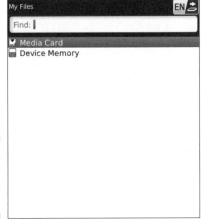

Figure 14-8: Explore your media files here.

Folders are in a tree hierarchy. You can get into child folders (subfolders) by selecting from the parent folder, starting from one of the root folders.

If you've set the property of a picture to hidden, Explore is the only place in your BlackBerry through which you'll be able to locate the file again. Do the following to find a hidden picture:

1. **Navigate to the folder where your picture file is located.**

   If you don't know exactly where the picture file is located, you may have to select different folders until you find the file.

2. **Press the Menu key and select Show Hidden.**

The default location for pictures taken by Camera is `/Device Memory/ home/user/pictures` or `/Media Card/BlackBerry/pictures`.

Changing the Media Flavor

As with the rest of your BlackBerry apps, you can customize some parts of the Media app. You do so through the Options screen in Media:

1. **From the Media screen, press the Menu key.**

2. **Select Options.**

   The screen shown in Figure 14-9 appears. Each media customization option is described in the following sections.

Figure 14-9: The Media Options screen.

Customizing Media

Starting at the top of the Media Options screen, in the General section, you can finesse the following options:

- ✔ **Device Memory Limit:** This option is the maximum amount of device memory that Media can use. This limit ensures that important apps, such as Messages and Phone, aren't affected even if you're a heavy media user.

  Leave Device Memory Limit set to the default value.

- ✔ **Close Media Player When Inactive:** The default is Off, but you can set this option to 5, 10, 20, 30, or 45 minutes. This option can save battery life if you get distracted and leave your BlackBerry on a table playing your favorite video.

- ✔ **Set Convenience Keys:** Change the settings for the right and left convenience keys, which are shortcut keys to an app. The right convenience key defaults to launching the Camera app, and the left convenience key defaults to launching Voice Dialing.

Going down the Media Options screen, in the Playback section, you can customize the following options:

- ✔ **Headset Equalizer:** The default is Off. If you want to have a different audio setting, your options are Bass Boost, Bass Lower, Dance, Hip Hop, Jazz, Lounge, Loud, R&B, Rock, Treble Boost, Treble Lower, and Vocal Boost.

- ✔ **Audio Boost:** This option allows you to increase the volume beyond the normal level. The default setting is Off. If you change the setting to On, you get a warning about possible ear discomfort when you're using headphones.

- ✔ **Turn Off Auto Backlighting:** Your BlackBerry includes a backlight feature, which provides additional screen lighting. The backlight turns on when you move the smartphone from shade to direct sunlight. If you find backlighting bothersome, such as when you're watching a movie, use this option to toggle backlighting off.

  Turn off backlighting when you need battery juice.

- ✔ **Display Closed Captions:** This option applies only to videos that support closed captions. The options are Yes (the default) and No.

- ✔ **Appearance:** Appears when Display Closed Captions is selected. This option changes the appearance of closed captions. Choose Style 1 (blue text with a black background) or Style 2 (the default, black text on a white background).

✔ **Position:** This option refers to the location of the closed captions and only appears when Display Closed Captions is selected. You can choose Top Left, Top, Top Right, Bottom Right, Bottom (the default), or Bottom Left.

✔ **Font Scale:** Choose the size of the font used in closed captions during playback, which appears only if Display Closed Captions is selected. Your choices are Largest, Larger, Large, Normal (the default), Small, Smaller, or Smallest.

The box that reads For your viewing pleasure works with the Display Closed Captions option. If you opt to display closed caption, this box illustrates where the closed caption will appear during playback.

Customizing Pictures

Toward the bottom of the Media Options screen, in the Pictures section, you can change the Pictures app in the following ways:

✔ **Sort By:** Toggle file sorting based on recent updates or name.

✔ **Slide Show Interval:** When you're viewing your files in a slide show, a picture appears for this many seconds before moving to the next picture.

✔ **Reserved Pictures Memory:** This setting makes sure that device memory is reserved for the Pictures app. The default setting is 0, or no reserved memory. We recommend leaving the default value because we don't see any difference in the Pictures app when we change this setting.

✔ **Exclude Folders:** Use this option when you don't want to display any pictures in a particular folder. Doing so makes the list of pictures load faster. This option hides the folder only from Pictures; you can still see excluded folders using Explore.

Chapter 15

Managing Media Files

*T*he ways that you can get your hands on media continue to evolve. Ten years ago, who would have thought that you could buy music from a tiny card or from an "all you can download" monthly subscription? Someday, you'll wake up with a technology that doesn't require you to constantly copy media files to your handheld music player. But for now, enjoying music while on the move means managing those files.

The Media app on your BlackBerry is a great music player, but without music files, it's as useless as a guitar without strings. In this chapter, we show you how to get your music library from your desktop computer to your Pearl. And to satisfy your quest for mobile media satisfaction, this chapter gives you good information on ways to manage your media files.

Using Your BlackBerry as a Flash Drive for a PC

The most common way to manipulate media files into and out of your BlackBerry is to attach it to a PC and use Windows Explorer. Just follow these steps:

1. **Connect your BlackBerry to your PC, using the USB cable that came with your BlackBerry.**

   Only folders and files stored on the microSD card are visible to your PC. Make sure to have the microSD card in your BlackBerry *before* you connect your BlackBerry to the PC.

   When connected, the BlackBerry screen displays a prompt for enabling mass storage mode.

2. **On the BlackBerry screen, select Yes.**

   A screen appears on your BlackBerry, asking for your password.

3. **On the BlackBerry screen, type your BlackBerry password.**

   The device is now ready to behave like an ordinary flash drive. On your PC, the Removable Disk dialog box appears.

4. **On your PC, in the Removable Disk dialog box, click Open Folder to View Files and then click OK.**

   You see the familiar Windows Explorer screen.

5. **Manipulate your media files.**

   You can do anything you typically do with a normal Windows folder, such as drag and drop, copy, and delete files.

6. **When you're finished, close Windows Explorer.**

Using Media Sync

BlackBerry Desktop Software's Media Sync program is your key to managing files between your BlackBerry Pearl and Windows PC. If you maintain a media library on your desktop machine at home, most likely you're using iTunes or Windows Media Player. Fortunately, Media Sync supports both programs.

If BlackBerry Desktop Software isn't installed on your PC, see Chapter 16 for details on downloading and installing the latest version for free.

Setting the music source (iTunes or Windows Media Player)

As mentioned, you can use BlackBerry Desktop Software with iTunes and Windows Media Player to locate media files to sync to your BlackBerry Pearl. Simply follow these quick and easy steps to configure BlackBerry Desktop Software to the music source of your choice:

1. **Connect your Pearl to your PC.**

2. **Click the Windows Start button.**

3. **Choose All Programs➪BlackBerry➪Desktop Software.**

   The BlackBerry Desktop Software screen appears.

4. **Click the Device menu, and then click Device Options.**

   The Device Options screen appears.

5. **Click the Media tab.**

   The screen shown in Figure 15-1 appears.

Figure 15-1:
Set your
music
source
application
here.

6. **In the Music Source drop-down list, select iTunes or Windows Media Player.**

7. **Click OK.**

After you set the music source, BlackBerry Desktop Software is smart enough to figure out the location of the music files stored by the app, as you see in the next section.

Synchronizing music files

After you've set your music source to iTunes or Windows Media Player (see preceding section), it's easy to get your music library into your BlackBerry Pearl. Simply use BlackBerry Desktop Software to select music files, as follows:

1. **Connect your Pearl to your computer.**

2. **On your PC, click the Windows Start button.**

3. **Choose All Programs⇨BlackBerry⇨Desktop Software.**

4. **Click the Music link (in the Media Sync section).**

   A screen similar to Figure 15-2 appears with your music library.

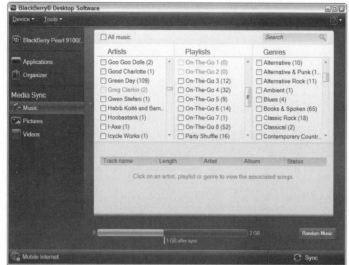

Figure 15-2:
Choose
music files
here.

5. **Select All Music or select music by artists, playlists, and genres.**

   When you make a selection, the bottom portion of the screen displays the amount of storage remaining on the microSD card.

   Get a big capacity microSD card. A 16GB microSD costs about $30 from Amazon.com and can hold thousands of music files.

Synchronizing picture files

You can copy your PC's folders that contain picture files to your BlackBerry Pearl. By the same token, you can also import pictures on your BlackBerry Pearl to your PC.

To set the folder location on your PC and select picture folders to copy to your BlackBerry Pearl, do the following:

1. **Connect your Pearl to your PC.**

2. **On your PC, click the Windows Start button.**

3. **Choose All Programs➪BlackBerry➪Desktop Software.**

4. **Click the Pictures link (in the Media Sync section).**

   A screen similar to Figure 15-3 appears, displaying the Device Pictures tab, which displays all the pictures on your Pearl. The second tab, Computer Pictures, displays the pictures on your computer.

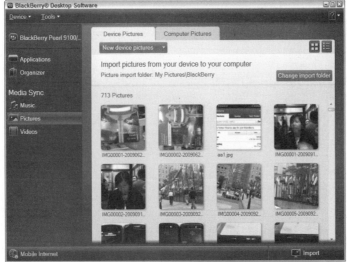

Figure 15-3:
View
images and
choose the
import loca-
tion here.

5. **To select a folder of pictures on your PC to import:**

   a. **Click the Change Import Folder button.**

   b. **Navigate to the folder, and then click Open.**

6. **To select picture folders to copy to your BlackBerry Pearl:**

   a. **Click the Computer Pictures tab.**

   The screen shown in Figure 15-4 appears, displaying all the picture folders you previously selected to be copied to your BlackBerry Pearl. The My Pictures folder on your desktop is listed here by default initially.

   b. **Click the Add Folder button.**

   c. **Navigate to the folder you want to add and then click Open.**

   You return to the Computer Pictures tab (see Figure 15-4), with the selected picture folder added to the list. Note that you can opt to not include this folder later by removing the check mark.

Synchronizing video files

Videos are synchronized and configured in the same way as pictures. You can copy PC folders that contain video files to your BlackBerry Pearl, and you can import pictures stored on your BlackBerry Pearl to your PC.

Figure 15-4:
Sync pic-
ture folders
from your
computer to
your device.

To set the import folder location in your PC and select video folders to copy to your BlackBerry Pearl, do the following:

1. **Connect your Pearl to your computer.**

2. **On your computer, click the Windows Start button.**

3. **Choose All Programs⇨BlackBerry⇨Desktop Software.**

4. **Click the Videos link (in the Media Sync section).**

   The screen shown in Figure 15-5 appears, with the Device Videos tab displaying the videos on your BlackBerry Pearl.

5. **To select a folder on your computer to import:**

   a. **Click the Change Import Folder button.**

   b. **Navigate to the folder, and then click Open.**

6. **To select video folders to copy to your BlackBerry Pearl:**

   a. **Click the Computer Videos tab.**

   BlackBerry Desktop Software appears, displaying the video folders you've selected to copy to your BlackBerry Pearl.

   b. **Click the Add Folder button.**

c. **Navigate to the folder you want to add, and then click Open.**

You return to the Computer Videos tab, and the selected video folder is added to the list. You can opt to not include this folder later by removing the check mark.

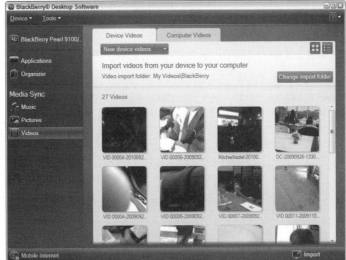

Figure 15-5:
View Device videos and choose the import location here.

Synchronizing media manually

With the effort you put into selecting media files, it's time to get those files into your BlackBerry Pearl. Simply do the following:

1. **From BlackBerry Desktop Software, click the Device menu.**

2. **Select the check boxes for the data you want to synchronize.**

3. **Click the Device menu and then click Sync All.**

    The synchronization starts, and you see a progress screen.

If you turned on automatic synchronization (see the next section), the items you select in Step 2 automatically sync every time you connect your BlackBerry Pearl to your PC.

Synchronizing media automatically

After you've configured Media Sync with the media files you want to sync, you don't have to navigate back to the BlackBerry Desktop Software screens and manually run media synchronization. The best way to keep your BlackBerry Pearl updated is to set BlackBerry Desktop Software to automatically sync your media files whenever you connect your BlackBerry Pearl to your PC. Set it up this way:

1. **From BlackBerry Desktop Software, click the Device menu.**

2. **Click Sync by Type.**

3. **Click Media.**

   The media synchronization starts, and you see a progress screen.

Part V
Getting Hooked with BlackBerry Desktop

CRICHTENNANT

Of course it doesn't make any sense, but it's our only chance! Now hook the BlackBerry Pearl into the override and see if you can bring this baby in.

In this part . . .

Here, you discover essential information about some behind-the-scenes yet integral processes. Read all about BlackBerry Desktop Software for Windows and BlackBerry Desktop Manager for Mac in Chapter 16. If you're a Windows user, you also find out how to switch from your old BlackBerry to your new Pearl. Find out how to monitor and control database synchronization in Chapter 17. You see how to back up your data in Chapter 18. And finally, in Chapter 19, you discover the many ways of installing third-party applications and upgrading your operating system

Chapter 16

Installing Desktop Software

*Y*our BlackBerry Pearl by itself is a standalone product, which means you can enjoy the benefits of having a smartphone by just having a BlackBerry Pearl. However, if you maintain personal information such as an address book or a calendar on your computer, it makes sense to synchronize this information with your BlackBerry Pearl. To do this synchronization business, you need software from RIM called BlackBerry Desktop Software (for the PC or the Mac). The program includes these main features:

✓ **BlackBerry Application Installation:** Installs BlackBerry applications and updates the BlackBerry OS.

✓ **Backup and Restore:** Backs up your BlackBerry data and settings. Check out Chapter 19 for details.

✓ **Synchronize Organizer Data:** Synchronizes BlackBerry Organizer data with your desktop.

✓ **Media Sync:** Uploads media files to your BlackBerry from computer and vice versa. See Chapter 15 for details.

✓ **Switching Device:** Available only for Windows, this feature helps you transfer data from your existing BlackBerry to a new BlackBerry.

The program is loaded on the CD that comes with your BlackBerry, but it's best to download the latest version at BlackBerry's Web site.

In this chapter, we introduce the program for Windows and the Mac, show you where and how to download them, and then provide instructions for installing them. And if you have a Windows machine, you find out how to back up data automatically from an old BlackBerry onto your new Pearl.

Using BlackBerry Desktop Software for Windows

BlackBerry Desktop Software for Windows has been around for many years and has been updated regularly. To make sure that you benefit from new features of the software, keep your copy updated. We describe how to get the latest copy later in this section.

Most companies have strict policies on what software can be installed on an employee's PC and have technical staff to install software. This section is intended for those who have a personal BlackBerry Pearl.

Downloading

You can find and download BlackBerry Desktop Software from RIM's Web site. Follow these easy steps:

1. **On your PC, open Internet Explorer.**

2. **In Internet Explorer's address bar, type** http://na.blackberry.com/eng/services/desktop/**.**

   If RIM has changed the download location, this address won't get you to the download page. Your best bet is to enter **BlackBerry Desktop Software for Windows Download** in a search engine such as Google. The top search results should lead you to the download page.

3. **Click Download for PC, and then click Download.**

   You see a prompt asking whether you want to run or save the file.

4. **Click Save.**

   A SaveAs screen appears so you can place the installation file in the folder location you want.

5. **Change the folder location of the installation file if you want, and then click Save.**

   Take note of the location and the name of the installation file. A progress screen appears. The installation file is large, so downloading should take a few minutes. After the file is downloaded, you see a confirmation screen.

6. **Close the confirmation screen.**

   You now have an installation file.

Installing

After you download the installation file for BlackBerry Desktop Software, as described in the preceding section, you need to install the software. Doing so is easy but requires a little patience. The process takes 15 to 20 minutes.

To install BlackBerry Desktop Software, follow these steps:

1. **On your PC, double-click the BlackBerry Desktop Software installation file.**

   An Open File — Security Warning screen appears.

2. **Click Run.**

   A Winzip Self-Extractor screen appears, quickly followed by the Choose a Setup Language screen.

3. **Select a language from the drop-down list, and then click OK.**

   An installation welcome screen appears.

4. **Click Next.**

5. **Select a country from the drop-down list, and then click Next.**

   A long license agreement appears. You have to accept the agreement before you can proceed.

6. **Select the license agreement terms, and then click Next.**

   The next screen allows you to choose the destination folder and whether you want BlackBerry Desktop Software available for all users of your computer. We suggest you keep the default settings.

7. **Click Next.**

   You see a screen similar to Figure 16-1, with the option to create a short-cut on your desktop already selected. We suggest that you keep the default and create a shortcut.

8. **Click Install.**

   The actual installation starts, and you see the progress screen shown in Figure 16-2.

9. **When you see the Installation Completed message, click Finish.**

   A screen appears telling you that some configurations take effect only after you restart the machine and prompting you to restart now or later.

   Before you click the Yes button to restart your machine, make sure you don't have any unsaved documents from other programs. You don't want to lose the edits you made on those documents, right? It's safer to close other programs manually.

10. **Click Yes.**

    Your machine restarts, and BlackBerry Desktop Software is fully installed.

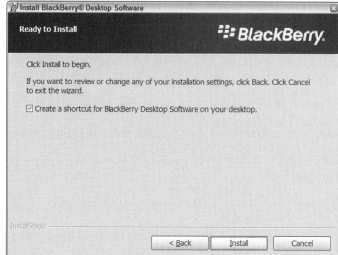

Figure 16-1: Create a shortcut on your desktop for BlackBerry Desktop Software.

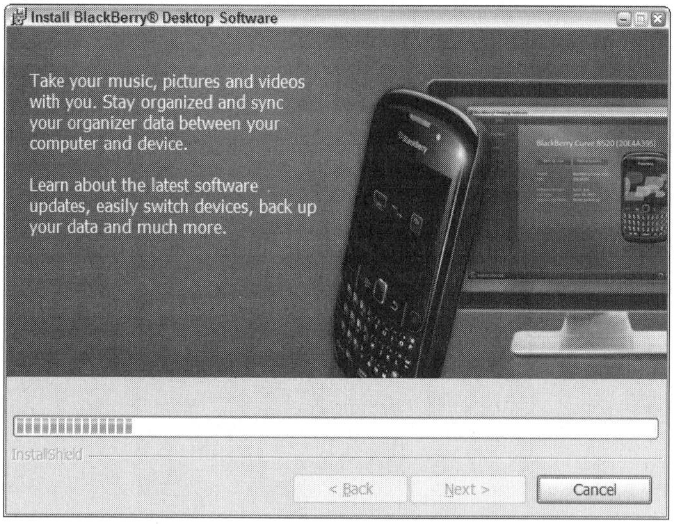

Figure 16-2: You see the progress of the installation.

Launching

If you kept the default settings during the installation, you find a shortcut to launch BlackBerry Desktop Software on your Windows desktop or in the Start menu. Launch the program by double-clicking the shortcut or by choosing Start➪All Programs➪BlackBerry➪BlackBerry Desktop Software. You see a screen similar to the one in Figure 16-3.

Figure 16-3:
BlackBerry
Desktop
Software
under
Windows.

On the left side of the screen are the following main links:

- BlackBerry Pearl (shows information of the connected BlackBerry)
- Applications (see Chapter 20)
- Organizer (see Chapter 17)
- Media Sync (see Chapter 15)

Connecting to your Pearl

After BlackBerry Desktop Software is running, it tries to find a BlackBerry (your BlackBerry Pearl) on the type of connection specified. The default connection is USB, so you shouldn't need to configure anything.

Follow these steps to connect your BlackBerry Pearl to BlackBerry Desktop Software:

1. **Use the USB cable to plug your Pearl into your desktop computer.**

   Keep your device on.

2. **Launch BlackBerry Desktop Software.**

   BlackBerry Desktop Software tries to find your BlackBerry Pearl on a USB connection.

3. **If your device has a password, enter your password at the prompt.**

   If your Pearl doesn't have a password, you won't see the prompt. You see a summary of your BlackBerry Pearl (refer to Figure 16-3).

If you're connecting your BlackBerry Pearl to the BlackBerry Desktop Software for the first time, the program displays the prompts shown in Figure 16-4.

Figure 16-4:
Set up your
Pearl with
BlackBerry
Desktop
Software.

These prompts allow you to

✔ Set up Organizer data synchronization options

✔ Customize the information about your device

✔ Transfer data from your older BlackBerry to your new Pearl

You can perform either task at any time. You don't have to do them now. See Chapter 17 for details on setting up Organizer data synchronization options. You find out how to transfer data from your old BlackBerry next.

Switching to a new BlackBerry Pearl

Switching from an older BlackBerry to your new BlackBerry Pearl is usually a painstaking task because you need to manually back up the data that you want from your old BlackBerry smartphone to your new BlackBerry Pearl. However, BlackBerry Desktop Software has a Device Switch Wizard that helps you with this process

Sorry Mac users. The wizard is not available in BlackBerry Desktop Manager.

Windows users can do the following to run the wizard:

1. **From BlackBerry Desktop Software, click the Device drop-down list and select Device Switch.**

   The Desktop Software screen appears, displaying Device Switch Wizard, as shown in Figure 16-5.

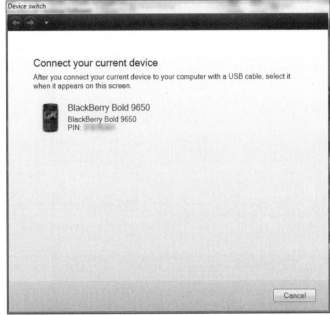

Figure 16-5: Device Switch Wizard helps you back up your data.

2. **Select the BlackBerry displayed in Figure 16-5.**

   The screen shown in Figure 16-6 appears so you can choose what to copy to your new BlackBerry Pearl 9100.

3. **Decide whether to include device data and third-party applications.**

   If you want to back up all the data, leave the screen untouched, and everything will be backed up. *Device data* consists of your contacts, calendar, call history, e-mail, configuration information, and lots more. *Third-party applications* are the programs you installed — the ones that didn't come with the device originally.

4. **Click Next.**

   A status screen appears, showing the progress of the backup. When the backup is finished, the screen prompts you to connect your new BlackBerry Pearl.

Figure 16-6:
Decide what
to copy to
your new
BlackBerry
Pearl 9100.

5. **Connect your new BlackBerry Pearl to your PC with the USB cable, and then click Next, see Figure 16-7.**

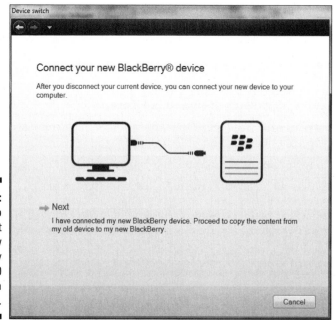

Figure 16-7:
Ready to
connect
your new
BlackBerry
Pearl 9100
for data
transfer.

6. **Confirm that the connected device is your new BlackBerry Pearl by clicking it on the screen.**

   Data transfer kicks off.

7. **When the Success screen appears, click the Close button.**

Using BlackBerry Desktop Software for the Mac

To perform data synchronization and data backup between a Mac and the BlackBerry Pearl, you use BlackBerry Desktop Software for the Mac. The program doesn't come with your BlackBerry packaging. No worries — you can download an installation program from RIM's Web site.

Downloading

Downloading BlackBerry Desktop Software for the Mac is as easy as following these steps:

1. **On your Mac, open Safari.**

2. **In the Safari address bar, type** http://na.blackberry.com/eng/services/desktop/desktop_mac.jsp.

   If RIM has changed the download location, this address won't get you to the download page. Your best bet is to enter **BlackBerry Desktop Software for Mac Download** in a search engine such as Google. The top search results should lead you to the download page.

3. **On the download page, click Download.**

   You see a progress screen as the installation file downloads. The process takes a few minutes.

When the file is downloaded, you see a screen on your Mac displaying two icons: BlackBerry Desktop Manager.mpkg and BlackBerry Desktop Manager Uninstaller. The file that ends with mpkg is the installation file.

Throughout this chapter, you've been seeing *BlackBerry Desktop Software,* not *BlackBerry Desktop Manager.* That's no typo in the preceding paragraph. RIM's Web site used the word *Software,* but after you download the program to your Mac, *Software* becomes *Manager.* So, whenever you see BlackBerry Desktop Software in this chapter, it's the same as BlackBerry Desktop Manager.

Installing

After you have downloaded BlackBerry Desktop Software (see the preceding section), you need to install it. (Remember, the program's name changes to BlackBerry Desktop Manager.) Follow these steps:

1. **Double-click BlackBerry Desktop Manager.mpkg.**

   A standard Mac warning message appears, telling you that you're about to run the installation of a program.

2. **Click Continue.**

   An installation welcome screen appears.

3. **Click Continue.**

   Another prompt appears, this time asking you to agree to the license agreement.

4. **Click Agree.**

   A screen appears so you can choose the location of the installation. The default is your Mac's hard drive.

5. **Click Continue.**

   You're prompted for your Mac password.

6. **Enter your Mac password and then click OK.**

7. **Click Continue Installation.**

   The installation kicks in. This process may take a few minutes.

   When the installation is complete, you are asked to restart your Mac. Before you proceed, save any unsaved files and close any programs manually.

8. **Click Restart.**

Launching

After installation, BlackBerry Desktop Manager may not be on the Mac's dock (the bottom bar with application icons on Mac OS 10.5 or later) or the Mac's desktop. If that's the case, do the following:

1. **Find BlackBerry Desktop Manager:**

   • **Mac OS 10.5 or later:** Click the Finder application (the leftmost icon) on your Mac's dock. In the search text box (top-right corner) of the Finder screen, type **BlackBerry Desktop**.

   • **Mac OS before 10.5:** Press Command+F to launch the Find utility. In the Find text box of the Find screen, type **BlackBerry Desktop**.

2. **Connect your BlackBerry Pearl to your Mac.**

3. **In the Finder or Find screen, click BlackBerry Desktop Manager.**

   The screen shown in Figure 16-8 appears, displaying the BlackBerry connected to your Mac.

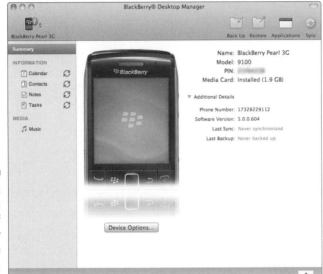

Figure 16-8:
The main screen of BlackBerry Desktop Manager.

Your newly installed BlackBerry Desktop Software is ready. Start enjoying your desktop media library on your Pearl (see Chapter 14) and be sure to check the next chapter if you want to update your Pearl with your desktop's organizer data.

Chapter 17

Syncing Organizer Data

· ·

· ·

*W*hat better way to keep your BlackBerry Pearl updated than to synchronize it with your desktop application's data? Arguably, most of the data you need to synchronize is from your Organizer applications: notes, appointments, contacts, and tasks. You use BlackBerry Desktop Software to synchronize your Organizer data and to upload and download media files between your PC and your smartphone.

In this chapter, you explore how to manually and automatically synchronize your Pearl with your desktop computer. You find tips about which options you may want to use. Before delving into all that, however, we have a section on BlackBerry Desktop Software.

If you're a Mac user, good news! The folks at Research in Motion have a Mac version of BlackBerry Desktop Software. In this book, we show you how to use BlackBerry Desktop Software on Windows PCs and on the Mac.

If you're using a corporate BlackBerry that's running under BlackBerry Enterprise Server, you can skip this chapter. BlackBerry smartphones running under BlackBerry Enterprise Server synchronize over the air (OTA), through serial bypass, or wirelessly.

Data Synchronization on a Windows PC

Organizer data synchronization has two parts: configuring how and what to synchronize and running the sync. We describe both parts in detail in this section.

Configuring Organizer data synchronization

With BlackBerry Desktop Software (for the PC), you do the configuration in the Organizer screen and run the sync by clicking Sync All or Sync by Type in the Device menu.

To configure Organizer synchronization, you click the Configure Settings button. When you do, the Select Device Application screen appears. This screen is the entry point for the entire synchronization configuration for Organizer applications. The names on the screen correspond to BlackBerry applications, except for Address Book, which the Pearl calls Contacts. Selecting an application on this screen allows you to pair the Organizer hand-held application with a desktop application (most likely Outlook).

From the Organizer configuration screen, select which application data you want to sync with your BlackBerry Pearl. The following popular Organizer applications can be synced to your Pearl: ACT!, ASCII Text File Converter, Lotus Notes, Lotus Organizer, Microsoft Outlook, Microsoft Outlook Express, and Microsoft Schedule.

You can synchronize the following types of application data with your BlackBerry Pearl:

- **Calendar:** The appointments and events stored in your favorite Organizer app
- **MemoPad:** Notes or text you've been storing in your Organizer app
- **Address Book:** Contact information, which syncs to Pearl's Contacts app
- **Tasks:** Your to-do list

Follow these steps to set up your device's synchronization:

1. **Connect your Pearl to your PC.**

2. **Double-click the BlackBerry Desktop Software desktop icon or click Start⟹All Programs⟹BlackBerry⟹BlackBerry Desktop Software.**

3. **Click the Organizer link, on the left side of the screen.**

   The screen shown in Figure 17-1 appears.

4. **Click the Configure Settings button.**

   The Select Device Application screen shown in Figure 17-2 appears.

5. **Select the check box next to the application data type (Calendar, MemoPad, Address Book, or Tasks) you want to synchronize.**

   For this example, we selected the Calendar application data type.

6. **Click the Setup button.**

   This step opens the screen for the application — in this case, the Calendar Setup screen.

Figure 17-1:
The
Organizer
screen.

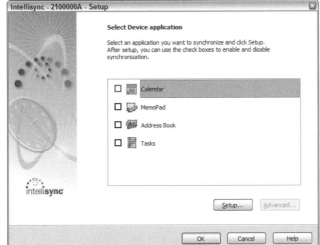

Figure 17-2:
Select the
Organizer
applications
to sync
here.

7. Select an Organizer application from which to retrieve application data, and then click Next.

BlackBerry Desktop Software will pull your selected application data from the application you select on this screen. In Figure 17-3, we selected Microsoft Outlook. When we synchronize the BlackBerry, BlackBerry Desktop Software will retrieve Calendar data from Microsoft Outlook.

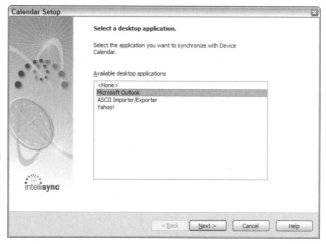

Figure 17-3:
Choose the
desktop
application.

8. **Select which direction the synchronization will follow.**

   The Synchronization Options screen, shown in Figure 17-4, provides three synchronization options:

   - Two Way Sync synchronizes changes in both your BlackBerry Pearl and in your desktop application.

   - One Way Sync from Device synchronizes only the changes made to your Pearl. Changes to your desktop application aren't reflected in your BlackBerry Pearl.

   - One Way Sync to Device synchronizes changes made in your desktop application with your BlackBerry Pearl. Any changes made in your Pearl aren't reflected in your desktop application.

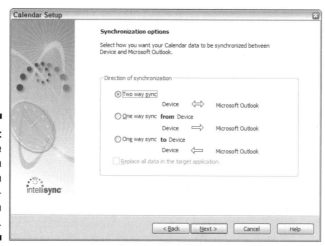

Figure 17-4:
Decide
which
direction
synchro-
nization
follows.

9. **Click Next.**

You see the Options screen for the Organizer application you selected in Step 5. Figure 17-5 shows the Microsoft Outlook Options screen.

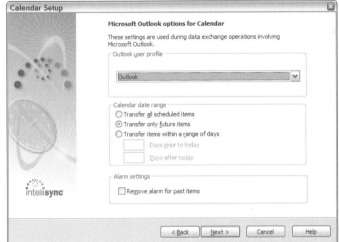

Figure 17-5: Select specific application settings.

For synchronization to Microsoft Outlook, make sure that you choose the correct user profile from the Outlook User Profile drop-down list. This is particularly pertinent if you have multiple user profiles in your computer. Choosing the wrong one may put the wrong data into your BlackBerry Pearl.

10. **In the Calendar date range section, select from three available options to limit the calendar data you want synchronized.**

You can control the amount of data that is reconciled or synchronized in a given application. For example, in Figure 17-5, you can specify whether to transfer all Calendar items, a set of appointments in the future, or items within a date range.

Select the Remove Alarm for Past Items check box if you don't want to keep the alarm setting for events that have already occurred.

11. **Click Next, and then click Finish.**

Clicking the Next button brings you to the Calendar Setup Finish screen, and clicking the Finish button completes the configuration of the Calendar synchronization you selected.

Mapping fields for synchronization

For all four Organizer applications, BlackBerry Desktop Software is intelligent enough to know which information — such as names, phone numbers, and addresses in Contacts — corresponds to information in Outlook. A specific bit of information, or attribute, is a *field*. For instance, the value of a home-phone-number field in Contacts needs to be mapped to the corresponding field in Outlook so that information is transferred correctly.

But not all fields on the desktop side exist on the smartphone (and vice versa). For example, a Nick Name field doesn't exist in BlackBerry Contacts but is available in Exchange (Outlook) Address Book. In some instances, BlackBerry Desktop Software provides an alternative field and lets you decide whether to map it.

If you ever need to change the default mapping, you can. The interface is the same for all Organizer applications. We use Contacts as our example in the following steps as we illustrate how to map and unmap fields:

1. **From BlackBerry Desktop Software, click the Organizer link.**

2. **Click the Configure Settings button.**

   The Organizer configuration screen appears (refer to Figure 17-2).

3. **Select the Address Book check box.**

   The Advanced button is enabled.

4. **Click the Advanced button.**

   The Advanced screen appears, as shown in Figure 17-6.

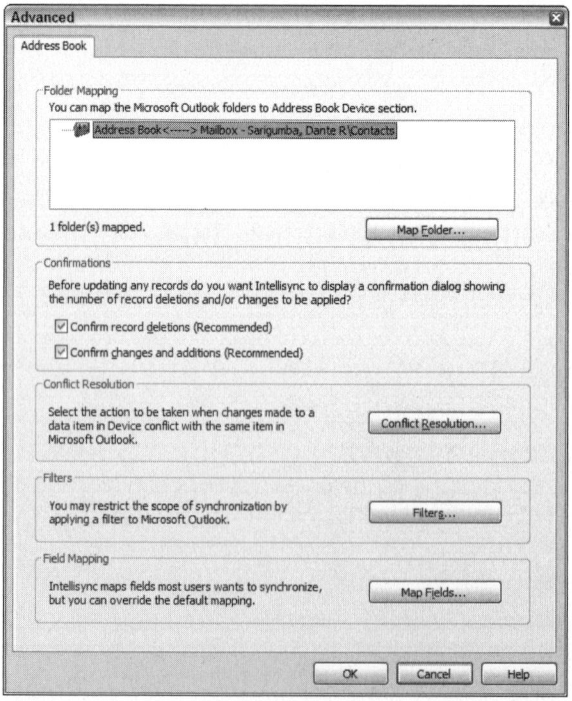

Figure 17-6: The Advanced screen for Address Book.

5. Click the Map Fields button.

The Map Fields screen for the Address Book/Contacts application appears, as shown in Figure 17-7.

Figure 17-7:
The Map Fields screen for Address Book.

6. To map or unmap, click the arrow icons.

If you aren't careful, you can inadvertently unclick a mapping (such as Job Title), and suddenly your titles aren't in sync. Double-check your mapping before you click OK. If you think you made a mistake, click Cancel to save yourself from having to restore settings.

7. Click OK to save your changes.

Confirming record changes

Face facts: Doing a desktop synchronization isn't an interesting task, and few people perform it regularly. You can tell BlackBerry Desktop Software to prompt you for any changes it's trying to make (or perhaps undo) on either side of the fence. The Advanced screen comes into the picture here. To get to this view, follow these steps:

1. From BlackBerry Desktop Software, click the Organizer link.

2. Click the Configure Settings button.

The Organizer configuration screen appears (refer to Figure 17-2).

3. Select the Address Book option.

If you want an Organizer application other than Address Book, select that application from the list.

4. **Click the Advanced button.**

The Advanced screen for Address Book appears (refer to Figure 17-6). The Confirmations section gives you two options:

- Confirm Record Deletions (Recommended)

- Confirm Changes and Additions (Recommended)

Regardless of whether you select the first option, BlackBerry Desktop Software displays a prompt if it detects that it's about to delete *all* records.

Resolving update conflicts

BlackBerry Desktop Software needs to know how you want to handle any conflicts between your BlackBerry Pearl and your desktop application. A conflict normally happens when the same record is updated on your BlackBerry Pearl and also in Outlook. Suppose that you change Jane Doe's mobile number on both the BlackBerry Pearl and Outlook on the PC. Where you resolve these conflicts is the same for all Organizer applications. Again, for illustration, we use Address Book as an example:

1. **From BlackBerry Desktop Software, click the Organizer link.**

2. **Click the Configure Settings button.**

The Organizer configuration screen appears (refer to Figure 17-2).

3. **Select the Address Book option.**

If you want an Organizer application other than Address Book, select that application from the list.

4. **Click the Advanced button.**

The Advanced screen for Address Book appears (refer to Figure 17-6). This screen has five sections, and the third section is Conflict Resolution.

5. **Click the Conflict Resolution button.**

The Conflict Resolution screen shown in Figure 17-8 appears. You can tell BlackBerry Desktop Software to handle conflicts in the following ways:

- **Add All Conflicting Items:** When a conflict happens, add a new record to the BlackBerry Pearl for the changes on the desktop and add a new record to the desktop for the changes on the BlackBerry.

- **Ignore All Conflicting Items:** Ignores the change and keeps the data the same on both sides.

- **Notify Me When Conflict Occur:** This option is the safest. BlackBerry Desktop Software displays the details of the conflict and lets you resolve it.

- **Device Wins:** This option tells BlackBerry Desktop Software to disregard the changes in the desktop and use handheld changes every time it encounters a conflict. Unless you're sure that this is the case, you shouldn't choose this option.

- **Microsoft Outlook Wins:** If you aren't using MS Outlook, this option is based on your application. This option tells BlackBerry Desktop Software to always discard changes on the smartphone and use the desktop application change when it encounters a conflict. We don't recommend this option because there's no telling on which side you made the good update.

6. **Select the option you want, and then click OK to save the settings.**

Figure 17-8:
Manage
conflicts
here.

Ready, set, synchronize!

Are you ready to synchronize? Previously in this chapter, we show you ways to define synchronization filters and rules for your e-mail and Organizer data. Now it's time to be brave and synchronize. You can do so in one of two ways:

- ✔ **Manually:** Select the Device menu, and then select Sync All or Sync by Type

- ✔ **Automatically:** Choose How Often on the calendar.

Using on-demand synchronization

On-demand synchronization is a feature in BlackBerry Desktop Software that lets you run synchronization manually. Remember that even if you set up automatic synchronization, actual synchronization doesn't happen right away. So if you make updates to your appointments in Outlook while your BlackBerry Pearl is connected to your PC, this feature lets you be sure that your updates make it to your BlackBerry Pearl before you head out the door.

Without delay, here are the steps:

1. **From BlackBerry Desktop Software, click the Organizer link.**

   The right portion of the BlackBerry Desktop Software screen is updated (refer to Figure 17-1).

2. **Select the check boxes for the data you want to synchronize.**

3. **Click the Device menu at the top left (see Figure 17-9), and then click Sync All.**

   The synchronization starts, and you see a progress screen. If you set up prompts for conflicts and BlackBerry Desktop Software encounters one, a screen appears so that you can resolve that conflict. When finished, the progress screen disappears, and you're back to the previous BlackBerry Desktop Software screen.

Figure 17-9:
Run
Organizer
data syn-
chronization
here.

If you turned on automatic synchronization (see the next section), the items you select in Step 2 automatically sync every time you connect your BlackBerry Pearl to your PC.

Synchronizing automatically

How many times do you think you reconfigure your Organizer synchronization setup? Rarely, right? After you have it configured, that's it. And if you're like us, the reason you open BlackBerry Desktop Software is to sync your Organizer data. So it's annoying having to open BlackBerry Desktop Software and click the Sync All Device menu item.

To make BlackBerry Desktop Software run automatically every time you connect your BlackBerry Pearl to your PC, simply make sure that you select the Organizer data check box on the Device Options screen. Here's how you get there:

1. **From BlackBerry Desktop Software, click the Device menu and then click the Device Options menu item.**

   A screen like the one shown in Figure 17-10 appears.

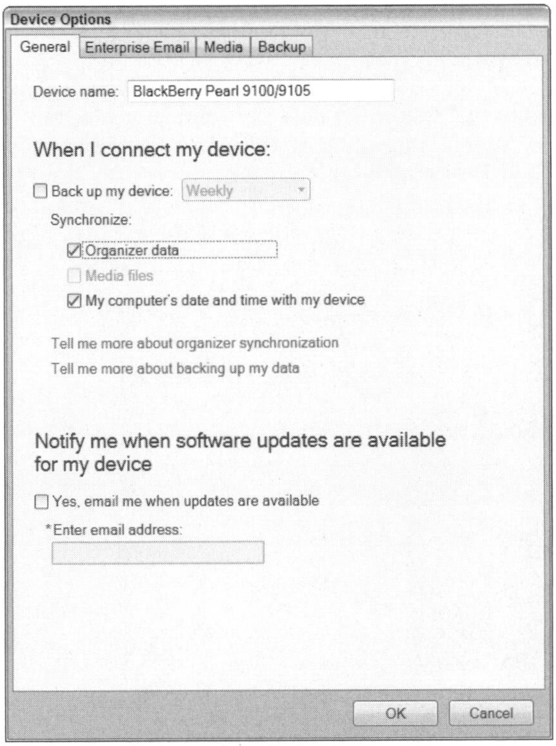

Figure 17-10: Sync automatically when you connect your Pearl to your PC.

> **Device Options**
>
> General | Enterprise Email | Media | Backup
>
> Device name: BlackBerry Pearl 9100/9105
>
> ### When I connect my device:
>
> ☐ Back up my device: Weekly ▾
>
>   Synchronize:
>
>   ☑ Organizer data
>   ☐ Media files
>   ☑ My computer's date and time with my device
>
>   Tell me more about organizer synchronization
>   Tell me more about backing up my data
>
> ### Notify me when software updates are available for my device
>
> ☐ Yes, email me when updates are available
>   *Enter email address:
>
> [   ]
>
> OK   Cancel

2. **Select the Organizer Data option.**

   This option is in the When I Connect My Device section.

3. **Click OK**

   That's it. Whenever you connect your Pearl to your PC, BlackBerry Desktop Software will automatically run a synchronization process.

You may be asking, "What items will autosynchronization sync?" Good question. BlackBerry Desktop Software automatically syncs the items you configured (see the previous section "Configuring Organizer data synchronization") to be synchronized.

Data Synchronization on the Mac

Synchronizing Organizer data and music files is what most of us look for when talking about BlackBerry Desktop Manager. Just follow these short sections as we delve in to the details on configuring the sync, doing a manual sync, and doing an automatic sync.

Setting synchronization options

You'll probably need to set synchronization options only once. Follow the steps in this section to make sure the data between your Mac and your BlackBerry Pearl are synced the way you want. To begin, connect your Pearl to your Mac. The BlackBerry Desktop Manager screen shown in Figure 17-11 appears. If you don't have BlackBerry Desktop Manager installed on your Mac, read Chapter 15 to find out where to get the software and how to install it.

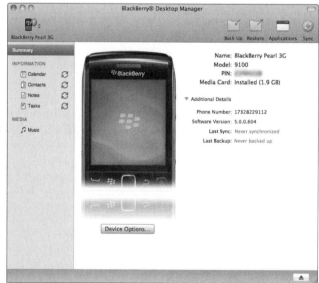

Figure 17-11: Default BlackBerry Desktop Manager screen showing a connected Pearl.

Device Options

At the bottom center of the BlackBerry Desktop Manager screen (refer to Figure 17-11) is a Device Options button. Click this button, and you see the screen shown in Figure 17-12.

An important option is This Device Is Synchronized. If you sync your BlackBerry Pearl with other machines or even if you have Google Sync for Calendars and Contacts, we advise that you select With Other Computers.

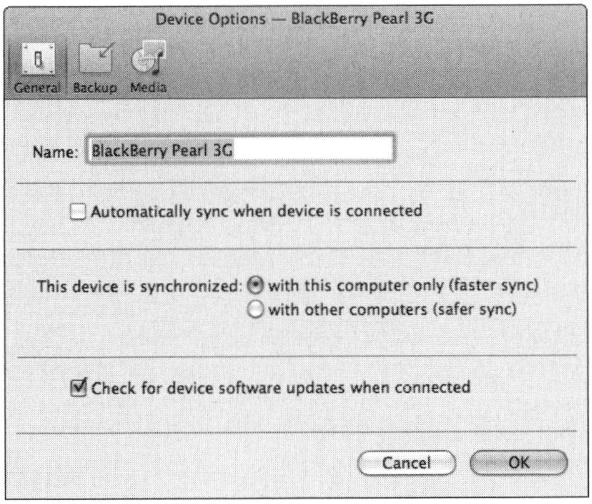

Figure 17-12:
Decide
whether you
want your
Pearl to
sync only on
this Mac.

This option ensures that the automatic sync option is disabled. One side effect of automatic sync is creating duplicate contacts on your BlackBerry Pearl and your other desktop machines. However, if you sync your BlackBerry Pearl only with the Mac currently running the software, select With This Computer Only.

The listing on the left (under the Summary heading) contains links for navigating to the option screens. We describe each option in the following sections.

Calendar

Clicking the Calendar link on the BlackBerry Desktop Manager screen displays the screen shown in Figure 17-13.

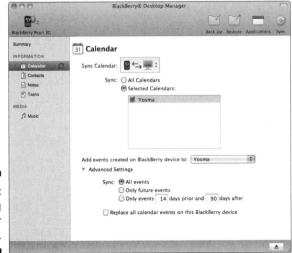

Figure 17-13:
Configuring
Calendar
sync.

You can configure how your appointments are synced as follows:

✔ **Sync Calendar:** Include Calendar in the sync by clicking the drop-down next to Sync Calendar. You can select Two Way (shown as two opposing arrows; refer to Figure 17-13) or Do Not Sync (the default, shown as an X).

A quick way to know that you set the Calendar app for Two Way sync is the appearance of two circular arrow icons next to the Calendar link on the left side of the BlackBerry Desktop Manager screen (refer to Figure 17-13). This is true for Contacts, Notes, Tasks, and Music as well.

✔ **Sync:** This section applies only if you have multiple calendar applications on your Mac. You can include all calendars or select one from the list. The BlackBerry Calendar app uses different colors to indicate which calendar an appointment belongs to.

✔ **Add Events Created on BlackBerry Device To:** The default Calendar on your BlackBerry Pearl doesn't tie directly to any Mac applications. Appointments you create in your BlackBerry Pearl aren't synced to any Mac applications. Setting this option tells BlackBerry Desktop Manager to sync those appointments or events to a particular Mac application.

✔ **(Advanced Settings) Sync:** Use this setting to limit the number of appointments or events to sync on your BlackBerry Pearl. After all, past events just occupy valuable space on your smartphone with no purpose but a record. Here, you can control which ones your BlackBerry Pearl carries. Choose All Events (the default), Only Future Events, or Only Events *n* Days Prior and *n* Days After. The last option allows you to have a range of dates relative to the current day. The default is 14 days in the past and 90 days after.

✔ **(Advanced Settings) Replace All Calendar Events on This BlackBerry Device:** Keep this option deselected unless you want a fresh start and want to copy to your BlackBerry appointments or events from your Mac.

Contacts

Click the Contacts link on the BlackBerry Desktop Manager screen to display the screen shown in Figure 17-14.

Here, you can do the following:

✔ **Sync Contacts:** Include Contacts in the sync by clicking the drop-down next to Sync Contact. You can select Two Way (shown as two opposing arrows; refer to Figure 17-14) or Do Not Sync (the default, shown as an X).

✔ **Sync:** Include all contacts and groups when syncing or click Selected Groups to sync only the groups you want.

✔ **(Advanced Settings) Replace All Contacts on This BlackBerry Device:** Keep this option deselected unless you want a fresh start and want to copy all contacts from your Mac to your smartphone.

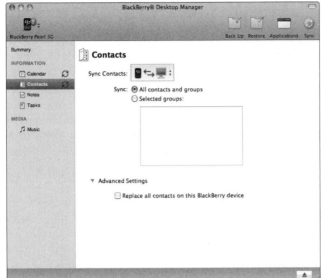

Figure 17-14:
Configure
Contacts
sync here.

Notes

The Notes link on the BlackBerry Desktop Manager screen displays the screen shown in Figure 17-15.

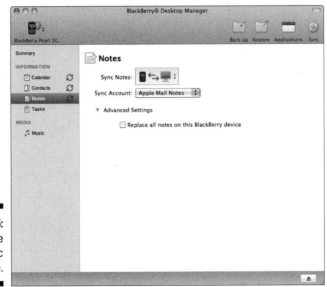

Figure 17-15:
Configure
Notes sync
here.

From this screen, you can configure the syncing of Notes or MemoPad items on your BlackBerry Pearl:

✔ **Sync Notes:** Configure whether or not you want Notes included in the sync by clicking the drop-down next to Sync Notes. Select Two Way (shown as two opposing arrows; refer to Figure 17-15) or Do Not Sync (the default, shown as an X).

✔ **Sync Account:** If you have multiple note-keeping programs in your Mac, this setting allows you to choose which one you want to tie the sync into. The default is Apple Mail Notes.

✔ **(Advanced Settings) Replace All Notes on This BlackBerry Device:** If you select this option, the Mac side becomes your master. Keep this option deselected unless you want a fresh start and want to copy to your BlackBerry Pearl all notes from your Mac.

Tasks

Clicking the Tasks link on the BlackBerry Desktop Manager screen displays the screen shown in Figure 17-16. Note that the screen is similar to Calendar because most of the Tasks items have associated dates and are essentially tied to your Calendar.

Figure 17-16:
Configure the Tasks sync here.

You can configure how your tasks are synced as follows:

✔ **Sync Tasks:** Include Tasks in the sync by clicking the drop-down next to Sync Tasks. Select Two Way (shown as two opposing arrows; refer to Figure 17-16) or Do Not Sync (the default, showing as an X).

✔ **Sync:** This section applies only if you have multiple calendar applications on your Mac. You can include all calendars or choose one of those listed. The BlackBerry Calendar app uses different colors to indicate which calendar an appointment belongs to.

✔ **Add Tasks Created on BlackBerry Device To:** The default Calendar on your BlackBerry Pearl doesn't tie into any Mac application. Tasks you created in your BlackBerry Pearl aren't synced to any of your Mac applications. Setting this option tells BlackBerry Desktop Software to sync those tasks to a particular Mac application.

✔ **(Advanced Settings) Sync:** Limit the tasks to sync on your BlackBerry Pearl so that completed tasks don't occupy valuable space on your smartphone with no real purpose. Select either All Tasks (the default) or Only Uncompleted Tasks.

✔ **(Advanced Settings) Replace All Tasks on This BlackBerry Device:** Keep this option deselected unless you want a fresh start, deleting current calendar items in your smartphone and copying all appointments or events from your Mac.

Music

You can easily sync your iTunes playlists to the BlackBerry Pearl by clicking the Music link on the BlackBerry Desktop Manager screen. You see the screen shown in Figure 17-17.

Figure 17-17:
Configure
Music sync.

You can choose the following:

- ✔ **Sync Music:** Decide whether to include Music in the sync or not. Just below this check box, you have options to sync All Songs and Playlists (the default) or Selected Playlists. If you have a big music library in iTunes, we recommend that you select the Selected Playlists option and then select only the music you want to carry with you, up to the capacity of your media card.

- ✔ **Add Random Music to Free Space:** If you want BlackBerry Desktop Manager to sync random songs from iTunes that aren't included in your playlist, select this option. You can find the songs in the Random Music playlist in the Music app of your BlackBerry Pearl.

- ✔ **Memory Settings:** Displays the free space of the media card, which stores your music in your BlackBerry Pearl.

Some useful information on this screen is related to the memory space of your smartphone, so you have some idea how much memory your playlist is occupying and how much free space is left on your device.

Deleting all music files on your Pearl

You might be wondering why we bother to include a section on deleting music files. What does deleting music files have to do with data synchronization? This is the first time you installed and ran BlackBerry Desktop Manager on your Mac. With BlackBerry Desktop Manager, you have the option to sync your BlackBerry Pearl with iTunes playlists, including album art. It makes sense to start fresh and clear your BlackBerry Pearl of whatever music files it has.

To do a one-time deletion of all music files on your Pearl:

1. **Connect your BlackBerry Pearl to your Mac.**

   The BlackBerry Desktop Manager screen appears.

2. **Click the Device Options button.**

3. **Click the Media icon.**

4. **Click Delete.**

   A confirmation prompt asks whether you really want to delete your music files on the device.

5. **Click OK.**

Syncing manually

Ready to sync? You've chosen the sync configuration you want. If you haven't, make sure to read the sections before this one.

To sync manually, click the green Sync button, which is located in the top-right corner of the BlackBerry Desktop Manager screen. If this is your first attempt at running the sync, you see the prompt shown in Figure 17-18. BlackBerry Desktop Manager needs to establish the latest copy of your data, and to do that, it needs to know how you want to proceed:

✔ **Merge Data:** Click this button if you want BlackBerry Desktop Manager to merge your Mac to your BlackBerry data. Merging is basically combining two sets of data with no duplicate checking. If you have synced your Mac before, using a different type of software such as PocketMac, you'll end up with duplicates.

✔ **Replace Device Data:** Click this button if you want to have a fresh copy of Mac data on your smartphone. After the sync, your BlackBerry data will be the same as what you have on your Mac.

Figure 17-18:
Doing a
manual sync
for the first
time.

Configuring an automatic sync

It's annoying to click the Sync button every time you want to sync. Simply follow these steps, and every time you connect the Pearl to the Mac, the sync occurs automatically:

1. **Connect the BlackBerry Pearl to the Mac.**

   The BlackBerry Desktop Manager screen appears.

2. **Click the Device Options button.**

3. **Select Automatically Sync When Device Is Connected.**

4. **Click OK.**

Chapter 18

Protecting Your Information

• •

• •

*I*magine that you left your BlackBerry Pearl in the back of a cab or on the train. You've lost your Pearl for good. Okay, not good. So what happens to all your information? Have you lost it forever? What about information security? Can anyone have unauthorized access to your personal information?

One thing that you *don't* need to worry about is information security — assuming that you set up a security password on your BlackBerry. With security password protection, anyone who finds your BlackBerry has only ten chances to enter the correct password; after those ten chances are up, it's self-destruction time. Although it's not as smoky and dramatic as what you see on *Mission Impossible,* your BlackBerry does erase all its information in such a scenario, thwarting your would-be data thief. Therefore, set up a password for your BlackBerry! For information on how to do so, refer to Chapter 3.

What you *do* need to worry about is how to retrieve all your information on your BlackBerry Pearl. If you're like us and you store important information on your Pearl, this chapter is for you. Vital information such as clients' and friends' contact information, notes from phone calls with clients — and, of course, those precious e-mail messages — should not be taken lightly. Backing up this information is a reliable way to protect information from being lost forever.

You can make sure your data is backed up properly in several ways. From BlackBerry Desktop Software (PC) and BlackBerry Desktop Manager (Mac) to third-party applications to BlackBerry Enterprise Server, you can be sure to find a way that works for you.

If your employer handed you a BlackBerry and the BlackBerry is part of BlackBerry Enterprise Server (BES), you don't need to do anything because all your information is stored on the corporate BES server. If you're part of a small business or you purchased your own BlackBerry, your best bet is

BlackBerry Desktop Software or BlackBerry Desktop Manager. (For installation instructions, please see Chapter 17.) The drawback of using BlackBerry Desktop Software or Desktop Manager is that you need to connect your BlackBerry to a PC or a Mac to back up your information.

In this chapter, we provide instructions for using BlackBerry Desktop Software on the PC. The steps for the Mac are similar.

Backing Up

BlackBerry Desktop Software (Windows) and BlackBerry Desktop Manager (Mac) allow you to back up all the sensitive data on your BlackBerry, including contacts, e-mails, memos, to-dos, personal preferences, and options. For most users, your e-mails are already stored in accounts such as Gmail or Yahoo! mail. But you can still back up your e-mails just in case.

Backing up manually

To back up information on your BlackBerry, follow these steps:

1. **Open BlackBerry Desktop Software on your PC by choosing Start⇨ All Programs⇨BlackBerry⇨BlackBerry Desktop Software.**

   If you haven't already installed BDS on your PC, see Chapter 17.

2. **Connect your BlackBerry to your computer with the USB cable that came with your BlackBerry.**

   A pop-up window on your computer asks you to type your BlackBerry security password. If you have set up a password on your BlackBerry, you need to enter a password. If you do not have a security password set up on your BlackBerry, then skip to Step 4.

3. **If you've set up a password on your BlackBerry, type it now.**

   If you haven't set up a security password, you can skip this step.

4. **Click the Backup Now button.**

   The Back Up Options screen shown in Figure 18-1 appears. You're ready to back up data from your BlackBerry.

5. **Type the filename for your backup, and select where to save your file.**

6. **Click the Back Up button.**

   The backup process starts and you see a screen similar to Figure 18-2.

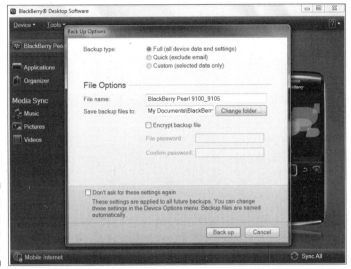

Figure 18-1:
Back up
your files
here.

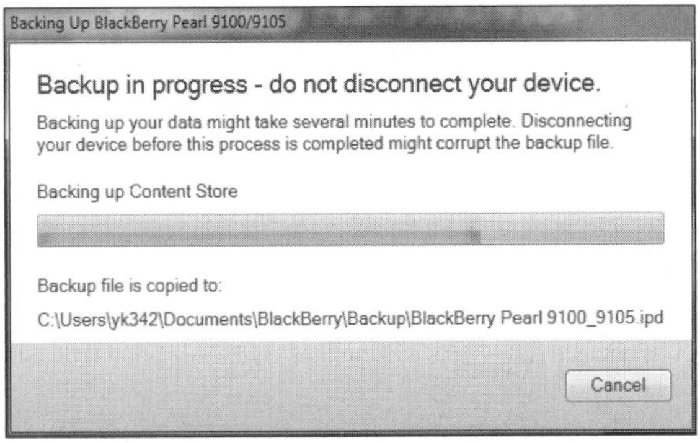

Backing Up BlackBerry Pearl 9100/9105

Backup in progress - do not disconnect your device.

Backing up your data might take several minutes to complete. Disconnecting
your device before this process is completed might corrupt the backup file.

Backing up Content Store

Backup file is copied to:

C:\Users\yk342\Documents\BlackBerry\Backup\BlackBerry Pearl 9100_9105.ipd

Cancel

Figure 18-2:
Data backup
in progress.

Backing up automatically

What's better than backing up your information once? Remembering to back
it up regularly! What's better than regularly backing up? You guessed it —
having your PC and BlackBerry run backups automatically. After you schedule automated backups of your BlackBerry, you can have peace of mind when
it comes to preventing information loss. To set up an autobackup:

1. **From BlackBerry Desktop Software, click the Device menu and choose
   Device Options.**

   You see the Device options screen.

2. **Click the Back Up My Device check box and then make a selection in
   the drop-down list that appears (see Figure 18-3).**

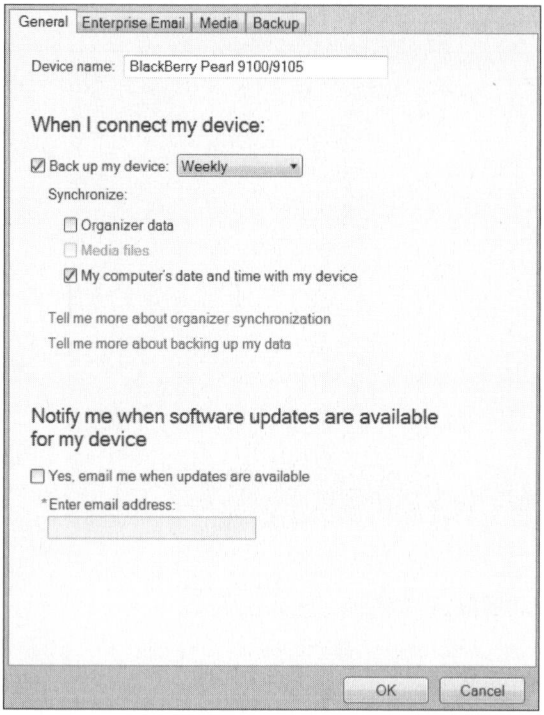

General | Enterprise Email | Media | Backup

Device name: BlackBerry Pearl 9100/9105

When I connect my device:

☑ Back up my device: Weekly ▼

Synchronize:

☐ Organizer data

☐ Media files

☑ My computer's date and time with my device

Tell me more about organizer synchronization

Tell me more about backing up my data

Notify me when software updates are available for my device

☐ Yes, email me when updates are available

*Enter email address:

[   ]

OK   Cancel

Figure 18-3:
Set auto-
backups
here.

3. **Click Okay.**

   Every time you connect your BlackBerry to your computer, your BlackBerry will be backed up according to the schedule you set.

Full Restore from Backup Information

We hope that you never have to read this section more than once. Why? Because it describes how to perform a full restore from backup, and every time you do that, it probably means that you've lost information that you hope to find from the backup you created on your computer.

To fully restore your backup information, do the following:

1. **From BlackBerry Desktop Software, click the Device menu and then choose Restore.**

   The screen shown in Figure 18-4 appears.

2. **Select a backup file to restore from.**

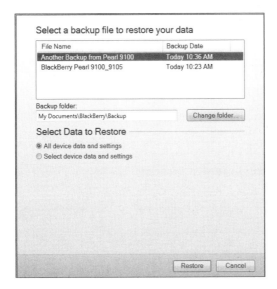

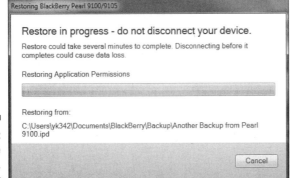

3. Select the All Device Data and Settings option.

This option restores all the settings and data from the backup file. If you want to restore only certain type of data, see the next section.

4. Click the Restore button.

A progress bar similar to Figure 18-5 now appears, showing the progress of the full restore. When the progress bar disappears, your BlackBerry Pearl is fully restored from the backup file.

It might take awhile for the full restore to finish. Do not unplug your Pearl from your PC during this time!

5. When the progress bar disappears, you're finished with the restore process and may unplug the Pearl from the computer.

Restoring, Your Way

Sometimes, you might want only a selective restore, not a full restore. For example, you might not want to override some of the new contacts in your address book and want to restore only your e-mail messages. To restore your way, follow these steps:

1. **From BlackBerry Desktop Software, click the Device menu and then choose Restore.**

2. **Select a backup file to restore from.**

3. **Click the Select Device Data and Settings option.**

   The screen shown in Figure 18-6 appears.

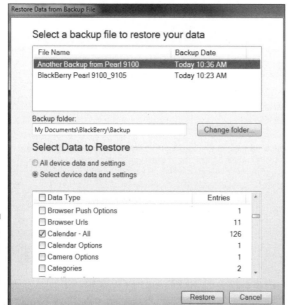

Figure 18-6: You can select different types of data.

4. **Select the data type(s) that you want to restore.**

   The different information categories, or databases, appear on the left.

5. **Click the Restore button.**

   A bar displays the progress of the restore.

6. **When the progress bar disappears, you're finished with the restore process and may unplug the Pearl from the computer.**

Chapter 19

Finding and Installing Apps

. . . .

. . . .

Think of your BlackBerry Pearl as a mini laptop where you can run preinstalled apps as well as install new apps. You can even upgrade the operating system (OS). Yup, that's right — your Pearl has an OS.

We start the chapter by introducing BlackBerry App World, which you use to load apps (who'd have guessed?) onto your BlackBerry Pearl. Next, we describe BlackBerry Desktop Software for the PC and BlackBerry Desktop Manager for the Mac, which you use to install and uninstall apps to and from your BlackBerry Pearl. Then we explore how you can upgrade the OS of your smartphone.

In Chapter 22, you find a few great games that make your BlackBerry Pearl that much more fun.

Using BlackBerry App World

Your BlackBerry comes with BlackBerry App World, an app store (or app store) that provides an organized listing of apps, both free and for purchase.

Navigating App World

What better way to describe BlackBerry App World than by opening the app and navigating to the screen? To launch the store, simply select BlackBerry App World from the Home screen. BlackBerry App World sports an icon similar to the one on the Menu key but enclosed in a circle. After you launch App World, you see a progress screen followed by a Featured Items screen similar to Figure 19-1.

Figure 19-1:
BlackBerry
App World
showcases
featured
apps.

If you don't have App World on your BlackBerry, you can download it from the Research in Motion (RIM) Web site at `http://na.blackberry.com/eng/services/appworld`.

The bottom of the screen in Figure 19-1 shows a few icons that you can use to navigate the store. From left to right, they are as follows:

✔ **Categories:** Apps are organized and showcased in a series of categories. It's easy to explore a certain type of app by going to this link.

✔ **Top Free:** Find it here first. If you're lucky, the type of app you're looking for is offered free of charge. This is the place to find the most popular free apps.

✔ **Top Paid:** Best-selling apps are listed here.

✔ **Search:** If you know the app that you're looking for, go here. The link allows you to enter the name and search for it from the store.

✔ **My World:** This lists the apps you've downloaded from the store.

If you're sitting at a desktop computer, you'll be glad to know that RIM created a Web version of App World. Using your desktop Internet browser, you can visit the site at `http://appworld.blackberry.com`. The site allows you to send an e-mail to your device with a download link for the app you're interested in.

Installing an app using App World

Find a free time-killing game at the store? Installing the app is easy, and you probably see all the links on the screen. Nevertheless, here's a quick run-down on how to do an installation:

1. **Select BlackBerry App World on the Home screen.**

2. **Navigate to the app you want to install.**

3. **Select the app's icon.**

   You see a screen similar to Figure 19-2, which shows a Download button for the free version of SmrtGuard, a security and backup app.

Figure 19-2:
Download
an app.

4. **Select the Download button.**

   The My World screen appears. At the top are the app you're downloading and a progress bar, as shown in Figure 19-3. When the download has finished, the installation kicks in, and a prompt appears as shown in Figure 19-4 after the app is installed.

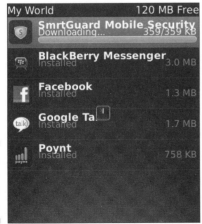

Figure 19-3:
The prog-
ress of the
download.

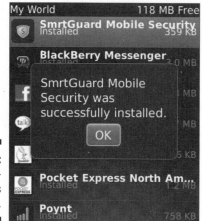

Figure 19-4:
App instal-
lation is
finished.

Any app you download is located in the Downloads folder on the Home screen.

Finding and Installing Apps from Other App Stores

BlackBerry App World is not the only app store out there in BlackBerry Land. Why do you need additional app stores? BlackBerry App World has a minimum price of $2.99 to be listed as a nonfree app, so this limits app developers who want to sell their apps for less. Check out the following pioneers:

- **Handango (www.handango.com):** Handango is one of the oldest storefronts that sell apps for mobile devices. It started selling apps through its Web site but eventually created an app store. Handango's app store can be downloaded from its Web site.

- **CrackBerry SuperStore (http://crackberryappstore.com):** Partnering with MobiHand, CrackBerry also provides an app store where you can find great apps to download.

Visit CrackBerry's app store before you decide to buy an app. There are many good reasons for doing this:

- Apps may be priced below App World's $2.99 minimum.

- Daily promotions provide discounts of up to 50 percent.

- CrackBerry offers refunds. App World doesn't.

✔ **BlackBerry Application Center:** This is software built by RIM, but the carrier has control over what shows up in the Application Center. The app is typically already installed on your BlackBerry, possibly under the brand name of your wireless carrier.

Finding and Installing Apps Directly from the Developer's Web Site

Most of the newly built apps as well as those that cost $2.99 and above are available in BlackBerry App World, but some of the free apps may not be listed there at all.

Publishing an app in BlackBerry App World (or any other app store, for that matter) requires effort from the developer. Of app developers who consider BlackBerry app development a hobby, few give the extra effort to publish apps some place other than their Web sites.

BlackBerry users' forums such as CrackBerry.com and BlackBerryForums. com are the best places to find useful apps. You'll get unsolicited feedback both good and bad from existing users about an app, which can be helpful when making a decision about which app to try.

If the app you find in the forums is not available in BlackBerry App World, simply do a Google search of the app name. Doing so will likely lead you to the app developer's Web site, which probably has an over-the-air installation using BlackBerry Browser. Chapter 11 shows how to use Browser to install an app.

Installing an App

In this section, you work closely with your desktop machine (Windows PC or Mac) and your BlackBerry for installing apps. On your desktop, you use BlackBerry Desktop Software (for PC) and BlackBerry Desktop Manager (for Mac), both of which can be downloaded from RIM's Web site.

For details on where to get and how to install BlackBerry Desktop Software and BlackBerry Desktop Manager, see Chapter 16.

For illustration purposes, in this section we show you how to install iSkoot for Skype for BlackBerry. iSkoot is a free app that connects to the Web directly and allows you to use Skype. You can download this app at www. download.com/iSkoot-for-Skype-BlackBerry-/3000-7242_4- 10797721.html.

Installing, Windows style

No matter what app you're installing from your PC to your BlackBerry, the steps are the same. Use the following steps to install the app of your choice:

1. Download the app's installation files to your PC.

Refer to the app publisher's instructions on how to download the installation files. This is the only part of the installation process that varies from vendor to vendor. Some vendors allow you to download a ZIP file, and other vendors do the extra effort of giving you a self-extracting file. After following their instructions, you should end up with a set of files, and one of those files should have an `.alx` extension.

2. Locate the app's ALX file.

You can usually find a file with the `.alx` extension in the folder where you installed the app on your PC.

The ALX file isn't installed on your BlackBerry. It tells BlackBerry Desktop Software where the actual app file is located on your PC.

3. On your PC, double-click the BlackBerry Desktop Software icon or click Start⇨All Programs⇨BlackBerry⇨BlackBerry Desktop Software.

4. Use the USB cable to connect the BlackBerry to the PC.

A screen prompts you to enter your BlackBerry password.

If your handheld isn't connected properly, the bottom-right portion of BlackBerry Desktop Software displays the word *Disconnected.* Connect your BlackBerry to the USB cable and then connect the USB cable to the PC.

5. If you set a password, enter it now, as shown in Figure 19-5, and then click OK.

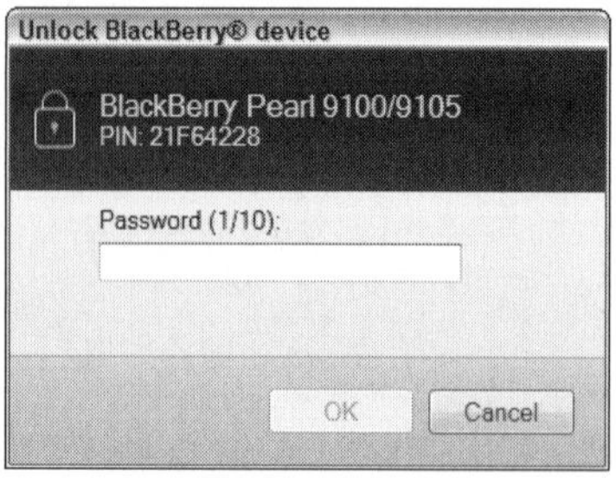

Figure 19-5:
Enter your
BlackBerry
Pearl pass-
word here.

> **Unlock BlackBerry® device**
>
> 🔒 BlackBerry Pearl 9100/9105
> PIN: 21F64228
>
> Password (1/10):
> [   ]
>
> OK   Cancel

6. Click the Applications link on the BlackBerry Desktop Software screen.

7. Click the Import Files button.

8. **Locate the ALX file you want to install.**

The default installation location of iSkoot is C:\Program Files\iSkoot\ iSkoot Skype for Blackberry. In this folder, you should find a file with an `.alx` extension. See Figure 19-6.

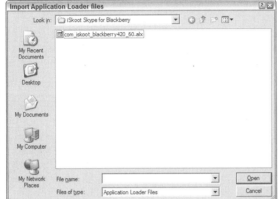

Figure 19-6:
Application installation file showing an .alx extension.

9. **Select the ALX file you want to install.**

iSkoot is now listed in the Application Summary section, as shown in Figure 19-7.

10. **Click Apply.**

The installation process starts, and a progress window appears. When the progress window disappears — and if all went well — the app will be in the Applications folder of your BlackBerry Pearl.

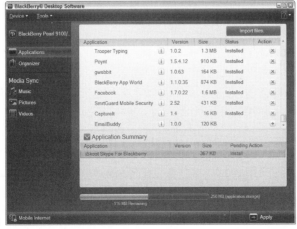

Figure 19-7:
Your app is added to the list of installed apps and can be installed on your BlackBerry.

If you get an invalid signature error after clicking the Apply button, the solution depends on how you received your BlackBerry:

- ✓ **If you didn't get your BlackBerry from your employer,** something is probably wrong with the app. You need to contact the software vendor.

- ✓ **If you got your BlackBerry from your employer,** you don't have permission to install apps on your BlackBerry. The IT department rules the school.

You don't have to use BlackBerry Desktop Software to get the goods onto your BlackBerry, though. You can install apps in other ways as well:

- ✓ **Wirelessly through an *over-the-air* (OTA) download:** See the section on installing and uninstalling apps from the Web in Chapter 11 for more on wireless installations.

- ✓ **BlackBerry Enterprise Server wireless install (if your employer provided your BlackBerry):** In this case, you have no control over the installation process. Your company's BlackBerry system administrator controls which apps are on your BlackBerry.

- ✓ **Through the PC via Microsoft Installer:** Some app installations automate the preceding steps. All you need to do is connect your BlackBerry to the PC and then double-click the installation file. The app installation file that uses Microsoft Installer bears the .msi file extension.

Installing, Mac style

For Mac users, a newly minted BlackBerry Desktop Manager allows you to add apps to and remove apps from your BlackBerry.

To install an app, follow these steps:

1. **Connect the BlackBerry to your Mac.**

2. **On your Mac, click BlackBerry Desktop Manager on the dock.**

    Can't find the BlackBerry Desktop Manager icon? Use the Finder, which is located at the left end of the dock.

    If you haven't installed BlackBerry Desktop Manager, refer to Chapter 16.

3. **In the BlackBerry Desktop Manager screen, click the Applications icon.**

    The next screen (see Figure 19-8) lists apps installed on your BlackBerry as well as those available for installation. Your next step is to add the ALX file for the app you want to install.

4. **Click the + button (on the bottom left), and locate and select the ALX file you want to install.**

   You return to the Install/Remove Applications screen (refer to Figure 19-8), where iSkoot is one of the apps in the list.

5. **In the Install column, select the app(s) you want to install.**

   For an installed app, deselecting it from the list uninstalls the app. Keep it selected if you want to keep the app on your BlackBerry.

6. **Click the Start button.**

   BlackBerry Desktop Manager starts installing your selected apps. This may take time, depending on the sizes of the apps.

Figure 19-8:
Install or uninstall apps here.

Uninstalling an App

You can uninstall an app in the following ways:

 ✔ Using BlackBerry Desktop Software on a Windows PC

 ✔ Using BlackBerry Desktop Manager on the Mac

 ✔ Using your BlackBerry

We use iSkoot as an example here and assume that you've already installed the iSkoot app. You can follow the same steps to uninstall other apps.

Uninstalling with BlackBerry Desktop Software on a Windows PC

To uninstall a BlackBerry app using BlackBerry Desktop Software on your PC, follow these steps:

1. **On your PC, double-click the BlackBerry Desktop Software icon or click Start⇨All Programs⇨BlackBerry⇨BlackBerry Desktop Software.**

2. **Use the USB cable to connect the BlackBerry to the PC.**

   A screen prompts you to enter your BlackBerry password.

3. **If you set a password, enter it now.**

4. **Click the Applications link in the BlackBerry Desktop Software screen.**

   The right portion of the screen is updated and lists apps currently installed on your BlackBerry Pearl (refer to Figure 19-7).

5. **Scroll to the app you want to delete. In the Action column, click the X button for that app.**

   The app is listed in the bottom part of the Application Summary section, with *Remove* in the Pending Action column.

6. **Click Apply.**

   An Updated Applications screen appears indicating the status of the uninstallation process. The process might take awhile if the apps you're uninstalling require a reboot of the device.

Uninstalling with BlackBerry Desktop Manager on the Mac

The steps for uninstalling an app using BlackBerry Desktop Manager on the Mac should be familiar because they use the same screen as the one for installing an app. Follow these steps:

1. **Connect the BlackBerry to the Mac.**

2. **On the Mac, if BlackBerry Desktop Manager does not automatically launch, click the BlackBerry Desktop Manager icon on the dock.**

3. **In the BlackBerry Desktop Manager screen, click the Applications icon.**

4. **Deselect the app(s) in the list that you want to uninstall.**

5. **Click the Start button.**

   A dialog box appears, asking whether you are sure that you want to remove an application from the device.

6. **Click Remove to uninstall the app, or click Cancel to stop the uninstallation.**

   A dialog box appears stating, "Updating the device. Do not disconnect your device until update is complete". A Stop button is provided in case you want to stop the uninstallation.

Uninstalling with the BlackBerry

When you don't have access to your PC, you can uninstall an app directly from your BlackBerry. Follow these steps:

1. **Locate the app icon on the BlackBerry Home screen.**

   By default, any apps you installed on your BlackBerry are filed in the Downloads folder on the Home screen. However, you always have the option to move the app to other folders or to the Home screen.

2. **Select the app icon, press the Menu key, and then select Delete.**

3. **In the confirmation dialog box that appears, select Delete to confirm the deletion.**

   You're given a choice to restart now or later. After the restart, the deleted app is uninstalled.

Upgrading the BlackBerry OS

The OS used by BlackBerry has gone through a few revisions. With BlackBerry Desktop Software (for Windows PC) and BlackBerry Desktop Manager (for the Mac), upgrading the OS is made so much simpler. The software detects whether a new version of BlackBerry OS is available and will prompt you for an upgrade the next time you connect your BlackBerry Pearl to BlackBerry Desktop Software or BlackBerry Desktop Manager. Refer to Chapter 16 for details on how to get BlackBerry Desktop Software and BlackBerry Desktop Manager.

Upgrading the BlackBerry OS, Windows style

If you're a Windows user, you'll be using BlackBerry Desktop Software and you can start the upgrade process by doing the following:

1. **On your PC, launch BlackBerry Desktop Software.**

2. **Using the USB cable, connect your BlackBerry Pearl to your PC.**

   A password prompt appears if you've set one on your Pearl.

3. **If you've set a password for your Pearl, enter it.**

   If there is a newer version of BlackBerry OS for your Pearl, you see the screen shown in Figure 19-9.

Figure 19-9: A newer version of BlackBerry OS is available.

4. **Click Get Update.**

   BlackBerry Desktop Software downloads the new OS, and the Check for Update screen appears, indicating the progress of download. When the download is finished, the Update Options screen appears, as shown in Figure 19-10, warning you that the upgrade process may take up to an hour. This screen also gives you options to back up your device data before the upgrade and to encrypt the backup file. We recommend that you keep the default setting, which is to back up the device data.

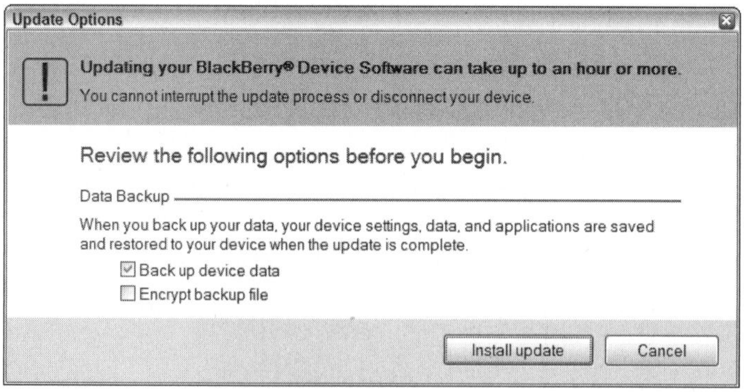

Figure 19-10: Always back up your device file before doing the upgrade.

5. **Click Install Update.**

   A screen displays the progress of the upgrade, as shown in Figure 19-11.

At times during the OS upgrade, your BlackBerry's display goes on and off. Don't worry; this is normal.

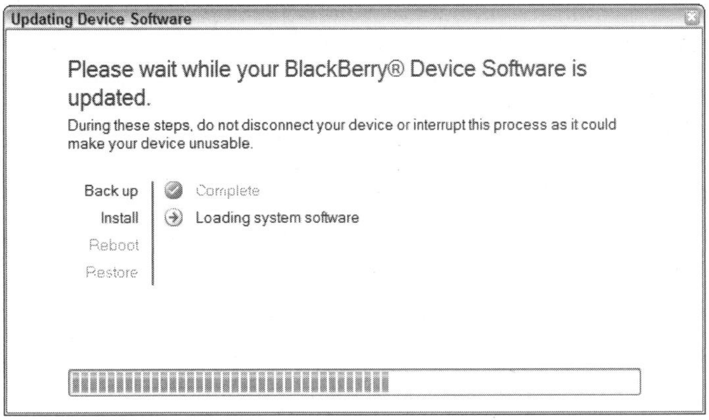

Figure 19-11:
You can
watch the
progress
of the OS
upgrade.

> **Updating Device Software** ⊗
>
> **Please wait while your BlackBerry® Device Software is updated.**
> During these steps, do not disconnect your device or interrupt this process as it could make your device unusable.
>
> Back up   ✓ Complete
> Install   ➔ Loading system software
> Reboot
> Restore

6. **When you see a message that the upgrade is finished, click Close.**

   The BlackBerry Desktop Software appears, showing the details of your Pearl with the new device software (OS) listed.

Upgrading the BlackBerry OS, Mac style

Upgrading your BlackBerry OS from your Mac is no different from installing an app. Here's how:

1. **Connect the BlackBerry to your Mac.**

2. **On your Mac, click BlackBerry Desktop Manager on the dock.**

3. **In the BlackBerry Desktop Manager screen, click the Applications icon.**

4. **Click the Check for Updates button (refer to Figure 19-8).**

   BlackBerry Desktop Manager checks online for any new versions of the OS for your BlackBerry. If it finds one, it downloads that update and lists it on the Applications screen.

5. **Select the check box next to the OS in the list.**

6. **Click the Start button to start the upgrade.**

Part VI
The Part of Tens

The 5th Wave   By Rich Tennant

"Of course your current cell phone takes pictures, functions as a walkie-talkie, and browses the internet. But does it shoot silly string?"

In this part . . .

If the earlier parts of this book are the cake and frosting, this part is the cherry on top. Delve into Chapter 20 to find out how to accessorize your BlackBerry. Use the ten programs listed in Chapter 21 to maximize your BlackBerry experience. Get into the fun stuff by checking out the ten popular games for your Pearl in Chapter 22. And find the top ten types of sites for easy Web browsing in Chapter 23.

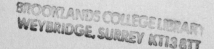

Chapter 20

Ten Great Accessories

*T*he BlackBerry retail box contains a few essentials: a battery, a charger, and a USB cable. If you're like us, though, you're not satisfied with just what's included in the box. In this chapter, we present the accessories that we think supplement your BlackBerry well and also where to shop for them.

Cases for Protection and Style

If your Pearl 9100 didn't come with a case (most don't), you need to get one so that your Pearl doesn't get scratched or damaged. Cases from the following places will set you back anywhere from $15–$35, which isn't too bad for looking hip. Check out CrackBerry.com (`http:// shop.crackberry.com/ blackberry-pearl-3g-cases.htm`) and BlackBerryStuff.com (`www.shop blackberry.com`).

BlackBerry Screen Protector

If the protector case described in the preceding section is a bit stressful for your wallet, try Invisible Shield for BlackBerry Pearl 3G, starting for about $15. You can get it at www.zagg.com/invisibleshield/blackberry-pearl-3g-cases-screen-protectors-covers-skins-shields.php /.

MicroSD Memory Card

If you want to store lots of music, pictures, or files on your BlackBerry Pearl, you definitely need to get a microSD memory card. The maximum microSD memory capacity is 32GB. You can get a card from almost all the online shops. We get ours from Amazon.com because of the free shipping.

If your laptop has an SD slot, make sure to buy a microSD card that comes with a card adapter. That way, you can use the same microSD card for your laptop. Two uses for the price of one. Nice!

Long Live Your BlackBerry

An extra battery for your BlackBerry comes in handy if you're a daily BlackBerry user. We recommend that you buy your battery only from Research in Motion (RIM), the maker of BlackBerry, and not from some other manufacturer because a faulty battery can seriously damage your BlackBerry beyond repair.

You can buy a battery manufactured by RIM from Shopblackberry.com (www.shopblackberry.com) or PocketBerry.com (http://store.pocketberry.com/homeAccessories.asp?deviceid=1152&hCategory=1009&hSubcategory=293).

Replenishing Your BlackBerry

If you're always on the go, you better have a portable charger on hand. The charger included with your BlackBerry is great to carry around town (and the world) because it has multiple adapters for different countries' electric plugs. The one we recommend is the BlackBerry Car Charger, which is great for all you road warriors out there. It will set you back around $30. Get your car charger from the official RIM online shopping store (www.shopblackberry.com).

Make sure that the charger you buy is for your BlackBerry model.

Bluetooth Hands-Free Headset

If you're a frequent phone user, we definitely recommend that you pick up a Bluetooth hands-free headset. Even though a wired hands-free headset comes with your BlackBerry, the convenience of a wireless Bluetooth hands-free headset is hard to live without. Plenty of Bluetooth headsets are on the market for you to choose from.

When choosing a headset, consider a comfortable fit, the voice quality, and whether it has a rechargeable battery.

You probably need to spend anywhere from $50–$150 for a hands-free headset. The best place to get your Bluetooth headset is good ol' Amazon.com (www.amazon.com).

BlackBerry Presenter

If you think you need your laptop to give a PowerPoint presentation, you're in for a surprise. For those presentations, you can replace your laptop with your slim BlackBerry Pearl 3G paired with BlackBerry Presenter. Although Presenter will set you back $200, it will save you from carrying a laptop and impress your clients at the same time. Get it at www.shopblackberry.com/us/presenter.

External Speaker Phone

Although some of you have a BlackBerry that comes with a speaker phone, sometimes the sound quality just isn't good enough for you to comprehend the phone conversation while in a car. Check out the wireless Bluetooth speaker phone by Motorola. It costs about $100, and you can get it from CrackBerry.com (http://shop.crackberry.com/motorola-eq5-wireless-travel-stereo-speaker/184A92A4040.htm).

BlackBerry Car Mount

To complete your BlackBerry car experience, you need a place to mount your BlackBerry in your car. With so many road warriors out there, the competition for your wallet has grown. We recommend the Motorola MOTOROKR T505 or the BlackBerry Bluetooth Premium Visor; both are just under $90. You can get them at Crackberry.com (`http://shop.crackberry.com/blackberry-pearl-3g-car-kits-and-mounts.htm`).

BlackBerry Pearl Cleaner

After you have your Pearl for more than a day, it's no longer clean and shiny. Instead, it's covered with fingerprints and smudges. The solution: Monster ScreenClean kit, which comes with a nonabrasive microfiber cloth. The ScreenClean kit work wonders not only on your BlackBerry Pearl but also on all types of surfaces — LCD, TV, and iPod. You can get it at `www.monster cable.com/productPage.asp?pin=2350`.

Chapter 21

Ten Must-Have Programs

The availability of BlackBerry software is growing at a dizzying rate. In this chapter, we introduce ten must-have apps that make your BlackBerry experience that much better.

We don't quote specific reviews. These choices are the results of our quest to find programs that people use, discerned from discussions with BlackBerry users, postings on message boards, and commentaries in the public domain. The apps featured here are just the tip of the iceberg. Feel free to surf the Internet, because by the time this book is published, more software will likely be available.

SmrtGuard, Your Smartphone Guardian

If you lost your BlackBerry, have you wondered what would happen to your data, such as your sensitive e-mails, phone call histories, contacts, and appointments? It's scary to think of a stranger getting to know you through your e-mails and knowing what you're going to do next. These same thoughts haunt us as well. Fortunately, there's SmrtGuard, which provides the following tools:

- ✔ **Locate and "LowJack" your BlackBerry:** With no GPS signal required, you can track your BlackBerry's approximate location to determine whether you simply misplaced it or someone stole it.

- ✔ **Wireless data backup:** Another must-have feature that SmrtGuard provides. If you self-destroyed your data and don't have a backup, the scheduled wireless backup of your PIM data will come in handy. From the SmrtGuard Web site (www.smrtguard.com), you can even see and browse through your backed-up data and export it to a CSV (comma-separated values) file.

- ✔ **Sound the audio ping:** If you simply misplaced your BlackBerry, but you can't find it by calling because you muted it, don't worry. Just send an audio ping, and your BlackBerry will emit a loud sound regardless of your profile setting. We wish our TV remote controls had this feature!

- ✔ **Self-destroy in five seconds:** Okay, perhaps not in five seconds, but you can decide when to destroy all your BlackBerry data. With SmrtGuard Remote Wipe, you can erase such data as e-mails, contacts, appointments, to-do's, memos, phone logs, text messages, and even all the files on your microSD card. SmrtGuard also uninstalls all your third-party apps (such as Facebook and MySpace apps), as well as native Phone and Message app. After a SmrtGuard Remote Wipe, your BlackBerry is rendered pretty much useless to others.

Always protect your BlackBerry with a password. That way, if your BlackBerry gets into the wrong hands, your data will be self-erased after ten unsuccessful password entries. However, the files on your microSD card aren't deleted, which is why SmrtGuard is so helpful.

With SmrtGuard by your side, you can concentrate on your business instead of worrying about your BlackBerry data being stolen. You can get SmrtGuard for $3.99 a month, or $49.99 for a year's subscription. There's also a free version of SmrtGuard. Check it out at www.smrtguard.com.

Tether

Subscribing to mobile broadband for your laptop is expensive. Tether provides an inexpensive solution for connecting to the Internet from your laptop by using your BlackBerry. You can check the details at www.tether.com.

On the Web site, you can order the app for a one-time fee of $49.95. That's spare change considering that you get connectivity to your laptop using your BlackBerry. There's also a 30-day money-back guarantee.

VibAndRing

Don't like the fact that you can't get your BlackBerry to alert you the way you want? Do you need custom vibration when a phone call comes in? Time to get your hands on VibAndRing. With it, you can customize how many vibrate bursts you get before your BlackBerry starts ringing and how long each vibration lasts. To download a free trial, go to www.mobihand.com, and search for *vibandring*.

Viigo for BlackBerry

Viigo is an app that you'll use daily. An RSS reader, Viigo is really a one-stop shop for almost all information you need, whether you want news, blogs, podcasts, weather info, entertainment, finance, or flight info. Download Viigo free from your BlackBerry at www.viigo.com.

SmrtAlerts

Ever find yourself in the middle of browsing or composing an e-mail, and all of a sudden, a new e-mail finds its way to your inbox? Instead of stopping what you're doing and heading to the inbox, get a preview of the e-mail or SMS message with SmrtAlerts. Then you can dismiss the message, mark it as read, go to your inbox, or delete the message — all from the alert pop-up. To find out more, go to www.smrtguard.com/smrtapps.jsp.

Google Talk Mobile and Yahoo! Messenger Mobile

If you use Google Talk or Yahoo! Messenger on your PC, both mobile versions are must-downloads to keep up with your buddies no matter where you are. To download, point your BlackBerry browser to the following:

- Google Talk Mobile: www.blackberry.com/GoogleTalk
- Yahoo! Messenger Mobile: www.blackberry.com/YahooDownload

Nobex Radio Companion

FM radio on your BlackBerry? That's right. With Nobex, you can get streaming radio on your BlackBerry free (for now)! More than a hundred stations are available for streaming. Nobex works best if you have a 3G or EvDo network (the faster the network, the better your experience with Nobex). To find out more, go to www.nobexrc.com.

Online Personal Music Players

Two apps, Pandora and Slacker, stream CD-quality music right to your BlackBerry. After you download and sign up for Pandora, you just search for the music that you like to hear, and Pandora will automatically feed you similar songs. If you indicate to Pandora whether you like or dislike a particular song that it feeds you, future Pandora selections should be more to your liking. Try Pandora free at www.pandora.com/blackberry. To try Slacker free, download it at www.slacker.com.

Neverfail

If you're a BlackBerry Enterprise Server (BES) administrator, The Neverfail app might help you monitor your BlackBerry population better. With Neverfail, you'll be the first to know about any problem that occurs in the BES infrastructure. Additionally, you can set up Neverfail so that your corporate BES has a hot-standby copy of the current production BES; if the production BES fails, the hot-standby BES can take over in no time. In short, your users will be able to carry out business on their BlackBerry smartphones no matter what. Find out more at: www.neverfailgroup.com.

ISEC7

ISEC7's B*Nator solution allows you to fine-tune and monitor your corporate BlackBerry Enterprise Server. You (as the administrator) can pinpoint the location of network bottlenecks and resolve problems quickly. Additionally, B*Nator provides extensive reporting features so your management team can understand how its money is being spent. Find out more at iSec7.com.

Chapter 22

Ten Fun Games

*W*ho says BlackBerry is all work and no play? True, you can get tons accomplished on your BlackBerry, but what you get accomplished doesn't necessarily need to be work related. Yes, you do have the BrickBreaker game that comes with your BlackBerry, but you can beat it only so many times before you get bored.

As the BlackBerry becomes increasingly popular, several BlackBerry game companies are making more and more fun titles. For example, you can play a game of online Texas Hold 'em with other BlackBerry users or an exciting match of Street Fighter. Whatever you play, you can find a huge selection of games out there. What's even better is that some great games are free.

After this chapter, you might play so many games on your BlackBerry that you'll have to watch your productivity level.

SmrtZodiac

SmrtZodiac is a simple yet addictive game in which you hear a satisfying "bing" when you match three or more cute animal figures. The best part is that your spouse and kids will enjoy SmrtZodiac as well. Try it for free by downloading it from www.smrtguard.com/smrtapps.jsp.

Bookworm

Warning: The Bookworm word game is addictive. It is part crossword puzzle, part word jumble, and part arcade puzzler. Your job is to make Lex, the hungry bookworm, well fed with words. If you're up to the challenge, you can buy it for $6.99 or download a free trial version. Point your BlackBerry to www.bplay.com and search for *bookworm*.

Crash Bandicoot Nitro Cart

Ever played Crash Bandicoot on PlayStation? Well, Crash Bandicoot Nitro Cart can be as addictive as the bigger version. With many racetracks to choose from, you can hone your driving skills and use weapons to fight opponents. You'll find no end of challenges to face as you discover advanced features for changing track designs. You can buy Crash Bandicoot Nitro Cart for $6.99 or download a trial version. Use your BlackBerry to go to www.bplay.com and search for *bandicoot*.

Who Wants to Be a Millionaire 2010

Who Wants to Be a Millionaire 2010 has the same sound effects as the TV show as well as the lifelines you would expect. With a tense and fun game, who wouldn't want to win a million? If you're ready to take the hot seat and make critical decisions, you can buy Who Wants to Be a Millionaire 2010 for $6.99. Use your BlackBerry to go to www.bplay.com and search for *millionaire*.

Texas Hold 'em King 3

Crave a game of Texas Hold 'em while away from your buddies? Practice your bluff with Texas Hold 'em King 3. We like this game because you can play an online tournament right from your BlackBerry. Buy the game for $5.99 or download a trial version. Point your BlackBerry to www.bplay.com and search for *texas holdem*.

Guitar Hero III Mobile

Guitar Hero is so popular and has gained so much success in the game-console space that it's now available for your BlackBerry. If you're into karaoke, this game brings you much closer to becoming a rock star. You play in a rock band and can choose the instruments you like. You can buy Guitar Hero III Mobile for $6.99 or download a trial version. From your BlackBerry, go to www.bplay.com and search for *guitar hero*.

Street Fighter II: Champion Edition

If you've ever played Street Fighter in the arcade, you'll love the Champion Edition of Street Fighter II on your BlackBerry. The graphics and background sounds are the same as the original arcade game. If only the BlackBerry keyboard was big enough to fit two hands so you could play against a friend. You get to choose from the usual characters, such as Chung Lee and Ken. To find out more, go to www.bplay.com and search for *street fighter*.

Chuzzle

Do you love Tetris, but tire of the same old thing every time? Try Tetris with a twist — Chuzzle. You aren't controlling blocks here but googly-eyed little balls of fur that giggle, squeak, and sneeze while you poke them across the board. A friendly warning: This game is simple yet addictive. And you get trophies. For $6.99, you can download Chuzzle. Just point your BlackBerry browser to www.bplay.com or http://handango.com and search for *Chuzzle*.

Nintaii

Nintaii is a puzzle game of rolling blocks and switches with more than 100 levels to challenge your brain. This game won the best game award of the 2008 BlackBerry Developer Challenge. A lot of brainpower went into this mind-twisting game. For $6.99, you can download Nintaii. Just point your BlackBerry browser to `www.bplay.com` and search for *Nintaii*.

Great Free Classic Games

Hundreds of free games are available. Following are our favorite classics:

- ✔ **Asteroids:** Avoid UFO attacks and obliterate the asteroids. Get the game at `www.mobilerated.com/asteroids-1839.html`.

- ✔ **Chess:** What's a smartphone without chess? Go to `www.mobilerated.com/chess-1878.html`.

- ✔ **Fear of the Dark:** Be a prince and rescue your princess. Here's an adventure game that you can get at `www.mobilerated.com/fear-of-the-dark-1700.html`.

- ✔ **Pacman:** Feeling nostalgic? Get Pacman at `http://bennychow.com/blackberry.shtml`.

- ✔ **Rubix Redux:** Sometimes, you just need a game that doesn't require a lot of thinking. In Rubix Redux, you push squares and align colors. Get it at `www.mobilerated.com/rubix-redux-1915.html`.

- ✔ **Space Invaders:** Really looks like the original Space Invaders. Get it at `http://blackberryfreeware.com/images_games/space_invaders.zip`.

- ✔ **Jet Fighter:** Feel the need to fly a fighter jet and shoot down enemy planes and tanks? Get Jet Fighter at `www.mobilerated.com/jet-fighter-2356.html`.

- ✔ **Zelda:** This is the classic Nintendo Zelda. Get it at `www.mobilerated.com/zelda-2417.html`.

Chapter 23

Top Ten Types of Sites

*W*eb surfing with a BlackBerry has improved dramatically with the newer models. With higher screen resolution and bigger real estate, your BlackBerry should give you a good mobile Web-browsing experience. And, with a 3G connection, your Web browsing should be faster. Remember that by using Page view on your BlackBerry, where the Web page displays the way it does in your PC Web browser, you can maintain the browsing habits you have on your PC but in a smaller package.

The Web site recommendations in this chapter are based on reviews in the public domain and sites that help when you're on the go.

Weather

You can keep up with weather changes at these sites:

- ✔ **AccuWeather.com (www.accuweather.com):** AccuWeather.com provides the local weather forecast.

- ✔ **Weather.com (www.weather.com):** Weather.com is smart enough to know that you're using a mobile device and displays a nice, trim version of its page with a few links to non-weather–related information.

If these two sites aren't enough, check out the "Search Engines, Directories, and Portals" section, later in this chapter. Major portals have weather information as well as traffic alerts and airport delays.

News

Most major news companies have mobile versions of their sites. This section gives you a sampling of what's out there. We list the same Web address you'd expect when browsing from your desktop. These sites detect that you're using a smartphone and redirect you to the mobile-friendly version of their sites:

- ✔ **ABC News (www.abcnews.com):** Get ABC News on your BlackBerry.

- ✔ **BBC News (www.bbc.com):** Read the BBC News right from your BlackBerry, even if you're not in the United Kingdom.

- ✔ **CNN (www.cnn.com):** This is CNN's mobile-friendly Web site.

- ✔ **Reuters (www.reuters.com):** This is a mobile-friendly version of the Reuters site.

- ✔ **The New York Times (www.nytimes.com):** This automatically points you to *The New York Times* mobile-friendly Web site, a site that's clean and easy to navigate, without a lot of advertisements.

- ✔ **USA Today (http://usatoday.com):** *USA Today,* one of the most popular newspapers, is now available free from your BlackBerry.

- ✔ **Wired News (http://mobile.wired.com):** Wired News is the mobile version of this tech-news Web site.

Search Engines, Directories, and Portals

In this section, we list *Web portals,* which are sites that contain various information or links to other sites:

- ✔ **Bing (www.bing.com):** This site is Microsoft's latest search engine. It's optimized for mobile searches and works great on your BlackBerry.

- ✔ **Google (www.google.com):** The king of search engines works like a charm on your BlackBerry.

- ✔ **MSN (www.msn.com):** You can access MSN Hotmail, MSN Messenger, and an online calendar. MSN has all the features that you can find in a Web portal, such as Web search, weather lookup, sports information, and news. Plus, you get MSN's finance-related pages, which give you up-to-the-minute stock quotes.

- ✔ **RIM mobile home page (http://mobile.blackberry.com):** This page is the default home page setting for most BlackBerry browsers. The service provider can customize it, though, so your BlackBerry browser may point to your service provider's home page. RIM's home page is definitely a place to start browsing the Web.

  You should definitely bookmark this site.

- ✔ **Yahoo! Mobile (www.yahoo.com):** Yahoo! is a smart portal because it knows you're using a mobile device and formats the page accordingly — meaning a smaller page with no advertisements. The portal site allows BlackBerry users to employ regular Yahoo! functions, such as Yahoo! Mail, Messenger, Finance, and Games, as well as driving directions and weather.

  This is another site you should bookmark.

Business

You can keep up with the latest news in the finance world from your BlackBerry. Visit the following sites for finance-related articles and news:

- ✔ **BusinessWeek Online (www.businessweek.com):** This site is a place to get great finance information.

- ✔ **Fidelity (www.fidelity.com):** Fidelity is an online investment brokerage firm.

- ✔ **Yahoo! Finance (http://finance.yahoo.com):** This site is great for checking the performance of your stocks.

Travel

Every site in the following list of BlackBerry-accessible travel sites features flight status and gate numbers. Some allow you to log in (if you're part of the airline's frequent-flier program) to access frequent-flier benefits:

- ✔ Air Canada: `www.aircanada.ca`
- ✔ American Airlines: `http://aa.flightlookup.com/omnisky`
- ✔ British Airways: `www.britishairways.com`
- ✔ Cathay Pacific: `www.cathaypacific.com`
- ✔ Continental Airlines: `www.continental.com`
- ✔ Delta: `www.delta.com`
- ✔ JetBlue: `http://jetblue.com`
- ✔ Northwest Airlines: `http://nwa.com`
- ✔ United Air Lines: `http://ua2go.com`
- ✔ Any airline: `http://flightview.com`

Also, check out these travel sites:

- ✔ **KAYAK (`www.kayak.com`):** Aggregates popular travel sites to find you the best deals on hotels, car rentals, cruises, and vacation packages. The Web site isn't formatted for mobile devices but works okay on the BlackBerry. You can also download its BlackBerry app with the download link that conveniently appears when you go to its site using BlackBerry Browser.
- ✔ **TripKick (`www.tripkick.com`):** Don't be so excited about getting a good deal on a hotel only to end up in a crummy room. TripKick tells you who has the best rooms and who doesn't.
- ✔ **WikiTravel (`www.wikitravel.com`):** This is one of the most up-to-date and complete travel guides on the Web.

Sports

Tired of missing updates on your favorite sport while on the go? You don't have to. Visit the sports-related sites that follow, and you'll get the scoop on what's happening with your favorite team:

- **CBS Sports Mobile (www.cbssports.com/mobile):** If you're active with a CBS Sports fantasy team, you'll be happy to know that you can log in and view your stats from this Web site. Popular U.S. sports are covered here.

- **ESPN (http://mobileapp.espn.go.com):** Everyone knows ESPN. This is the mobile version of its Web site.

Advice and Self-Help

Looking for ways to save time and get your questions answered? Check out these sites:

- **HowCast (www.howcast.com):** With a dose of humor, this site is a world of how-to videos.

- **Omiru (www.omiru.com):** This site offers practical fashion advice for the common person.

- **Yahoo! Answers (http://answers.yahoo.com):** Here, you can get all sorts of creative, amusing, and helpful responses to your questions — advice that's free.

- **Zeer (www.zeer.com):** No need to stand in the supermarket comparing nutritional labels; do it here.

Social and Virtual Networking

For those of you who are (or aren't yet) addicted to social networking sites, we list a few of the most popular ones here. If your favorite site isn't listed, don't fret; just search for it with a search engine:

- **Friendster (www.friendster.com):** This site is popular in Southeast Asian countries and is open to people 16 and older.

- **LinkedIn (wwwlinkedin.com):** LinkedIn caters to professional and business relationships. You'll find people publishing their bios on their profiles.

- **Multiply (www.multiply.com):** This site claims to focus on real-world relationships and is open to anyone 13 and older. It's a popular site for teenagers.

- **Orkut** (`www.orkut.com`): Orkut is a social networking site run by Google. It's open to anyone 18 and older, and it requires Google login credentials. This site is popular in Latin America and India.

- **Windows Live Space** (`home.spaces.live.com`): Microsoft runs this social networking site. It's open to everyone and requires a Hotmail or Windows Live login.

MySpace and Facebook both have an app you can download from BlackBerry App World or RIM's Web site. Point your browser to `mobile.blackberry.com` and navigate to IM & Social Networking.

Shopping and Shipping Information

Shopaholics can keep it up online even when they're not in front of the PC. Check out these sites:

- **Amazon** (`www.amazon.com`): With Amazon Anywhere, you can shop and check your account information right from your BlackBerry.

- **eBay** (`www.ebay.com`): You can bid on goods from the convenience of your BlackBerry.

- **FedEx tracking** (`www.fedex.com`): This mobile version of the FedEx Web site allows you to track packages from your BlackBerry.

- **Gas Buddy** (`www.gasbuddy.com`): You can find the nearest gas station that sells the cheapest gas.

- **ILikeTotallyLoveIt.com** (`www.iliketotallyloveit.com`): This site is shopping with a twist. Shoppers post things they like, from wasabi gumballs to DeLorean cars, and solicit opinions on posted sale items from other members.

- **UPS tracking** (`www.ups.com`): Like FedEx, UPS has a mobile version of its Web site that allows you to track packages from your BlackBerry.

Other Browsing Categories

You can visit the following sites from your BlackBerry to get more information on various topics:

- **BlackBerry Cool (`www.blackberrycool.com`):** A competitor to CrackBerry (see the upcoming bullet), BlackBerry Cool is one of the pioneers in providing great reviews of BlackBerry apps.

- **CrackBerry (`http://mobile.crackberry.com`):** Go here to discover the latest BlackBerry news, communicate with other BlackBerry users, find BlackBerry accessories, and read app reviews and BlackBerry-related articles. This Web site is optimized for BlackBerry browsing. Without a doubt, this site is one of the most active BlackBerry communities.

- **DataOutages.com (`www.dataoutages.com`):** From time to time, RIM's network operation center or a mobile network operator undergoes maintenance or some mishap causes e-mails to stop flowing to your BlackBerry. This is not an official RIM Web site, but the site does list any planned or unplanned data outages.

- **MiniSphere (`www.minisphere.com`):** You find useful links designed for mobile devices here.

- **MizPee (`www.mizpee.com`):** When you gotta go, you gotta go. This site locates the nearest clean public bathroom.

- **MyBlackBerry (`my.blackberry.com`):** RIM's official Web site dedicated to BlackBerry owners. You can find BlackBerry related news, blogs, tips and tricks, featured apps, and a forum where you can share your BlackBerry experience or post your questions.

- **Starbucks Locator (`www.starbucks.com`):** This site helps you locate the nearest Starbucks so you can meet your buddies or get a dose of caffeine.

- **YourShortCut.mobi (`www.yourshortcut.mobi`):** This site shows a list of popular mobile-friendly Web sites in nice and easy-to-understand categories.

Index

• **C** •

• *N* •

• R •

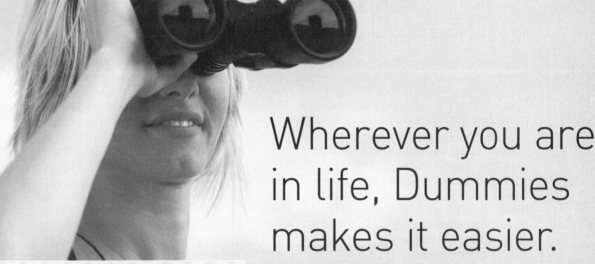

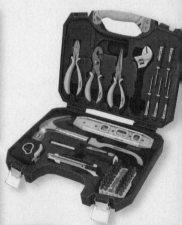